Mindful
Leadership

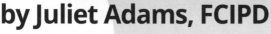
for
dummies®
A Wiley Brand

by Juliet Adams, FCIPD
Director, A Head for Work Ltd

Technical Editor:
Marina Grazier, MBPsS
Owner Director, The Mindfulness Exchange Ltd

for
dummies®
A Wiley Brand

Mindful Leadership For Dummies®

Published by: John Wiley & Sons, Ltd., The Atrium, Southern Gate, Chichester, www.wiley.com

This edition first published 2016

© 2016 by John Wiley & Sons, Ltd., Chichester, West Sussex

Registered Office

John Wiley & Sons, Ltd., The Atrium, Southern Gate, Chichester, West Sussex, PO19 8SQ, United Kingdom

For details of our global editorial offices, for customer services and for information about how to apply for permission to reuse the copyright material in this book, please see our website at www.wiley.com.

For general information on our other products and services, please contact our Customer Care Department within the U.S. at 877-762-2974, outside the U.S. at 317-572-3993, or fax 317-572-4002. For technical support, please visit www.wiley.com/techsupport.

Wiley publishes in a variety of print and electronic formats and by print-on-demand. Some material included with standard print versions of this book may not be included in e-books or in print-on-demand. If this book refers to media such as a CD or DVD that is not included in the version you purchased, you may download this material at http://booksupport.wiley.com. For more information about Wiley products, visit www.wiley.com.

A catalogue record for this book is available from the British Library.

Library of Congress Control Number: 2016940590

ISBN 978-1-119-06877-8 (pbk); ISBN 978-1-119-06879-2 (ebk); ISBN 978-1-119-06880-8 (ebk)

Printed and Bound in Great Britain by TJ International, Padstow, Cornwall.

10 9 8 7 6 5 4 3 2 1

Contents at a Glance

Table of Contents

Introduction

Mindfulness is a mental discipline that has been practiced for thousands of years. Modern science has researched the impacts of mindfulness on health and well-being over the last 40 years. In recent years, researchers have turned their attention to exploring the benefits of applying mindfulness to the way people work.

Nowadays, hundreds of corporate organisations, from Google to General Mills, from Dow Chemicals to the UK Parliament, use mindfulness to help their employees boost their resilience, productivity, emotional intelligence, focus and well-being. Leading business schools now recognise that mindfulness provides the foundation for effective leadership and routinely offer mindfulness training to MBA students and those in search of new approaches to the challenges of the modern-day workplace.

A lot of hype and myth surrounds mindful leadership. Simply put, mindful leadership = mindfulness + leadership.

A mindful leader is simply a leader who uses mindfulness to gain deeper knowledge of himself and makes a conscious effort to use this knowledge to manage himself better, taking personal responsibility for his actions and striving to be the best leader he can be.

Mindful leaders provide calm, clarity and a clear sense of direction, carefully balancing the needs of the organisation with the needs and aspirations of the workforce. Mindful leaders monitor themselves to maintain a focus on present- moment reality, their impact on other people, and their reactions to stressful situations.

Mindful leaders experience the reality and vividness of what's going on in any given moment, without knee- jerk reactions based on negative mind states (such as anxiety, fear or anger) responding with a calm awareness and care for themselves and others.

Mindful Leadership For Dummies offers a highly accessible and practical guide for busy professionals. It includes all the basics you need to know, such as what mindfulness is and how it works (Chapter 1) and the underpinning neuroscience (see Chapter 3). It includes a full six-week WorkplaceMT course (Chapters 8 through 13), which you can use to teach yourself mindfulness or as a course workbook if you decide to attend a WorkplaceMT course. It includes practical guidance on improving your presence and influence (Chapter 14), leading in a digital age (Chapter 15) and mindfully leading change (Chapter 16). For those looking for ways to introduce mindfulness to their organisation, you can find pragmatic advice and guidance in Chapter 17.

We hope you enjoy reading *Mindful Leadership For Dummies* and that it leads to improvements in the way you work, your happiness and well-being.

About This Book

Whatever your reason or level of engagement, you'll find something in this book for you. It's designed to be practical and accessible, full of real-life examples that you can start applying straightaway. For some, this book will prove the catalyst for major change; for others, the messages in this book may be less resonant.

This book provides you with the information and guidance you need to make up your own mind and decide how mindfulness can help you become a better leader. We encourage you to read with an open mind and a sense of exploration. In the spirit of mindfulness, suspend judgment as you read and experiment with some of the concepts and techniques described in these pages, and then take from it what works best for you.

Foolish Assumptions

When writing this book, we have made a number of assumptions about you, the reader:

>> You've picked up this book because you're committed to becoming a more mindful leader.

>> You have experience working in a professional role.

>> You're ready to change the way you work for the better.

>> You're just curious, or even sceptical, about mindfulness.

> » You've read about mindfulness in the business pages of your newspaper or an article in your trade journal and you want to know whether the hype is justified.

Icons Used in This Book

Like other *For Dummies* books, this one has icons in the margins to guide you through the information and help you zero in on what you want to know. The following paragraphs describe the icons and what they mean.

REMEMBER

Information flagged with this icon is useful and worth keeping in mind when working with your experience of low mood and depression.

TIP

The text next to this icon offers quick and effective ideas to support your leaning about mindfulness.

WARNING

This icon flags text that you need to take heed of.

TECHNICAL STUFF

This icon points out interesting bits of information that goes beyond need-to-know. You can skip paragraphs marked with this icon if you're pressed for time, but reading them will further enhance your understanding.

PLAY THIS

When you see this icon, you can download an MP3 to guide you as you practice a formal mindfulness exercise.

Beyond the Book

In addition to the material in the print or e-book you're reading right now, this book also comes with a free access-anywhere Cheat Sheet that provides top tips on becoming a mindful leader, the most recent research into mindful leadership and developing a leadership approach that works best for you. To get this Cheat

Sheet, simply go to www.dummies.com and search for "Mindful Leadership For Dummies Cheat Sheet" in the Search box.

We also offer further resources that go with this book.

>> Visit the Resources page of www.aheadforwork.com for leadership, productivity and mindfulness resources. You can also use this website to get in touch with Juliet about the programmes offered.

>> Go to www.workplacemt.com to find out more about WorkplaceMT mindfulness training, its research base, teachers and teacher training.

>> Check out The Mindfulness Exchange Ltd. (TME; www.mindfulness-exchange.com). Marina is the owner of TME, which is a spin-off from Oxford University's Oxford Mindfulness Centre (OMC) that provides mindfulness training for the workplace. You can use this website to contact Marina.

>> To find out more about mindfulness and its research basis and to browse books and resources, check out www.mindfulnet.org, the mindfulness information website.

We've recorded MP3s to guide you when you practice the formal mindfulness exercises as detailed in Chapters 8 through 13. Download them from www.dummies.com/go/mindfulleadershipfd.

Where to Go from Here

This book is designed so that you can dip in and out as you please. You're invited to make good use of the table of contents (or the index) and jump straight into the part or chapter that grabs your attention. You're in charge, and it's up to you.

If you're new to mindful leadership, or not sure where to start, begin with Part 1, and you'll have a better idea of how to proceed. If you're ready to start your mindfulness development, start at Chapter 7, and then work through Chapters 8 to 13 in order.

We wish you all the best in your quest to be a more mindful leader and hope you find lots of valuable ideas and information within these pages. Above all, see this book as an exploration with nothing to lose but everything to gain.

1

Breaking the Mould

IN THIS PART . . .

Explore what mindful leadership is and how it can work for you.

Examine the leadership challenges of the modern workplace.

Discover the potential and limitations of your brain and become aware of your unconscious drivers.

Chapter 1

Exploring Mindful Leadership

M indful leadership is about flexibility of thought and actions, breaking out of autopilot and habitual behaviours and being the best you can be in any given moment. Mindfulness certainly isn't a silver bullet or a quick fix; it takes time and practice. But every great journey starts with one step, and this book will be your companion and guide every step of the way.

Establishing the Facts about Mindfulness and Leadership

In this section, we start with the basics and establish a shared understanding of what mindfulness is and how it can enhance your leadership capability.

Understanding mindfulness

Mindfulness is all about your ability to focus attention on the situation at hand with the intention to observe the judgments you make and choose how to respond appropriately. Developing this ability helps you to step away from automatic habitual responses to observe present-moment reality with an open mind and to make smarter decisions.

Everyone has the capacity to be mindful, but like anything worthwhile, it takes time, effort and practice. In the section 'Deconstructing Mindfulness' you'll find a more succinct definition of mindfulness and how to develop it for yourself.

Redefining leadership

The definition of *leadership* varies subtly from theory to theory. At its most basic, leadership is a process of social influence where a person (the leader) secures the help and support of others to accomplish a shared task.

In recent years, leadership theory has started to focus on the leader as one human being, leading other human beings. Recent discoveries in neuroscience and psychology have transformed our knowledge of how the human brain learns, reacts to different stimulus, and interprets what's happening.

On a daily basis, as a leader, you're involved in changing people's brains – literally! Everyday ordinary and extraordinary life events are the catalysts for thoughts, decisions and learning, which in turn change the structure of the brain physically. Understanding your brain, and how and why others do what they do, helps you use your brain more effectively. Applying neuroscience to your actions and behaviours as a leader helps make you a more effective, adaptive and resilient leader. You can find out more about this in Chapter 3.

Mindfulness is now recognised as a foundational skill for effective leadership. Peter Drucker once said that we can't manage others unless we learn to manage ourselves first. Mindfulness increases self-awareness, which enables you to manage yourself better. *Mindful leadership* combines the practice of mindfulness with practical management and leadership techniques, enabling leaders to engage a wider range of their capacities to the challenges at hand. Check out Chapters 15, 16 and 17 for the practical application of mindfulness to everyday work challenges.

Exploring the Benefits of Mindful Leadership

Having considered the meaning of both mindfulness and leadership (see previous section), you may be asking yourself, 'What's in it for me?' The following sections drill deeper into the role of leadership today, the evolution and modern-day uses of mindfulness, and practical ways to apply mindfulness to your work as a leader.

Refreshing your knowledge of leadership

Ideas about what makes a good leader have changed and evolved dramatically over the years. In the 1920s and 1930s, trait theories argued that leaders were born. From the 1940s to the 1960s, behavioural theories argued that you can be taught leadership – it's just a matter of adopting the right behaviours when attempting to lead.

In more recent times, contingency theories (such as situational leadership) argue that no one leadership style is correct and that as a leader you need to adopt the correct leadership style for the situation. Transformational theories view leaders as agents of change. As a transformational leader, you can *transform* the workplace via teamwork or team development, or by acting as an agent of change or a strategic visionary.

One of the most recent approaches to leadership is *authentic* leadership. It's an approach that encourages honest relationships with followers, whose input is valued. Authentic leaders tend to be positive people with truthful self-concepts who seek clarity and promote openness. By building trust and generating enthusiastic support from their followers, authentic leaders are able to improve both individual and team performance. Authentic leadership is a growing area of study in academic research on leadership, and mindfulness is a core element. Read more about authentic leadership in Chapter 14.

Investigating human nature

If you want to be a good leader, you need to have some understanding of what makes people tick. At a deep level, most humans have a natural desire to be led, fuelled by a primeval desire to survive, have a purpose in life, and achieve. Abraham Maslow described this in his hierarchy of needs (see Figure 1-1).

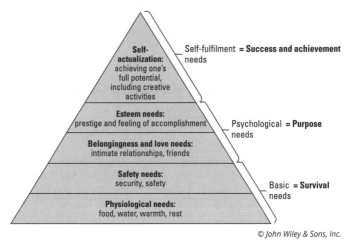

© John Wiley & Sons, Inc.

FIGURE 1-1: Maslow's hierarchy of needs.

Located at the foundation of Maslow's triangle are basic needs – needs for survival. Like most animals, humans will do anything and everything to survive and sustain life. Challenging situations may result in a feeling of threat. Threats to pride, integrity and future success may lead to seeking guidance, support and leadership from others to minimise threats. In a work context, if your ability to complete a task is threatened, it can have a negative impact on your future success and progress, which is why people are naturally predisposed to need leaders.

Good leaders help individuals to gain a meaningful sense of purpose by helping them align their thoughts and clarify the reasons behind their work. Humans need understanding to fully engage, and good leadership meets this need.

According to Maslow, after basic needs (survival) and psychological needs (purpose) are met, humans strive for self-fulfilment. In a work context, leaders can greatly enhance individuals' potential for success and achievement. Good leaders help individuals work towards their full potential and maximise their performance.

Deconstructing Mindfulness

As a human being, you perform at your best when you're authentic to yourself and lead in a way that resonates with your values. Of course, doing so is often easier said than done. It takes time and effort and an acceptance of personal responsibility for your actions. Unravelling and revealing your true self involves self-awareness and reflection, which is where mindfulness comes in.

Defining mindfulness

When you strip away the hype and well-worn catchphrases, mindfulness is simply the cultivation of metacognition and maintenance of an optimum mind state (see Figure 1-2).

>> *Metacognition* can be described as the ability to observe what's going on in your mind. When developing mindfulness, you cultivate an open monitoring state where you're aware of your thoughts, feelings and bodily sensations in any given moment of time.

>> An *optimum mind state* can be described as a feeling of ease, when you feel safe and secure, and your body and mind is functioning in its optimum state. In other words, an optimum mind state occurs when you're free from anxiety, anger and fear and are feeling secure, happy and comfortable with your surroundings. This state allows you to be the best you can and reach your full potential.

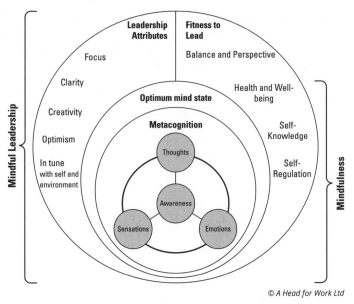

© A Head for Work Ltd

FIGURE 1-2: Mindfulness and mindful leadership.

The following sections explore these terms and what they mean in more detail.

Maintaining metacognition and an optimum mind state

Cultivating metacognition enables you to become more aware of your automatic tendencies and responses. This awareness allows you to make decisions and act appropriately based on present-moment reality instead of being hijacked by strong emotions and impulses triggered by past experiences and predictions of the future, which often lead to inappropriate actions and reactions.

Maintaining an optimum mind state is important. When you experience a negative emotional mind state, such as anger and fear, even to a small degree, your brain responds automatically. Your brain senses something is wrong and responds quickly to safeguard you.

For example, if you were standing in the middle of a road with a lorry hurtling towards you, you wouldn't want to have to take a moment to decide what to do, would you? In this situation, it's wholly appropriate that your brain should take control, quickly and efficiently evaluating the threat and the options and deciding on the right course of action. If this happened to you for real, you would almost certainly automatically jump out of the way without any conscious thought to avoid death or injury. In this instance, engaging in conscious thought would slow you down, but engaging autopilot allows you to live to tell the tale.

This lightning-fast, efficient, unconscious response has helped humans to survive and evolve into arguably the most successful species on the planet. But it does have its downfalls.

Exploring the Evolution of Mindfulness

Figure 1-3 shows a timeline of the evolution of mindfulness.

Mindfulness, as cultivated in the WorkplaceMT exercises you find in Chapters 8 through 13, originated from ancient practices, which were a component of Buddhism. In the late 1890s to early 1900s, mindfulness practices were simplified and westernised in an attempt to safeguard their future survival in a time of colonialism.

This more secular version of mindfulness was popularised by the pioneering work of Jon Kabat-Zinn, who developed Mindfulness-Based Stress Reduction (MBSR) in 1979. MBSR blended Jon's scientific training with his Buddhist and yoga training. His work sparked the interest of the scientific community who started researching the impact of mindfulness. In the 1980s, about one scientific research paper on mindfulness was published each year.

In the 1990s, John Teasdale Zindel Segal and Mark Williams blended MBSR with Cognitive Behavioural Therapy (CBT) to form Mindfulness-Based Cognitive Therapy (MBCT) as a treatment for recurrent depression. In the 1990s, about ten research papers on mindfulness were published each year.

Mindfulness at work timeline

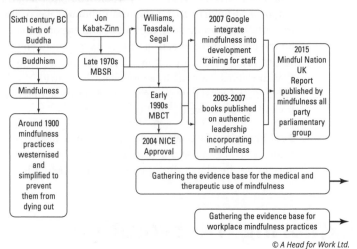

FIGURE 1-3: Mindfulness evolution timeline.

In 2004, the National Institute for Health and Clinical Excellence (NICE) recommended MBCT as a treatment of choice for recurrent depression. This accelerated scientific interest in mindfulness further, and by 2013 about 500 papers on mindfulness were published each year.

Identifying the foundations of mindfulness in the workplace

Exactly who first applied mindfulness to the challenge of the modern-day workplace is unclear. In recent years, a number of prominent leaders have come forward and admitted that they've been practicing mindfulness for a number of years, and they've claimed that it's been invaluable in their work as a leader.

In 2007, Google started to integrate mindfulness into its development programmes for staff. The success of Google's Search Inside Yourself programme may have been one of the catalysts for mindfulness gaining increasing traction in the workplace.

In 2011, Professor Mark Williams (co-creator of MBCT) and Dr Danny Penman published *Mindfulness: A Practical Guide to Finding Peace in a Frantic World* (Piatkus) as a self-help guide.

This best-selling book marked a turning point for mindfulness at work. Although written for the population as a whole, it was the first book on mindfulness that was aimed at teaching a *well* population to be mindful.

Recent research into the use of shortened mindfulness exercises like the ones used in WorkplaceMT mindfulness training indicates similar benefits to the longer, widely researched practices developed as part of MBSR and MBCT, respectively. More research is needed, but initial research data looks promising.

Starting your own mindful leadership journey

Every journey really does start with a first step. You've taken that first step by looking into mindful leadership. The next steps are up to you. You may want to find out more about mindfulness and its practical applications before committing to learning it yourself. Chapters 2 through 6 will help you to do this. You may want to learn mindfulness through self-study as detailed in Chapters 8 through 13, or via an app (see Chapter 22 for some suggestions) or attending formal training. If you are considering introducing mindfulness to your organisation, Chapter 17 is for you. Whatever it is, do is something. Your mindful journey starts right here, right now!

Chapter 2

Discovering Why Mindfulness Matters to Leaders

Media interest in mindfulness has exploded in the last few years. In parallel, the research base that connects mindfulness with decreased anxiety, depression and stress and increased resilience has become relatively well known. As the popularity of mindfulness has increased, interest has grown in the potential of mindfulness to transform the way people work. As interest and uptake of training has increased, researchers have started to explore its impact on workplace productivity, creativity and employee well-being. Research suggests that mindfulness aids focus, concentration and decision-making and improves relationships.

This chapter explores the role of mindfulness in modern leadership. It offers you some practical tips to help you improve your leadership by applying a little mindfulness.

Leadership Challenges of the Modern Workplace

To discover why mindfulness matters, you need to consider the leadership environment you're currently operating within. Are you working in a VUCA world? Is change now the norm, rather than the exception? Its also wise to consider the sources of workplace pressure that can lead to stress. Doing so can help you develop mindful ways to increase resilience and maintain well-being.

Leading in a VUCA world

The concept of a 'VUCA world' first originated in the U.S. military. In recent years, it's become a popular management acronym, used to describe the difficult business environment many people lead within. It stands for *volatile, uncertain, complex* and *ambiguous.* Some use the VUCA world as a scapegoat to delegate all responsibility for leading their organisation out of crisis.

Mindful leaders are self-aware and take personal responsibility. They know that although they can't necessarily control the VUCA nature of the modern workplace, they can take full responsibility for their actions and control their response to it.

The following sections explore the meaning behind the VUCA acronym in more detail.

Volatility

Volatile work challenges are unexpected, with an uncertain duration. The good news is the information is usually out there – you just need to find it. An example of a volatile work challenge may be share prices falling rapidly following a natural disaster.

Uncertainty

Uncertainty at work may result from you knowing that something bad is coming but not knowing exactly what form it will take, how bad it will be or how long it will last. An example of this is the UK Government's attempts to reduce the deficit. The public sector knew that cost-cutting measures would result in major budget cuts, but they didn't know exactly which services would be impacted and by how much their budgets would be reduced.

Complexity

Complexity can be caused by situations with interconnected parts or interdependencies and variables. Information is available, but the volume or nature of the information may be overwhelming or difficult to process. Global working is a good example of complexity: trying to deliver a good service to a business in many countries all with different cultures, currencies that fluctuate, and wildly differing legislation.

Ambiguity

Ambiguity involves those 'unknown unknowns' that are difficult to predict and have no precedents. An example of this may be moving into a newly emerging market with a new product range unlike anything you've manufactured in the past.

Leading when change is the norm

In the past, many leadership models were largely based on the principle that although organisations would experience times of change and transition, eventually they would settle into a stable 'business as usual' state. For most modern organisations, change is now the norm.

Of course, change is nothing new. In reality, change is the only constant in life. The difference is the pace of change. The pace of change has accelerated dramatically in recent times, fuelled, at least in part, by the digital age, shifting away from industrialisation towards an economy based on information shared digitally via computers. Access to and the control of information are key elements of business success. Indeed, for many companies, such as Google, the ownership and control of information is their business.

Humans hate uncertainty and are predisposed to feel uncomfortable in new situations. Mindful leaders recognise their inbuilt fear and resistance to change and how it manifests within them. They recognise their own patterns of avoidance and fear when confronted by unexpected change and have mastered techniques to stop them from sliding into negativity, fear and procrastination. You find more about the human negativity bias in Chapter 3.

Identifying Sources of Pressure

The ability to work under pressure is an important leadership attribute. Although you can't micromanage the curve balls that life throws at you, you can manage how you deal with them.

The following sections differentiate pressure from stress, help you identify how excess pressure can lead to stress and explore specific aspects of leadership stress.

Defining pressure

Pressure, up to a certain point, can have a positive impact on your performance. It provides the motivation to get out of bed in the morning. It can make you more alert, motivated and engaged, encouraging you to become the best you can and to reach a level of work that constitutes your peak performance. For those in leadership positions, levels of pressure experienced can be great. When holding a position of responsibility, everything that you say and do has the potential to influence the lives of others. Each decision you make affects not only your organisation but the people around you.

Defining stress

When pressure becomes excessive or unmanageable, it leads to stress. Stress can damage your health, performance, and even your business. Arguably, stress has been the cause of more poor business decisions than poor judgment or inexperience.

REMEMBER

Stress experienced for short spaces of time is normal and to be expected. In recent times, the combination of the economic downturn and unstable financial markets has increased workplace stress for many leaders. Every decision and action can become even more critical as the pressure grows to do more with less while maintaining the current level of performance.

Stress can affect all staff at all levels. In the United Kingdom, the Health and Safety Executive reported that in 2014, stress, anxiety and depression accounted for 39 per cent of workplace absence. In the United States, the current cost of workplace stress is estimated at $300 billion a year, 73 per cent experience the psychological symptoms of stress, with around 33 per cent living with extreme stress.

WARNING

Stress can cause impaired judgment, a lack of foresight, detachment from reality, irresponsibility, and strong egoism. This impaired brain function can prevent leaders and decision-makers from making good decisions and cause them to neglect the interests and needs of the business and wider society in pursuit of personal egoistic benefit.

Identifying sources of pressure that can lead to stress

Knowledge is power. If you want to reduce your stress, start by identifying possible causes of excess pressure at work. In the United Kingdom, the Health and Safety Executive (HSE) identify a number of factors, which, if not managed correctly, can lead to workplace stress.

Consider whether any of the following may be potential sources of workplace stress for you:

>> **Demands:** A feeling of inability to cope with the demands placed on you by your job

>> **Control:** A feeling of lack of control in the way you do your work

>> **Support:** A feeling that you're not receiving adequate information and support from your colleagues and superiors

>> **Relationships:** A feeling that you're being subjected to unacceptable behaviours from those you work with

>> **Role:** A feeling that you don't adequately understand your role and responsibilities

>> **Change:** A feeling that you're unable to contribute to or shape organisational changes that impact you

REMEMBER

Although you may not always have control of situations you encounter at work, you do have control of how you respond to them. Consider what you can change and the things you can't, see whether you can identify your thought patterns around them, and actively work to find alternatives that invoke less stress and help you function better as a leader.

Recognising power stress

A recent research study suggests that leaders experience less stress than their subordinates because they tend to have more control over situations, however, leadership can have its own unique stresses. One leader confided in Juliet that he only ever experienced stress at two points in any given 24 hours: night and day!

Leadership involves increased responsibility, working with ambiguities, pressure to achieve results by influencing others, and loneliness, each of which can take its toll. As a result, leaders may experience *power stress*, a term coined by Boyatzis and McKee. Power stress can result from the exercise of influence and sense of responsibility experienced in many leadership positions. If it isn't identified and addressed adequately, it can lead to physical and emotional exhaustion.

The chronic stress that can accompany leadership has been connected to a wide range of diseases and dysfunctions. It can also lead to a state of dissonance, which can drain your enthusiasm and energy. Power stress experienced as a result of being in a leadership position isn't really the problem; a lack of a sense of completion when you complete tasks and projects and insufficient recovery time are.

Although work pressure and stresses may not relent, you can take steps to change the way you choose to respond to them. Mindfulness is a key component of the renewal process.

Mindful Ways to Improve Your Leadership

The following sections discuss various ways you can improve your leadership mindfully.

Letting go of the stereotype

How do you become a more mindful leader, you ask? You may have already formed a mental image of how mindful people conduct themselves. Maybe thinking about this is conjuring up an image for you? Perhaps you think a mindful leader is a person with real presence, a person who is at ease with himself or herself, is open, wise, insightful, patient, kind and benevolent and has the strength of character to make ethical choices.

A mindful leader can of course be all these things, but this almost saintlike combination may feel unattainable or may foster a sense of inadequacy – neither of which is particularly helpful. The simple tips and techniques contained in this book will help you to develop metacognition (awareness of thoughts, emotions and bodily sensations), and maintaining an optimum state of mind, which are core components of mindfulness.

We encourage you to throw away any preconceived stereotypes of how a good leader should or shouldn't be. Be authentic to yourself and your values. Strive to be the best you can in your own unique way. Good leaders come in many different guises – one size does not fit all.

Although academics may seek to capture and define the essence of mindful leadership, within this book the definition of a mindful leader is simply a leader who knows himself, takes personal responsibility for his actions, and makes a conscious effort to manage himself to be the best leader he can be.

By putting some effort into developing metacognition, treating yourself with kindness like a true friend, and trying to maintain an optimum state of mind, you'll be better able to be the best you can in any given situation. Remember: as a human being, you will probably always be a 'work in progress'. Cultivating mindfulness is a journey, not a destination. It can take a lifetime, but you can feel the benefits very quickly if you practice as you work through this book.

Recognising your stress levels

To reduce your stress levels, you need to first identify your current level of stress. There are numerous stress tests online that can help you to gauge your current level of stress. You can find a very simple stress indicator on the Resources page of my (Juliet's) website – www.aheadforwork.com.

Mindful strategies for leading in a VUCA world

Working in a VUCA world may be inevitable, but suffering as a result optional. When faced with volatility, try to build in some slack to allow for unexpected volatile eruptions. Develop staff to be able to deal with a broad range of circumstances, and keep your workforce as flexible and nimble as possible.

When faced with uncertainty, collect, interpret and share information. Pool resources and support easy sharing and access to information. The more information you can gather, the less uncertainty for all concerned.

When working with complexity, you may need to reconsider your organisational structure. Do you have adequate specialists located in the right parts of the organisation to analyse, make sense of and inform action on the volume of incoming data? Allow time to stand back and evaluate which information is key and which isn't worth the investment to make else of.

When working with ambiguity and the absence of any information, approach the challenge with an open mind and experiment. Test hypotheses, gather information, learn lessons, and eventually ambiguity will become certainty.

Mindfully Reducing Leadership Stress

Leadership can be a lonely, isolating job. It can also be exhilarating and rewarding. Although you can't always predict or control the cards that life deals you, you can learn to control your response to them. A core component of mindfulness is learning to observe your own unique patterns of thought and behaviour. This allows you to take control and become a wiser, more considered leader.

Minding the gap

Awareness of your patterns of thoughts and behaviour are essential to being a good leader. Thoughts can trigger emotions and tension in the body, which lead to stress. Until recently, these were largely overlooked by leadership and executive education programmes. Over the past few years, leading business schools have added mindfulness training to leadership and MBA programmes.

Basic instruction in mindfulness helps you to develop awareness of the impact of your thoughts on your actions as a leader. In addition, it can improve focus, decision-making and relationships with peers and subordinates.

As you learn to reduce the flow of incoming information into the brain (more about this in Chapter 8), you may start to notice that a considerable gap exists between how you think things are, or how you wish they were, and how they actually are (see Figure 2-1). In order to be a mindful leader, it's useful to consciously 'mind the gap'. The thoughts we think are not necessarily facts, but our brain often responds as if they are.

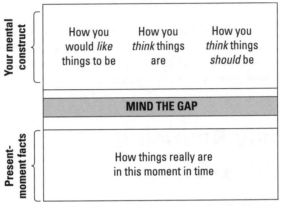

© John Wiley & Sons, Inc.

FIGURE 2-1: Mind the gap.

Mindful leaders learn to observe thoughts as simply mental processes that come and go without knee-jerk reactions.

To help you start to 'mind the gap', try the following:

TIP

>> See whether you can start to consciously 'mind the gap' in your daily life. Remember: you control your thoughts – your thoughts shouldn't control you!

>> Practice treating thoughts simply as mental processes that come and go rather than facts.

>> See whether you can notice how thoughts can evoke strong emotions or sensations in the body.

>> When you notice your thoughts spiralling down and depressive or negative thinking creeping in, take three minutes to do the three-step breathing space (see Chapter 10) to help you retain your equilibrium and consider things from a more objective viewpoint.

Gaining a sense of completion

Gaining a sense of completion can be a good way to diffuse stress.

At work, one task or project can easily merge into another, giving you the feeling that you're on a never-ending treadmill and are achieving nothing. The truth of the matter is that you've probably achieved a lot during the day; you have just failed to register a sense of completion.

TIP

To gain a better sense of completion, try the following:

>> Break down complex or lengthy tasks into subtasks. Consciously acknowledge completion of each subtask, activating your brain's feel-good reward circuitry.

>> Pair up small tasks with larger projects or tasks. As you complete these small tasks, acknowledge how they've contributed to the advancement and achievement of your larger project or task.

>> Celebrate each and every small win.

>> At the end of each workday before you go home, pause to reflect on and consciously acknowledge all the things you've accomplished in the day.

Engaging your recovery and renewal circuitry

Power stress, like any stress encountered over extended periods of time, makes the body susceptible to serious illness, digestive complaints and disturbed sleep patterns. It can drain your energy and capability to function and innovate.

Recovery and renewal can come from several sources. Small acts of kindness to yourself, others or even random strangers can have a hugely beneficial impact on your brain chemistry. Brain scans have revealed that even imagining an act of kindness, using virtual reality technology, can have the same positive impact on the brain as doing it for real.

Prioritise time to do things that you love doing that you may have stopped doing because you became 'too busy'. Go dancing, do stand-up comedy, go to the theatre, or just enjoy quality time with friends, family or pets. This time will help you to reduce stress and renew yourself, making you fitter to lead.

TIP

Make mindfulness part of your daily mental hygiene routine. It will help you to recover from the stresses and strains of the day and renew yourself by helping your brain chemistry to return to a rest and maintenance state.

Understanding that Mindfulness Is Not a Panacea for All Ills

Consider the following conversation:

> Sally: We've got a problem with Jim's leadership style. He's insensitive to the emotional needs of his team and thinks they should just 'get on with it'; his staff are feeling bullied.
>
> Bill: So are we going to sort out the bullying?
>
> Sally: No. We'll make Jim take a mindfulness course so he gets better at controlling his emotions.

REMEMBER

Mindfulness training shouldn't be made a mandatory part of a leader's development programme. Mindfulness training alone may not fix unwelcome behaviours at work. If leaders are open to learning about emotions and how they inform their behaviour and relationships at work, then it may help. However, mindfulness is not a panacea for all leadership ills.

Mindfulness alone is unlikely to fix systemic workplace or personality problems. In the same way that you can't force someone to lose weight by giving them a Weight Watchers membership, behavioural change can only occur if leaders are willing to rewire their brain by engaging in the exercises with curiosity, self-compassion and discipline.

Don't shoot the messenger

For a rare few, unexpected effects sometimes surface when they explore their experience by using mindfulness exercises. A lot of people keep themselves distracted and busy as a way of coping, maybe because they're afraid to look closely at their experience, so shining a light on emotions and bodily sensations during mindfulness exercises may bring up feelings of anxiety or even panic.

Natural emotional responses can be pleasant, unpleasant or neutral. This doesn't mean you're doing it wrong but may indicate that you need to explore your unpleasant emotions in an especially safe and compassionate way, particularly if they involve feelings of dissociation and enduring discomfort. This means seeking the advice of your doctor, occupational health team, or, if you have one, your mindfulness teacher.

The mindfulness meditation exercises aren't meant to be relaxing, but nor are they intended to cause unnecessary alarm or discomfort. If that is your experience, pull back from the edge of discomfort and seek professional support where you can discuss these side effects.

Be mindful of your breath

For a small minority, exercises that place focus on the breath may be disturbing, especially if you've had a history of breathing difficulties, asthma or panic attacks. If the latter or exercises involving breathing are a concern for you, seek medical support from your doctor and consider getting a mindfulness teacher. If you still want to explore the exercise, you can make the point of focus the sensations in your feet rather than the sensations of breath.

When to seek professional help

If you have a history of depression, alcohol or drug abuse, psychotic episodes, PTSD or any other clinical issues, you should check with your doctor before engaging with these exercises. If in doubt, pay attention to your concerns and check with your doctor. This advice is the same as if you had acute asthma and wanted to train to run a marathon – you'd be wise to seek medical and professional support first.

Chapter 3

Harnessing the Neuroscience of Mindful Leadership

T ake much of what you know about how the best leaders operate and forget it. Much of what we 'know' about the best way to get things done at work is being called into question by the latest neuroscience research. A basic knowledge of a few aspects of how the brain works and its hidden rules can prove invaluable if you want to improve your leadership impact while retaining your sanity!

This chapter offers you the basics you need to know in a practical and accessible format.

Grasping the Potential and Limitations of the Executive Brain

If you hold a position of power and authority within your organisation, you have responsibility for making key decisions upon which the future success of your organisation depends. With this comes responsibility for your employee's prosperity, not to mention your supplier's prosperity and the people who supply goods and services to your suppliers.

Recent neuroscience research is shining a spotlight on how the brains of the most effective leaders differ from the norm. It's still early days for this research, but studies indicate that many of the things you may think enhance performance are probably the opposite. We talk more about this in the final section of this chapter.

Setting aside these neurological differences, in the main, the executive brain is very much the same as anyone else's brain. This means that as a leader, you're blessed with the same incredibly powerful brain as the rest of your workforce – a brain more powerful than the most powerful super computer ever built, that's ever changing and evolving from the day you're born until the day you die, that's capable of re-authoring its own internal operating system and figuring out how to put man on the moon and how to split the atom.

Despite the unlimited potential of your brain, it does have a number of limitations. First, it doesn't come with an instruction manual. And unless your leadership education was very recent or you have a particular interest in neuroscience, you may have very little knowledge of what your brain is doing or why. So here's a little introduction to the human brain, its complexities, adaptability, and limitations.

The human brain 101

Humans have big brains. In the last 7 million years, the human brain has tripled in size. The fossil skulls of ancestors around 1.9 million years ago had an average brain size of 600 millilitres. More recent 500,000-year-old fossil skulls show a huge increase to around 1,000 millilitres. Modern brain size is around 1,200 millilitres, weighing around 1,300 grams or more. In comparison, a gorilla's brain is around 500 grams, and a chimp's brain, around 420 grams. The modern human brain evolved to have much larger regions devoted to planning, communication, problem solving and other more advanced cognitive functions.

To manage your mind better and understand its hidden rules, it's important to gain a basic understanding of how the brain is structured. See Figure 3-1.

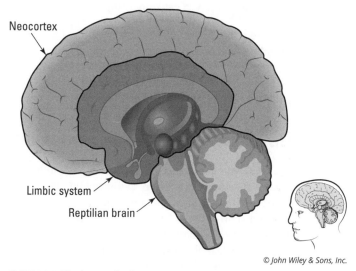

© John Wiley & Sons, Inc.

FIGURE 3-1: The human brain.

At the base of the brain is a cluster of structures referred to as the *reptilian brain*. This part of the brain controls your most vital functions, such as sleep, heart rate, breathing and the like. Its innate and reflex control programs help you to survive.

Above this is a cluster of structures referred to as the *limbic system*, which are associated with social and nurturing behaviours. While reptilian brain structures rely heavily on instinctive behaviours, the limbic system adds an emotional dimension. Emotions are the brain's way of remembering how different situations affect you.

The limbic system and reptilian brain combined are often described as the *primitive brain.*

At the top of the brain, the *neocortex* (the wrinkly bit you see in pictures) is a cluster of brain structures involved in advanced cognition — the mental process of acquiring knowledge and understanding through thought, experience and the senses. These structures are responsible for special human traits, such as planning, decision-making, reasoning language, thought and impulse control. They enable you to move from reaction to reaction so you not only respond to external stimuli but also are able to take action to get something to happen.

The neocortex gives you the ability not to take action in specific situations and equips you with the opportunity to reflect on your feelings and thus suppress or inhibit more impulsive reactions that are activated lower down in the brain. The neocortex brain structures give you awareness of yourself.

Boosting your neuroplasticity

The term *neuroplasticity* is derived from the root words *neuron* and *plastic.* It's a term that refers to the brain's ability to change and adapt as a result of experience. Up until the 1960s, researchers believed that changes in the brain could only take place during infancy and childhood. It was thought that by early adulthood, the brain's physical structure was permanent. Modern research has proven that the brain continues to create new neural pathways and alter existing ones to adapt to new experiences and learn new information until the day you die.

Neuroplasticity has two forms:

>> Your brain's ability to move functions from a damaged area of the brain to other undamaged areas is referred to as

functional plasticity. After a stroke, for instance, your brain can reorganise itself to move functions to undamaged areas.

>> Your brain's ability to actually change its physical structure as a result of learning is called *structural plasticity.* An example of this might be an increase or decrease in grey matter in specific brain areas as a consequence of experience and learning

The human brain is composed of approximately 100 billion nerve cells called *neurons.* Neural pathways transmit data from one neuron to another quickly by passing an electrical or chemical signal from one neuron to another neuron via the synapse (see Figure 3-2). Neurons that fire together wire together, forming strong connections over time. Each time you repeat a particular thought or action, you strengthen this connection, making it easier to repeat in the future.

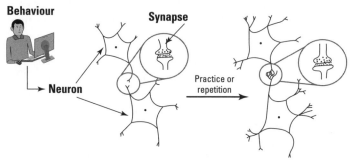

"Neuron's that fire together, wire together"

© John Wiley & Sons, Inc.

FIGURE 3-2: Neuroplasticity in action.

A good example of neuroplasticity has been found in London taxi drivers. A cab driver's *hippocampus* (part of the limbic system that holds spatial representation capacity) is measurably larger than that of a bus driver. By driving the same route every day, the bus drivers don't need to exercise this part of the brain as much. The cabbies, on the other hand, rely on it constantly for navigation.

REMEMBER

You can no longer solely blame your parents or genes for the way you behave – you are also a product of your experiences and thoughts so take responsibility for yourself!

Habits are formed by repeating an action or thought many times, creating neuropathways that act as information superhighways. Habits are never really erased from the brain, but they can be replaced by new, more dominant ones that you can consciously cultivate.

Becoming conscious of your unconscious

How much of your brain's activity are you actually aware of? Many neuroscientists estimate 98 per cent or more of all brain activity is completely unconscious. Unconscious brain activity includes housekeeping functions, such as breathing, keeping your heart beating, digesting food, and controlling and coordinating muscle action. It also includes repetition of activities you've done many times before, such as using a computer keyboard or flicking a light switch on. These functions are largely the responsibility of the primitive brain, which is highly energy efficient and very fast to respond.

Many higher functions that you'd typically associate with thought and reasoning also remain unconscious. The very highest level of brain activity is thoughts that you're aware of – *conscious thoughts.* Conscious thoughts represent a minute amount of overall brain function.

Conscious thought emerges from the neocortex. The neocortex is incredibly powerful but very energy hungry. This explains why when attending a training course to learn something new, or maybe reading this book, you may feel very tired. In comparison to the primitive brain, the neocortex is slow to respond.

If faced with a mortal threat, such as a car hurtling towards you, your primitive brain will take control, weigh the options, decide on the best course of action, and get you to a place of safety rapidly. Only afterwards might you consciously think "what happened?" or "I nearly died!" Most would agree that in this circumstance, the primitive brain taking control is a good thing. The downside of this is that your brain will often default back to habits or old ways of responding stored in the primitive brain, which may not be appropriate to the task in hand.

To maintain your precious energy reserves, your brain will always default to old tried and tested ways of doing things, stored in the energy-efficient primitive brain, and conscious effort is needed to engage the neocortex to stand back and see the big picture. Knowledge of this inbuilt brain tendency is invaluable for leaders. Becoming a more mindful leader raises your awareness of what's going on in your mind and provides you with tools to manage it.

REMEMBER

Many leaders are under the delusion that they're always consciously in control and their decisions are based on logic and weighing all the facts. This is frequently not the case. The brain will default back to habits and old familiar ways of thinking and behaving, and it takes conscious effort to do things differently. Awareness of the brain's default mode will help you to break out of old patterns of behaviour and become more creative and effective as a leader.

Recognising Your Hidden Drivers

A little understanding of the brain can go a long way. In this section, you find information on four of your brain's key drivers and tendencies which can have a big impact on your whole life.

Maximising reward, minimising threat

One of the brains primary functions is to maximise reward while minimising threat. Our ancient ancestors faced regular threats to their life from animal and, at times, human attacks. The brain's strategy to maximise reward and minimise threat has been highly successful in evolutionary terms, arguably making humans the most successful species on the planet. Despite this, when faced with things that you find challenging or threatening, your response may be primitive or instinctive rather than logical.

Despite the evolution and growth of your neocortex, which is responsible for planning, decision-making and reasoning (see the earlier section 'The human brain 101'), when faced with challenging situations, your primitive brain is usually in the driving seat. Situations like challenging meetings, making important presentations, or dealing with conflict, are frequently perceived as a threat by the brain.

To understand more about this, it's useful to understand a little more about what goes on in your body when faced with situations your brain thinks are threatening.

Exploring fight, flight or freeze

Instincts are inbuilt mechanisms. They're not something you have to learn because they're inbuilt. They're there to help you survive. Whether you're fending off a lion or delivering a best man's speech, fear responses are hard-wired in your brain. When threatening stimuli are received by your eyes or ears, signals are sent straight to the *amygdala* – your fear system, located in your limbic system – which uses its bank of conditioned responses, the most common of which is fight, flight or freeze. Here's an example of how it works.

Say that you're asked to make a presentation to a new client. It gets off to a poor start when your computer fails, and the client looks impatient and starts looking at his watch. Your brain generates thoughts about looking stupid, about showing your company in a bad light, of what your colleagues think of you, and possible negative repercussions.

Your amygdala detects a threat. Unfortunately, it doesn't differentiate between a life-threatening situation and the non-life-threatening situation of making a presentation. It simply detects a threat. In response, the amygdala triggers your *sympathetic nervous system* (SNS), triggering a chain reaction designed to help you sprint away from the type of mortal dangers your ancient ancestors faced. You freeze on the stage, as your *thalamus* (a junction for a number of survival-related responses) decides what to do.

Your brain decides that fleeing from the stage (flight) isn't a viable option and instead urges you to confront the situation (fight). Your blood flow to muscles increases, along with your breathing and heart rate and blood sugar levels, so you can run faster. Blood-clotting agents are released into your bloodstream to help stem bleeding if you're injured. At the same time, your digestion, your cell repair and regrowth, and your immune system switches down or off. This is because digesting food and warding off bugs are unnecessary when you're facing death.

The latter physiological response is disproportionate to the actual threat faced (struggling to make a presentation). Despite the non-threatening nature of the situation, you're still likely to default to fight or flight mode. All this occurs long before logic kicks in and your neocortex regains control.

The length of time that you are in 'fight or flight' SNS activation depends on how quickly you detect what's going on. Practicing mindfulness helps you to detect this faster, stopping your thoughts and emotions from spiralling out of control. Doing so triggers your parasympathetic nervous system (PNS), associated with mental clarity, rest, and repair, sending messages to the brain to relax and return to normal and that everything is okay. This puts your neocortex back into the driving seat, and rationality and logic return.

Recognising the human negativity bias

The other thing to consider when facing challenges is the human negativity bias. In ancient times, when our ancestors faced mortal threats, they had to be constantly vigilant to avoid sudden death. In response, the brain devoted more of its resources to look for potential dangers rather than potential opportunities. The same is still true today.

Hundreds of scientific studies confirm this negativity bias. A good day has little lasting impact on the following day, but a bad day is likely to be carried over to the next day or even longer. The human brain processes negative data faster and more thoroughly than positive data. Socially, people invest more in avoiding a bad reputation than in building a good one. Emotionally, people go to greater lengths to avoid a bad mood than to experience a good one. Becoming a more mindful leader helps you to recognise negative thought patterns and put things back into perspective and balance.

Of all the cognitive biases, the negativity bias has a huge influence over people's lives. Although times have changed, and you're no longer braving the harsh retribution of nature, the instinct that protected humans over millions of years of evolution is now a drag, threatening your intimate relationships and destabilising teams at work.

Recognising the wandering mind

A final human brain trait that's worth exploring is the mind's tendency to wander. Recent Harvard research by Killingsworth and Gilbert published in 2010 explored the extent to which the mind wanders. The research involved 2,250 adults living in the United States and concluded that, on average, the brain wanders around 47 per cent of the time. On average, people were unhappier when their mind wandered. The report also concluded that what people were thinking was a better predictor of their happiness than what they were doing.

REMEMBER

Becoming a more mindful leader won't stop your mind from wandering. What it will do is help you to quickly recognise that it has wandered, enabling you to refocus your attention more quickly, stepping out of autopilot and back into control. This in turn can make you more focused and productive. It can also help you maintain an optimum state of mind by stopping your thoughts from spiralling into negativity.

Establishing How Mindfulness Works

Until relatively recently, books about mindfulness have focused on how to practice rather than why or how it works. As we outline in Chapter 1, mindfulness involves the development of metacognition. By observing your patterns of thoughts, emotions and bodily sensations and their interplay with one another, you're better able to maintain a positive state of mind (calm, focused, creative and optimistic), enabling you to be the best you can.

Mindfulness training has four elements. Formal and informal daily practice help the brain embed and develop mindfulness capabilities including the ability to focus and maintain attention, observe without reactivity, suspend judgment, accept and move on and adopt an approach orientation. This is coupled with practical psychological tools to apply to life and underpinning knowledge, which helps the brain link to existing knowledge and strengthen neuro-pathways. Figure 3-3 illustrates how these four elements come together and develop mindfulness.

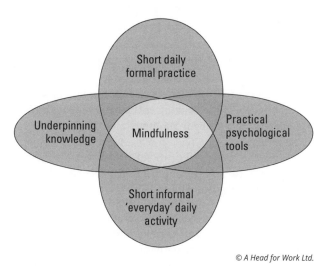

© A Head for Work Ltd.

FIGURE 3-3: How mindfulness is developed.

At a very basic level, when you sit down to formally practice mindfulness, the following happens.

Stage 1: Setting intent

You start by setting the intent to be mindful by sitting in an upright, open, relaxed posture that embodies confidence, self-acceptance and wakefulness. This is important for two reasons. Firstly, it's difficult to remain open-minded, curious and accepting when your body is uncomfortable. Secondly, by adopting this position every time you formally practice, you signal to the brain your intention to focus on present experience, observing and accepting whatever arises without triggering habitual responses, or triggering a spiral of judgments, thoughts and emotions.

TECHNICAL STUFF

Research into body posture reveals that how your body feels has a profound impact on your decisions. Researchers have discovered that when sitting up straight, people are more likely to remember positive memories. In comparison, another experiment concluded that slumping does the exact opposite, draining you of your energy. Another study used saliva samples to show that open, expansive postures positively altered participants' hormone levels, decreasing cortisol (a hormone responsible for stress).

Stage 2: Focused concentration

By focusing on one thing, such as the breath or sensations in different parts of the body, over time you reduce the flow of incoming information. Your thoughts about your work, career or that argument you just had slow or stop, and in response the brain detects that the level of threat has reduced, switching down the SNS response and switching up the PNS rest, relaxation and mental clarity circuitry.

FMRI brain scans reveal that contrary to popular belief, when practicing mindfulness, the brain's metabolic activity increases, making you more aware of what's going on. As you focus your attention and become less aware of sensory information stemming from your external environment, you become less aware of your orientation in space and time, and you experience a decrease of activity in the right parietal lobe. This explains why when you sit down to practice mindfulness, ten minutes can feel like either five minutes or an hour.

Stage 3: Open monitoring

When your brain settles into a more relaxed state, you're able to openly monitor what's happening, moment by moment. It becomes possible to observe cognitive processes, along with the bodily sensations that they trigger, increasing your self-knowledge and ability to self-regulate. You learn to observe thoughts simply as mental processes, observing them arising and dissipating.

Recognising the importance of kindness and acceptance

Two key principles than underpin the practice of mindfulness are kindness (trying not to be so hard on yourself and others) and acceptance (acknowledging the facts and moving on). We explore each in turn and bust some myths.

Kindness

Kindness is an important element of mindfulness, not because it's nice to be nice but because it's impossible to be in fight or flight (threat response) at the same time as being accepting and kind to yourself. In addition, recent research conducted in a virtual reality suit concluded that even by thinking about being kind to others, you experience positive benefits, such as activation of your PNS and reduction of your SNS.

Without kindness, the concentration phase of mindfulness practice becomes merely a means of self-control. In addition, you may experience dissociation, which can range from a mild detachment from your immediate surroundings to more severe detachment from physical and emotional experience.

Acceptance

When practicing mindfulness , the application of non-judgmental acceptance of your brain's unique patterns and behaviour, and simply accepting your current transient mind state, you increase your confidence.

In more general terms, the act of acceptance is a method of parking things and stopping them from escalating in your head – more about this in Chapter 12.

Mindfulness without self-acceptance and kindness can lead to frustration and increased, rather than reduced, brain chatter. Increased self-acceptance and kindness help you to understand others and treat them with kindness, helping both you and your work colleauges to be the best you can be.

2

Learning from Mindful Leaders

Discover how a market trader became managing director of Marks & Spencer and is now a member of the UK Parliament, thanks to mindfulness training.

Identify practical ways that a naval commander incorporated mindfulness into his work.

See how a senior leader developed mindfulness to overcome depression and find new, more productive ways of working.

Chapter 4

Case Study 1: Andrew Stone, Baron Stone of Blackheath

I n the next three chapters, you find three case studies, each featuring a leader who practices mindfulness. The case studies provide information on how these leaders developed their mindfulness, the practical ways that it helps them, and tips for leaders like you, who are just starting your mindfulness journey.

This chapter tells the fascinating story of Andrew Stone – a market trader who is now a member of the House of Lords.

The Impact of Mindfulness on Andrew's Work

As a child, Andrew Stone suffered from dyslexia, which at that time was seldom recognised in schools. As a result, he became rebellious and was expelled from school with no qualifications at the age of 16. He had two brothers who were academically gifted, and he felt that his failure in school had consigned him to, in his own words, 'a life in the gutter'. He started working on a street market in the 1950s, regarding himself as a 'hardened spiv'. Luckily, others recognised his potential to be a brilliant retailer.

In 1977, Andrew came to the attention of the chairman of Marks & Spencer (M&S), Sir Marcus Sieff, who took him on as his personal assistant and became his mentor. Andrew worked for M&S for 33 years, rapidly progressing in the company, despite his lack of education. In 1982, he was promoted to head of menswear, a department then worth £450 million.

Andrew became director of M&S from 1990 to 1994 then joint managing director from 1994 to 1999, overseeing a time of financial prosperity and retailing success.

In the 1990s, Prime Minister Tony Blair was keen to reduce the number of hereditary peers in the House of Lords. He created a number of new life peers from a range of backgrounds. Andrew became a life peer as Baron Stone of Blackheath on 29 October 1997.

While working in Parliament, Andrew has been tasked with a number of highly sensitive Middle Eastern negotiations, one of which we describe shortly. Mindfulness has had a significant impact on his life. Andrew strongly believes that mindfulness has given him the courage to take on tasks he would never have believed himself capable to do and has changed the way he thinks and works, and he feels more productive and happier as a result.

In this section, you find a number of examples of how mindfulness has impacted Andrew's ability to lead.

Mindful negotiations in the Middle East

In 1977, Israel and Egypt had fought four wars, and Israel occupied the Sinai Peninsula, part of Egypt that it captured in 1967. At that time in 1977, M&S executives thought that Egypt may make peace with Israel, and M&S wanted to support and encourage this. It was already buying 5 per cent of its stock from Israel and started to investigate what it could buy from Egypt. Andrew was sent to the Middle East to source goods to buy and, over time, developed a good understanding of Middle Eastern culture and sensitivities.

When Andrew became managing director of M&S, he reasoned that by M&S trading with different Middle Eastern countries, peace might be encouraged. He encouraged M&S to start buying from Morocco, Tunisia, Egypt and Lebanon. He reasoned that if all these countries in the Middle East and North were doing business, peace might prevail. Although this didn't work, Andrew gained a reputation for someone who understood the Middle Eastern culture, was curious, and had everyone's best interests at heart.

On 3 July 2013, Egyptian Army Chief General Abdel Fattah el-Sisi led a coalition to remove the President of Egypt Mohamed Morsi. El-Sisi wanted a new constitution, elections, and a new parliament and wanted a number of prominent external people to oversee the process. The U.K. government was struggling to engage with officials, and Andrew was posted to Egypt to help. He became a key link in the communication between the orthodox British parliamentarians and those in power in Egypt.

At that time, Israel wanted to strengthen its links with Egypt. General el-Sisi of Egypt was also keen to do so. Andrew played a key role as an intermediary in many delicate conversations, being invited to private meetings with General el-Sisi and Benjamin Netanyahu, the Prime Minister of Israel.

Andrew found himself becoming nervous and apprehensive because so much was at stake. After practicing mindfulness one day, he recognised that he needed to 'stop being Andrew' and 'see the people involved as simply human beings, part of the human race'. He reasoned that if the people negotiating could see each other's narratives and he could approach everyone involved with openness, setting aside his personal judgments and prejudices, he could make a difference.

Andrew also recognised that the people he was negotiating with were in a state of fear and that their primitive brain could be forcing them into fear-based, autopilot responses. Until he could make them feel safe and secure, they would be unlikely to think creatively about the way forward. This helped him to have the courage to move things forward as, in his own words, 'I had nothing to lose or gain – only my life and I don't care because I am 74. I was simply there to help the meetings happen and to help them to communicate'.

Being mindful, Andrew felt able to set aside his ego and encourage others to do the same – offering himself to do whatever was needed. Working towards a higher purpose of helping humanity as a whole, he was able to approach the negotiations from a place of care and compassion for his fellow human beings rather than from an ego-fuelled state, looking only at what he or his country could gain from the negotiations.

Mindful leadership at M&S

How was it that a kid of 27 joined M&S with no education and became the managing director of a £10 billion company with 37,000 employees? Possibly because he applied mindful principles to many aspects of his leadership at M&S, although at the time he was often unaware he was doing so.

Andrew was lucky to have a number of people who believed in him, even when he didn't fully believe in himself. At M&S, his first manager, the then Chairman of M&S Sir Marcus Sieff, encouraged him to contribute and share his ideas and opinions, even though he was working at a very junior level. This helped him gain promotion to the executive of menswear.

As the new executive of menswear, people asked Andrew what to do and how to drive the department forward. Andrew realised that he didn't know. Having worked with the chairman, Andrew realised that Marcus didn't know either, and neither did the board or other members of the executive team. Many people in his position would have embarked on an ego-driven rampage to make their mark, adopting the control-and-demand leadership style commonly in use at that time.

Instead, Andrew realised that the best thing to do was to 'drop [his] ego, stop being Andrew and be the 14 million customers and 37,000 employees and the suppliers'. Andrew simply told his team that he didn't know what to do and wanted to hear their ideas. He then sat back and listened with an open mind and eventually (sometimes after hours, other times after days), the answer would emerge. This honest, open, people-centric, mindful approach to leadership was very unusual at the time.

Only later did Andrew realise that during these meetings when he sat back to listen he was actually getting himself into an approach-oriented, mindful state of mind, looking for new possibilities with openness and a sense of curiosity and wonder. He later recognised that at these moments he stopped being "Andrew's thoughts and emotions" and instead tapped into his higher consciousness, entering a state of flow, seeing things more holistically, and viewing M&S as a living organisation.

Andrew believes that his daily mindfulness practice helps him to tap into this state of mind whenever he needs to pay close attention to something complex during the day.

Mindful work in parliament

When Andrew became a peer in 1997, he immediately noticed the aggressive, combative, protectionist nature of being in parliament. Initially he hated it because he liked to get things done by collaboration, and he became frustrated.

Andrew recognised that mindfulness was much needed in parliament, but this did not fully come to fruition until parliamentarians were offered mindfulness training based on the best-selling book *Mindfulness: A Practical Guide to Finding Peace in a Frantic World*, by Professor Mark Williams and Danny Penman (published by Piatkus). A growing number of people have attended mindfulness training (so far around 130 Members of Parliament [MPs] and 180 parliamentary staff), and they are slowly starting to change the way that they do business in parliament.

For example, when an argument occurs in the debating chambers, MPs and parliamentary staff from all parties who have attended mindfulness training now swap sympathetic glances and try to ensure that they get their viewpoint across firmly but in a less hostile and combative manner. They make a conscious effort to try to understand each other's points of view.

Mindful self-management

Mindfulness allows Andrew to see his own anxiety, anger and patterns of behaviour. He believes that this helps him to be kinder to himself and to others around him.

If Andrew sees someone holding an opposing political view becoming angry and argumentative, he takes a moment to pause and try to understand where that person is coming from, where he is now and the emotions he may be experiencing. He recognises that when in the grip of strong emotions, others' actions may be driven by their primitive brain and that they may be unable to tap into higher brain creative thinking. In response, Andrew tries to find ways to help them become calmer and move towards a more optimal state of mind, in which they're more likely to achieve the outcomes they desire.

Andrew monitors and regulates his impulses. When emotive issues (such as flood defences and the Middle East) are up for debate, in the past he would have responded in an 'argumentative aggressive confrontational manner'. He now takes a moment to put himself in a more mindful state of mind and focuses his energy on finding a solution that is good for everybody, including those with opposing viewpoints.

Cultivating happiness

In 2012, Andrew shared an office with fellow parliamentarian Baron Richard Layard who was co-editing the World Happiness Report. Richard is an economist and professor who works as programme director of the Centre for Economic Performance at the London School of Economics.

One day Richard entered the office and said, 'Andrew, you are driving me mad. I'm trying to write a publication on happiness, and I'm miserable, and every time you walk in the office you are happy. You go to work, and you are happy; you go home, and you are happy – what the hell's going on?' Andrew explained to Richard that he practiced mindfulness and as a result woke up happy. Richard told him 'don't be so stupid'. Andrew and Richard's wife later persuaded Richard to attend mindfulness training. He is now a strong advocate of mindfulness and speaks on the importance of clarity of thinking and mental and physical health.

Andrew's Mindfulness Experience and Practice

In this section, you discover why Andrew was motivated to become more mindful. You also find out how he practices mindfulness and makes it part of his everyday life.

Finding the motivation

Despite Andrew's lack of education and lack of life skills, in 1977 the chairman of M&S, Sir Marcus Sieff, recognised his potential and employed Andrew as his personal assistant. He took Andrew under his wing and started to mentor him. For the next ten years or so, Andrew was rapidly promoted. He worked long hours and eventually suffered a burnout. His doctor prescribed time off work and recommended that he learn mindfulness.

Developing mindfulness

Andrew first attended an intensive mindfulness retreat, practicing for four hours a day. As a result, he was able to gain some perspective on his life. Andrew came to recognise the importance of balancing the following needs:

» His basic needs in life (shelter, money, a sense of belonging)

» The demands of business (planning and strategy)

> **»** His need for a higher sense of purpose (ethics, principles, making people happy, helping humanity)

Mindfulness helped Andrew to balance the demands placed on him by the first two needs (the base and middle of Abraham Maslow's hierarchy of needs; see Chapter 1) while striving towards making a real difference in the world and being the best human being he could be (the top of Maslow's hierarchy of needs).

From that point forward, mindfulness became a part of Andrew's life, and he now practices mindfulness every day.

Andrew has attended various mindfulness trainings over the years and has read a number of books on the subject. Most recently in parliament, he attended eight weeks of MBCT mindfulness training based on the book *Mindfulness: A Practical Guide to Finding Peace in a Frantic World.* He attends weekly mindfulness drop-in sessions in parliament with other MPs and parliamentarians.

Incorporating mindfulness every day

Despite being in his 70s now, Andrew still works for around 12 hours a day. He usually gets to bed around 11 p.m., falling into a deep sleep. Whereas in the past he would have woken early and started worrying and ruminating about the day ahead, Andrew now wakes at around 4 a.m. and gets up to practice mindfulness. He usually practices for around 40 to 50 minutes then goes back to sleep for around 2 hours, having cooled his mind, and then, as he reports, he wakes up happy.

Andrew's Hints and Tips

Andrew believes that the way in which many people live their lives today is unsustainable, not good physically or mentally and not conducive to being fully effective at work. He recognises that getting out of a rut and changing the way you think, behave and respond to life can be very difficult on your own. Mindfulness can provide you with a structure to learn and a better way to live and work in the following ways:

>> Being mindful can help you develop a state in which you recognise the interconnectivity of everything and everyone.

>> Mindfulness will help release you from the ego-driven behaviour and enable you to work with others rather than against them.

>> Practicing mindfulness will help you to stop seeing everything as against you and separate from you and help you to monitor your thoughts, emotions and bodily responses to the challenges and pleasures of life. Doing so will allow you to maintain an optimum brain state and be more productive while at the same time improving your well-being.

REMEMBER

Everyone deserves to live a happy life, and your role as a leader is to help others around you to be as happy as possible. Happy people are more productive and engaged – and making people happy can make you happy, too. Remember that goodness is not weakness, and you can overcome fear. Mindfulness can help you to become the best person you can be.

Leadership Insights

Mindfulness helps Andrew to manage himself better. By learning to observe his emotional responses and thoughts, he can prevent himself from being drawn into inappropriate and unhelpful responses and diffuse negative emotions, even when under immense pressure in critical Middle Eastern negotiations.

Mindfulness has helped Andrew to work more effectively with those who may have sharply opposing views. By viewing angry colleagues as fellow human beings, Andrew is able to interact with them in a less combative manner and bring out the best in them.

No leaders have all the answers, although some may think they do! Mindful leaders let go of their ego and provide the right environment for others to help them to find the answers and creatively solve problems.

By focusing on the 'greater good' and thinking further than their balance sheet, businesses can find sustainable and profitable new ways to do business while making a positive impact on their communities.

To date, around 310 MPs and staff have taken part in mindfulness training. By being an informal advocate for mindfulness, Andrew is playing an important role in making the UK parliament a more mindful place to work.

Andrew first learnt mindfulness in a retreat setting and now practices mindfulness for 40 to 50 minutes a day early in the morning. How and where you learn mindfulness, along with how long you practice for and where, is up to you. Find a way that works for you.

Andrew discovered mindfulness when he experienced burnout at work. By developing a regular mindfulness practice now, a burnout won't become an inevitable part of your future.

Chapter 5

Case Study 2: Tim Neild, Royal Navy Commander

Tim's career spans 25 years in the Royal Navy as a Warfare Officer, at the sharp end. He has spent the majority of that time at sea, all over the world in various operational scenarios, which have included Iraq, Libya and other hotspots around the world. He has commanded warships on operations, as well as held senior staff positions in the United Kingdom Task Group, protecting his nation's interests worldwide.

Recently Tim spent a year at Cranfield University undertaking an MBA programme before returning to the Royal Navy Headquarters to take up a staff position in acquisition.

The Impact of Mindfulness on Tim's Work

Tim has lots of examples of how mindfulness is helping him in his work as a naval leader. He feels that 'the net effect of mindfulness is that my performance has increased and the quality of my output has improved'.

Mindfulness has become an integral part of Tim's daily routine: 'I use it all the time. It's not something where I specifically say, "and now I am deploying mindfulness to do this". I've just got into a space now where it's just part and parcel of my everyday life'.

When Tim compares his life now, post mindfulness, to his life pre mindfulness he says, 'I genuinely think it's had a positive effect on my performance. I liken it to having a volume button for your brain'.

Working under pressure

Military operations present a number of different scenarios on a daily basis. Although Tim has never been one to buckle under stress, he recognises that when you operate in a high tempo environment, it's very easy to allow your mind to race, to want to answer the problem as quickly and as efficiently as possible and move onto the next problem that presents thereafter.

When the going gets tough, rather than just gritting his teeth and getting through a situation using a combination of courage, commitment, determination and know-how, Tim is able to 'take a more objective view with much greater clarity' and this allows him to 'plot a more efficient course of action to achieve the same outcome, but in a much more thoughtful, less stressful manner'.

Tim thinks that mindfulness allows you to 'just pause two marching paces and think with greater clarity. You get the same result but lead in a much more measured fashion'.

Maintaining balance and perspective

Tim reports that 'mindfulness gives me a much more balanced view of life. I'm definitely more engaging and I think I am equally more engaged in the situation as a result, because I'm more in the present. My attitude to risk and stress is improved and as a result of that, my net performance has increased. I think these techniques should not be underestimated'.

Remaining focused in meetings

Tim also reports that he is now better able to remain focused during meetings. He says, 'At the first glimmer of mind wandering, I can very quickly refocus my attention on the breathing spot, take a few seconds to focus simply on breathing, and then I'm able to bring my attention straight back to the meeting in a heartbeat. My performance has definitely improved as a result of practicing these mindfulness techniques'.

When in a meeting or interacting with colleagues or clients, mindfulness techniques allow Tim to be 'much more in the present and therefore give a much better account of yourself in personal interactions'.

Improving personal effectiveness and productivity

Tim reports, 'Without a shadow of a doubt, I think mindfulness techniques have a positive effect on everything including interactions with colleagues and clients. They make negotiations more efficient, they bring clarity to decision making and it definitely increases your awareness of risk and therefore make you a more resilient and less encumbered person when operating in a stressful environment. There is something in these techniques that everybody can take away'.

Improving sleep quality

A Naval Officer's sleep pattern can be very broken. When on patrol, Senior Officers may be frequently woken in the night by more junior watch-keeping officers to make important decisions about how the ship should manoeuvre to avoid risk of collision, or regarding other matters of ship safety. Trying to sleep whilst having the expectation that your sleep might be broken at any moment to take a report and make a decision, with potentially life-changing consequences, isn't necessarily a recipe for a good night's sleep.

As a consequence, Tim was a fairly light sleeper until he encountered mindfulness. Once he'd got used to 'clearing his head and generating some headspace', he found the impact 'absolutely amazing. I've never slept so well in my life'.

Despite being woken up, Tim was able to get back to sleep more quickly and sleep more deeply. Even when Tim is working hard and has as little as three or four hours a night 'thanks to mindfulness I get good quality sleep which in turn has a positive effect on the next day's performance'.

Becoming more self-aware

Tim feels that 'the most compelling part' of learning to be a more mindful leader is the 'self-awareness and the confidence that you can generate knowing that you've got a technique in your armory for every situation that arrives. I think as a result of being more mindful, I am certainly a much more attentive person to be around'.

Tim's Mindfulness Experience and Practice

Tim first discovered the discipline of mindfulness whilst studying for an MBA at Cranfield University's School of Management in 2013/14. The MBA at Cranfield majored heavily on self-development, so Tim spent much of his year introspectively analysing himself, supported by the Cranfield team.

Finding the motivation to learn about mindfulness

As part of his MBA programme, Tim had an executive coach for a year who encouraged him to try out new techniques for self-improvement. A member of the lecturing team at Cranfield, Dr Jutta Tobias, inspired Tim to consider mindfulness as a technique that might assist his leadership.

Halfway through the MBA, Jutta presented Tim and his fellow MBA cohort with an opportunity to try out mindfulness, through a visiting lecturer, mindfulness teacher Per Norrgren. Per presented a short session about mindfulness, which culminated with the opportunity to give mindfulness a try. Tim left the presentation thinking, 'Do you know what, there might just be something in this'. It was then that, in his own words, 'the penny dropped for me. I started to understand what Jutta was talking about and the techniques that Per was advocating. It was somewhat of an epiphany!'

Developing mindfulness

Per's introductory presentation at Cranfield revolved around improving leadership performance through focusing on the present and raising your awareness of yourself through mindfulness techniques. Tim concluded that after years of training and operating in the Royal Navy he had a unique opportunity to try something different and decided to pay attention to these techniques, as they might deliver unknown benefit.

Through Cranfield, Tim then had the opportunity to undertake a mindfulness course with his MBA cohort, again led by Per Norrgren, The mindfulness course focused on balancing thoughts and using mindfulness techniques to be more in the present. Per taught a specially adapted six-week course for one hour a week, with the requirement to formally practice mindfulness each day for a short period of time. Tim said, 'that is when the discipline was really cemented for me'.

Incorporating mindfulness into every day

Since completing the MBA in 2014, Tim has been posted to a new assignment, developing Naval Warships of the future. He is now working in the Royal Navy Command Headquarters, running a £2.5 billion equipment portfolio, setting the strategy and conducting the planning to efficiently deliver, effective, agile and coherent maritime capability to meet future needs of a World-Class Navy. In his own words, 'I have come from high tempo operations on the front line to high tempo operations in the rear echelon. It's all consuming in terms of my time, but incredibly rewarding!'

Since attending mindfulness training, he continues to reinforce it, researching and practicing regularly 'to optimize the benefits gained from it'. Tim has backed his training up with the Headspace app on his smartphone, which he finds 'very, very useful. It's ideal for sitting on a train in the morning or taking ten minutes for a little bit of down time. I will go to Headspace and Take Ten within my daily routine'. Tim further reports:

> When I get up in the morning, I spend ten minutes in the shower. I've got to a place with mindfulness now where I use my shower time to effectively conduct what you might call a body scan and really bring my sensory perception alive through the feeling of the water on my head. This may sound odd, but it really works.

> I also use my dead time in the car driving to work, using a steering wheel tapping technique advocated by Per. By tapping the steering wheel and feeling every single tap, I free up space in my mind and align my thoughts.

> When I go to bed in the evening, I usually spend the first 10 or 15 minutes just lying in bed winding down and clearing my head using mindful techniques before getting an amazing night's sleep as a result.

> I try to weave mindfulness into my daily routine. Whilst walking, I try to really focus on every single step, from heel to toe, and the feeling of the foot hitting the ground. That generates the same effect as some of the more formal mindfulness techniques that I practice.

If Tim does not find ten minutes to practice mindfulness during the day, he kicks himself. He says, 'I think we should all be able to find ten minutes in a day at some point, even if it's just whilst you're sitting on the sofa in the evening, having a cup of tea! I'm married, I've got two children and sometimes life just passes me by in a heartbeat as I'm sure it does for most people, but ten minutes of mindfulness can make a huge difference'.

Tim's Hints and Tips

Tim likens mindfulness to the activity of running. Technically we can all run, but some of us are better at it than others. The more you practice it, the better you become and the fitter you get, and more it adds value elsewhere in your life. Mindfulness is a bit like this. We can all do it, some will find it easier than others, but the more we practice it, the greater the benefits that can be gained.

In business, we talk about profit and loss. Whether it's the military or a commercial setting, all organisations deal with profit and loss in some way, shape or form. If somebody told you that you could positively impact your profit and loss figures through a free technique, you'd be a fool not to do it. Mindfulness is that free tool – available to everyone.

People can be put off by the title 'mindfulness'. Some are aware of what it is and get it the first time, whilst others have no idea and you need to demystify it or challenge their misconceptions. Tim says, 'I think the more that we as leaders demystify mindfulness and get this out in the public domain, the better. There really are some super benefits to be had from these techniques'.

Tim's advice for leaders considering mindfulness is 'don't knock it till you've tried it'. Start with something basic like the Headspace app, for instance, give it a try and see whether or not you can eke some benefit out of it. Equally, books like this give people an opportunity to experience and hear firsthand of the benefits of this discipline, in order to decide for yourself whether or not there's some benefit to be had from it. 'The bottom line is that by investing ten minutes a day, you can increase your performance and output markedly by having a much more attuned mind'.

Leadership Insights

Unlike Marion and Andrew, the other mindful leaders featured in the mindful leadership case studies in this book, Tim attended a short, work-focused mindfulness training course. The up-skilling that Tim gained from just six hours of mindfulness training and practicing for a short time each day illustrate the benefits to be gained from work-focused mindfulness programmes. This case study illustrates that work-focused mindfulness programmes such as the one taught by Per Norrgren (www.inmindsight.com.) or WorkplaceMT (http://workplacemt.com) have the potential to produce highly desirable workplace outcomes.

The quality of your sleep has a direct impact on your ability to focus, be productive and make good decisions whilst at work. Leaders like Tim who have attended mindfulness training often report that mindfulness helps them to sleep better.

Working as a Warfare Officer 'at the sharp end' in operational locations worldwide is about as stressful as any job could get. Tim used to deploy a combination of courage, commitment, determination and professional know-how. In conjunction with this, mindfulness now helps him to take a more objective view, getting things done in a more thoughtful and efficient manner, with a more resilient attitude to risk and stressful situations thanks to being able to draw upon a new skill set.

Like Marion, Tim has found ways to weave mindfulness into his day in no time at all! By doing things that you normally do on autopilot (such as commuting, walking, showering or driving), in a mindful way, you can practice mindfulness on the go. Doing so is a very time-effective way to benefit from mindfulness throughout the day, and the effects remain long after you have finished practicing.

Chapter 6

Case Study 3: Marion Furr, Director of MBPA

Marion Furr is director of Ministerial Business and Parliamentary Accountability (MBPA) in the Department of Health (DH), providing private office support to the permanent secretary and ensuring timely and appropriate responses to public and parliamentary representations to ministers and the department. For the past five years, in addition to her day job, Marion has led the staff health and well-being programme at the department with an explicit agenda of 'Practicing What We Preach'. She has personally practiced mindfulness for the past four years. She champions mindfulness in government and has contributed to the All-Party Parliamentary Group (APPG) on Mindfulness.

This chapter takes a look at the impact of mindfulness on Marion's work, how she practices mindfulness, and her tips on mindfulness for leaders.

The Impact of Mindfulness on Marion's Work

This section discusses some examples that show how mindfulness has aided Marion in her career. It includes an overview of Marion's mindfulness journey, along with tips and leadership insights to help you find ways that mindfulness could work for you.

Leading a major restructuring programme

The Department of Health (DH) has undergone a number of significant restructuring programmes in recent years and is currently going through an exercise that will reduce staff numbers by one-third over the next year. As part of the leadership team, Marion has been engaged in making numerous announcements to staff across the department. Staff survey results have suggested that the DH could improve on handling change; in response, the leadership team has worked hard to improve on past restructuring and change initiatives and to ensure that the process is fair.

All the top team members were available across different locations to conduct face-to-face briefings. They spent long days briefing packed rooms of staff, explaining that the department was changing and that there'd be a third fewer jobs in the new department. They emphasised that they were going to make the process fair, and as fast as they could, and had taken on board the feedback that people didn't want a long, drawn-out process.

Following the briefings to all DH staff, the team launched a separate consultation on terms and conditions for redundancy payments for all civil service staff. The timing of the consultation could have the effect that senior staff in the department might leave on potentially different – more favourable – redundancy terms than more junior staff.

This put Marion and her fellow leaders in a difficult situation. Having just completed general briefings the previous week, Marion had planned follow-up meetings with her own teams, some of whom now felt hostile and mistrustful.

In the past, when faced with a potentially hostile meeting like this, Marion recognised that she would feel very defensive. 'I think I would probably have been personally very angry about it, and I may have come across as quite defensive to staff, sticking to corporate lines and perhaps appearing unemotional about it all'. Instead, Marion was able to use mindfulness to help her to get into a calmer state, tapping into her higher brain circuitry to do the best she could for her team, given the circumstances.

Marion was aware of how her own strong personal feelings might impact how she responded to questions from staff members. So she focused on how *they* must be feeling and was really honest about how she felt, telling them, 'Look, I really wish I had the answers to your questions. I don't, and I am really sorry about that. If I were in your shoes, I would be cynical. This new consultation is a challenge to our process, making the whole thing really difficult, and for that I can only apologise'.

Marion's honesty, emotional intelligence and empathy helped staff to see that she was being genuine, and she felt she had gained some of their trust in difficult circumstances.

Being a less frantic, more authentic leader

Marion believes that her mindfulness training has really helped her to cope with difficult situations and to be a better leader. She says, 'I feel more real; I act with authenticity. I didn't have to work at that; all I had to do is what my mindfulness practice has taught me: take a few minutes before you go in, have a pause, settle, and be clear about what it is that you're trying to achieve through this meeting. I feel less frantic, less defensive'.

Mindfulness has helped Marion to become more authentic and true to herself, improve her clarity of thought, and develop a sense of calmness, a sense of being less frantic. 'People still see me as a busy person', she says, 'but I think I would possibly come across as less frantic'.

Introducing mindfulness to the Department of Health

Marion chairs the Staff Health and Well-Being programme at the DH. She started to wonder whether staff members could practice mindfulness as a preventative health method alongside drinking eight glasses of water, eating five fruits and vegetables a day, and exercising three times a week. Marion reasoned that maybe others should be applying mindfulness to their work. Since then, she has acted as a mindfulness champion within the DH. Marion says, 'At that time, it was still very taboo to talk about mental health and things like that, so I sold it based on its benefits for promoting health and well-being'.

Marion decided that if she wanted to raise awareness about mindfulness within the DH, running eight-week programmes wasn't an option, and introductory sessions was the way to go. The introductory programmes, offered in London and Leeds, were opened up to cross-government staff. Marion's aim was to give people enough practical information and a few tools and direct colleagues who wanted to go further to other resources or courses. To date, around 1,500 people have participated through the introductory programme. A number of staff has gone on to participate in other mindfulness training programmes in DH and elsewhere. The department continues to offer introductory programmes and staff weekly open drop-in sessions.

Marion's Mindfulness Experience and Practice

In this section, you discover how Marion first became aware of mindfulness, what inspired her to try it herself, how she developed her technique, and how she fits it into her life.

Finding the motivation

Marion first heard about mindfulness in 2011 at a Coaching in Government session. She quickly recognised how it might contribute to her corporate coaching work. But then she sort of ignored it for a while – until her partner became interested in mindfulness and attended an eight-week programme. Marion watched with interest from the sidelines, not really thinking about it or being interested in it, except showing interest in what her partner was doing.

Shortly after this, Marion moved out of London and had quite a lot of stressful things going on. Her department was going through a very significant change programme, which meant lots of people were about to lose their jobs. Marion's own job was at risk, and she, like other leaders, was applying for her own job. Her mother was diagnosed with dementia and had a very sudden and rapid decline, and she and her partner were buying a house together, moving in together and moving out of London.

During this time, Marion says, 'I found myself struggling emotionally and [feeling] depressed; I found myself, very strangely, setting off for work and not being able to face going through the front door. I used to sit in McDonald's, because it was the only place in Whitehall that was open, and have a cup of tea, putting off the moment I would head into the office. I wasn't even sure at the time why, but I was just struggling. Of course, I could get away with it because I was a director, so I would just send a text message to my PA and say, "I'm caught up in traffic", or, "I'll be in a little bit later", or whatever'.

Marion wasn't sleeping well and was flying off the handle and bursting into tears for what seemed to be no reason. She felt that she could justify all of these things because she had a lot going on and was not sleeping – being worried about her job and her mum and the long commute. She could always find reasons to justify it.

It wasn't until this had been going on for a few months that Marion actually realised that this behaviour wasn't right. It was like depression.

Marion went to see her doctor, who confirmed that she was suffering from depression. They discussed sleeping tablets, antidepressants, and time off work. Marion told her doctor, 'I don't really want to do any of those. . . . I need a routine, so I'm going to continue going into work, and actually I think I'll try this mindfulness stuff'. Her doctor agreed it was a good idea but was unable to advise her on where to go or what to look for. Marion set about finding her own course. She was sceptical; the only reason that kept her going was because her partner had been constantly telling her about all the evidence and reading all the books on it.

Developing mindfulness

Marion found a mindfulness course in London. After attending the eight-week MBCT course, she realised that although she had approached the course with a fair degree of scepticism, she felt that it had really worked. She says, 'I did actually feel better. Just being in that kind of space with other people and taking time out to focus on me, do the practices, and reflect on my experiences, I did actually feel better after each session of the course'.

Even though the course took up two-and-a-half hours each week, didn't start until 7 p.m., causing her to get home really late, Marion kept going and didn't miss any sessions. She was quite astonished about the advantages it gave her, both in terms of dealing with the current issue, her actual depression, but also with other things going on in her life. It gave her the space to see things more clearly and the capacity and a toolkit to remain calm.

When Marion feels fear or panic arising, she simply focuses her attention or does whatever is needed to address her fight-or-flight reaction. She says, 'As a psychologist, I did have quite a double mind most of the time during the course. There was the bit of me that was doing the experiential learning for myself, the bit of me that was observing me doing this, and the bit of me that was the psychologist saying, "I wonder what's actually going on here. How can you use this kind of stuff?"'

Marion has since learned of the neuroscience behind the mindfulness practices, showing how the brain physically changes with practice, creating the benefits that many studies repeatedly show. She now understands how these simple exercises affect her mood and behaviour.

Incorporating mindfulness every day

Marion now practices mindfulness on a regular basis. Some days, she formally practices for 40 minutes; other days, she practices for a shorter time. She also has a number of informal daily practices.

Marion practices mindfulness while standing on the bus and the tube. She says, 'I actually started to look forward to my short-hop bus journey and my 20-minute tube journey, because if I can stand where I can hold on lightly and just close my eyes or defocus, then I can really pay attention to all of the body movements. I can really feel all the muscles involved in keeping me upright'.

One of the government buildings Marion works in has a grand staircase, and she does a mindful walking exercise every morning as she climbs the stairs and again in the evening as she walks down the stairs. 'This mindful walking exercise is very short, but nevertheless I feel the benefits'.

The buildings Marion works in have long corridors and lots of stairs. Marion finds walking mindfulness exercises to be the best way to build mindfulness into her working day. She makes a conscious effort to be mindful when she moves between meetings during the day.

Marion is a warm, energetic, enthusiastic person. In the past, she used to rush down corridors and in and out of things. People who have worked with Marion for a little while have noticed that she now walks more deliberately. They now tell her, 'You seem so calm', and she replies, 'That will be the mindfulness'.

Marion's Top Tips for Leaders

Marion believes that a good way to integrate mindfulness into your life is to take a mindful pause, because it's something you're entirely in control of. It can take 30 seconds or 5 minutes, but if you can possibly find time to notice and schedule time between meetings, to have that mindful pause when moving from one thing to another, it can make an amazing difference. Here are a few other ways Marion suggests practicing mindfulness throughout the day:

> **» Introduce a little mindfulness at the start of meetings.** In Marion's own words, 'It doesn't have to be a bell-ringing, Buddhist session – it could just be as soon as the meeting is called to order, suggesting that everyone takes a few minutes, a few deep breaths, and reflect on what they want to achieve'.

When entering a difficult meeting, take a few minutes before you go in to have a pause, settle, and be clear about what it is that you're trying to achieve and the best way of achieving it during this meeting.

>> **Use eating and drinking as a way to squeeze some mindfulness into your day.** You don't have to eat a whole meal mindfully; you can just have three mindful mouthfuls. If you have a glass of wine after a long, difficult day, drink it mindfully.

Leadership Insights

Marion was drawn to mindfulness when she suffered from depression but found its impacts were much wider than simply health and mental well-being. Mindfulness can be a powerful preventative measure rather than simply a cure. There is no need to wait until you desperately need mindfulness. Learning it early in your career can be a wise investment.

Marion uses mindfulness to help her remain calm when facing challenging meetings. Mindfulness has taught her how to accurately and objectively observe how she is thinking or feeling at any moment. This capacity helps her to defuse negative emotions before they spiral out of control and remain open and vigilant of the dynamics at play in the room.

Marion is a warm, engaging and energetic leader with a busy and demanding job. Mindfulness helps her to feel more comfortable in her own skin – being true to herself and her values while still delivering the outcomes expected of her. Despite being very busy, she still finds ways to squeeze a little mindfulness into her working day. By focusing on walking when she walks down the corridors of government, she reduces her sympathetic nervous system activation, regains her equilibrium, and enters each meeting or interaction in a calmer, more objective state of mind.

Mindfulness helps Marion to manage herself better. She notices any thoughts, emotions or bodily sensations that might indicate that she needs to take better care of herself. By noticing signs at an early stage, she has remained free from depression while at the same time becoming happier and more productive during her working hours.

Developing
Mindfulness

Chapter 7

Setting the Stage for Transformation

Today's leaders face a number of expanding challenges. Technological, social, and economic forces compel leaders to address these issues to stay ahead of the competition. As organisations become less hierarchical and increasingly lean and flat in structure, workloads have increased and more skills are required. Daily technological innovations are accelerating the avalanche of information, freely available not only to leaders but also to their competitors

In response to these challenges, many employees are working increasingly long hours. While little evidence suggests that cultures with long working hours benefit the bottom line, plenty of evidence suggests that stress is reaching epidemic proportions.

In 2010 and 2011, the UK's Health and Safety executive (HSE) conservatively estimated the cost of stress, depression and anxiety at £3.6 billion. In a 2013 EU-funded project carried out by Matrix, the cost to Europe of work-related depression was estimated to be €617 billion annually.

New challenges demand new solutions. Mindful leadership is a new way of leading that can help you to become more productive, resilient and a better leader in times of rapid change. Becoming a mindful leader requires fortitude, commitment and a genuine desire to be the best leader possible. It's a journey of self-discovery, applying insights gained to manage yourself better.

Understanding Self-Authoring

Chapters 8 through 13 guide you through a WorkplaceMT course, which, if worked through and practiced as directed, will give you a firm introduction to mindfulness. This, in turn, forms the basis for your mindful leadership. To get the most from your WorkplaceMT mindfulness training, you need to undertake some *self-authoring*.

Self-authoring is a process that helps you to start to loosen the reins of others' expectations. It is a developmental process that can help you to re-write your own identity.

Leaders need to be able to adapt quickly and effectively to the world around them. Self-authoring is a phase when you become the author of your own identity. The ability to self-author is becoming recognised as a critical leadership skill.

REMEMBER

Becoming more mindful – that is, being present and aware of your-self, others and the world around you – helps you to self-author, recognising at any given moment your own perceptions, resulting potential biases, emotional reactions and the actions needed to deal with what's going on in the moment more effectively.

Many stories tell of people with glittering careers who experi-ence bad luck and misfortune and tumble into a negative spiral of thoughts, dwell on negativity, and start to think that they're useless, stupid or a loser. The problem is that the more you think it, the more you believe it. The more you believe it, the greater the impact on your actions and decisions. You can literally become what you think. Other people experience rags-to-riches success largely because they strongly believe and reinforce the fact that they can achieve anything. Working with this mindset, they overcome all the barriers and hurdles ahead of them.

Your thoughts, of course, are simply mental processes within your brain. You and you alone are responsible for your thinking. If you view the latest round of change initiatives at work as a bad thing, your brain will pay a lot of attention to things that further substantiate this view. It may even reject or ignore information to the contrary. Your thoughts about the change being a bad idea will become hardwired into your head. The more you reinforce these thoughts, the stronger the physical neural pathway in your brain and the more dominant and influential this thought becomes, thus impacting your decisions and perspectives. Conversely, you may see the change as offering you new and exciting possibilities, and your brain will pay extra attention to the benefits of the change.

REMEMBER

If a pattern of thinking is no longer serving you well, the good news is that you can replace that pattern of thinking and behaviour with one that serves you better. The trick to cognitive and behavioural change is recognising dominant patterns of behaviour and thought. This awareness gives you choices and allows you to consciously take control and change the way you think.

Developing the Tools for Self-Authoring

The ability to self-author and to change the way you lead starts with self-awareness. Six weeks of mindfulness training, as detailed in the next six chapters, can help you to enhance your self-knowledge and use this to manage yourself better. The next few pages provide some hints and tips about how to improve your awareness of your leadership preferences, decide what's working and what's not and use this knowledge as a basis for self-authoring.

Understanding your leadership style and preferences

Gaining a clear idea of your leadership preferences is a great basis for developing mindful leadership. If you haven't completed a self-diagnostic or psychometric on your leadership style and preferences recently, now would be a good time to do it.

TIP

Check out a free, simple leadership style and preferences diagnostic, designed for readers of this book, on the Resources page of my website (www.aheadforwork.com), along with some other handy tips for self-authoring.

Deciding what's working and what's not

The old adage 'if you always do what you have always done, you always get what you always got' is very true, especially when applied to your leadership. Different results require different ways of thinking and behaving.

Having gained a clearer indication of your current leadership preferences, it's worth asking yourself if they are currently serving you well. In some cases things that worked in the past are no longer effective. Are you comfortable to self-author your future leadership self, or is your acceptance within your social group a restricting factor?

Feel free to create your own unique hybrid that allows you to be the most authentic, effective leader you can be.

Setting your intention

Good leadership is about leading your people – coming up with the best solutions with the resources available to you. What often gets in the way is the desire to be accepted – your place within your social group.

Experienced mindful leaders know that your intention shapes what you consciously or unconsciously pay attention to. If your intention is to be the best leader you can be, this shapes your lens on the world. Your brain starts to pay more attention to approaching this challenge, making you aware of barriers that need to be overcome and new ways of achieving your goal. Your position and status within your social group remains important, but it becomes less of an influence on your decision-making. You start to become more comfortable at stretching the boundaries of your leadership, and at times standing outside your social group, acting as a lone voice for what you believe in.

Your **intention** drives your **attention**. Your attention influences your **awareness**. Your awareness gives you increased **choices**. Choices drive **actions**, and actions drive **results**.

Harnessing the power of neuroplasticity

Self-authoring is a process of change. Neuroplasticity, as we discuss in Chapter 3, is a process of hard wiring change into your brain. Anyone can harness the power of neuroplasticity. It's simple and straightforward but does require some effort. The following five-step model gets you started.

1. **Define what you want to change.**

Be realistic, and be specific. For example, say that you want to change your mindset about a proposed change at work.

2. **Approach and explore.**

What are the facts about the thing you want to change? Seek out information on exactly what's proposed, including costs, facts, figures, and who will be impacted. Research what worked and, more importantly, did not work for other companies in similar situations. Ask yourself, what opportunities does this change offer? How might this help me and my team develop?

3. **Suspend judgment.**

Make a conscious effort to suspend judgment without getting annoyed or blaming yourself. Suspending judgment allows you to be more objective, seek further information and gain a clearer picture of what's going on.

4. **Link with positive emotions.**

Emotions release powerful hormones in the brain, so they have a powerful impact on neuroplasticity. If possible, try to link your desired change to something positive, fun or rewarding. Pause to soak in and fully experience any positive emotions generated. If you're a visual person, try to visualise your desired change. Focus on each specific positive aspect of the change, and try to attach it to a positive emotion. Picture the positive changes and all they'll bring as vividly as possible.

5. **Reinforce regularly.**

   Repeat all or part of this exercise as many times as possible. The more you practice, the stronger and more dominant the neural pathways become. The more dominant patterns of thought and behaviour then become the norm, and previous neural pathways become less dominant with lack of use.

Taking Your First Step Towards Mindful Leadership

If you're a leader who is new to mindfulness, your mindful journey starts here. If you've practiced mindfulness in the past or do so sporadically, this six-week mindful leadership programme should prove to be an excellent catalyst for success.

WorkplaceMT training structure and rationale

Your Workplace Mindfulness Training (WorkplaceMT), detailed in Chapters 8 through 13, is structured as follows.

Week 1: Focusing your attention

The first week is about recognising how autopilot is currently ruling your life, noticing habitual patterns of thought and behaviour that are no longer serving you well, starting to train your attention and identifying autopilot in action.

Week 2: Observing the mind-body connection

This week focuses on understanding the interplay of thoughts, emotions and your body on your leadership and harnessing these to improve your leadership and life quality.

Week 3: Minding the gap

In Week 3, you discover how to use mindfulness to observe your hidden patterns, build on your successful strategies, and proactively work to replace unhelpful patterns of thought and behaviour with more helpful ones.

Week 4: Recognising that thoughts are not facts

Using mindfulness to observe the storytelling mind, the techniques you explore in Week 4 help you to better manage your emotions, recognise your inner bully and deal with frustration.

Week 5: Turning towards difficulties

In Week 5, you discover how to use mindfulness to help you approach and explore things you find difficult in a more productive way and decide how to pick your battles more wisely.

Week 6: Developing intention

The final week is about harnessing the power of mindfulness to gain balance and perspective and become more resilient, intentionally cultivating happiness. Mindfulness becomes part of your daily routine.

WorkplaceMT training requirements and expectations

Your WorkplaceMT course has been designed specifically with the busy people in mind, irrespective of sector seniority or executive education to date. We've pared it down to the bare minimum to ensure that it's accessible to all – however busy you are. It contains the core components of a standard eight-week MBCT course but is pared down to six weeks with new shorter practices that research suggests produce desirable workplace outcomes. Each week builds on the preceding one to help you progressively develop mindfulness, which, when applied to your leadership, will help you to review and refine your leadership and become a more mindful leader.

Each week, you will need to read a chapter, give the suggested activities a try, and practice both formal and informal mindfulness each day. It's simple and straightforward and should not take you more than 20 minutes a day. Here's an overview:

» Five minutes informal everyday mindfulness practice spread across the day: In reality, you don't need to make time for this because all you need to do is everyday things that you normally do – just more mindfully.

» Eight to 15 minutes formal brain training practice and reflection at home or in a quiet place where you won't be disturbed for at least 15 minutes: We encourage you to use the MP3 recordings provided to guide you and keep you on track.

TIP

Feel free to practice longer than 15 minutes, but be sure to practice formally for a minimum of 8 to 15 minutes a day. If you do miss a day, don't give up; just start with a clean slate the next day.

Don't fall into the trap of thinking that mindfulness is a Band-Aid or magic cure-all. You need to find time to work, reflect, recharge (have fun!) and get sufficient sleep. Although you can take steps to make your working hours more productive, sustain your attention for longer, make fewer mistakes and better decisions, don't think mindfulness will fix problems caused by toxic working environments. Be the change you want to see. Start a gentle mindfulness revolution to change working practices and culture for the better. If this doesn't work, maybe it's time to reconsider what's really important in life.

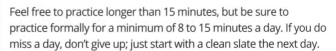

A PLEA FROM THE AUTHOR

Please learn from my mistakes. When I first attended mindfulness training, I was a busy department leader. I immediately recognised the possibilities that it offered me and in my haste to share it with others I failed to practice, so I did not gain full benefit. A year later I attended another course, and it all fell into place. I started practicing daily and reaping the rewards.

Nowadays, I work with leaders and notice a direct correlation between time spent practicing and positive outcomes. If you think you can't find 20 minutes in your busy day, it's time to take a serious look at your life before you're forced to do so.

If you practice each day using the suggestions in this book, you'll almost certainly see an improvement in both your productivity and well-being. If that isn't a strong enough incentive to give yourself the gift of 20 minutes of mindfulness a day, I don't know what is!

Chapter 8

Week 1: Focusing Your Attention

The significant problems we face cannot be solved at the same level of thinking we were at when we created them.

ALBERT EINSTEIN

I n this chapter, you find Week 1 of your WorkplaceMT learning and exercises.

Mindfulness or Mindlessness: Discovering the Difference

The following story illustrates how clever people can behave in mindless ways.

James had always been a high achiever. His father was a serial entrepreneur, and it was expected that he would follow in his father's footsteps. James worked hard, excelled at school, and later completed his MBA at Cambridge University's Judge Business School. Despite his father's repeated executive-level job offers, James was determined to make his own way and secured an executive position in a global financial organisation.

For the first year, all went well. James exceeded all his targets and was rewarded with a pay increase and greater responsibilities. In response, James worked harder, a strategy that had served him well in the past. His days were filled with web-based meetings at all hours of the day and night, travel, working on his computer, and evenings out with colleagues and business contacts. To make time for his work, James set aside his membership at the gliding club and prioritised a two-week fact-finding mission in Hong Kong over his annual break in the lakes with family and friends.

With so much to do and multiple tasks to juggle, James started to find it increasingly difficult to concentrate, so he did what he'd always done – worked harder. James worked into the early hours with increasing caffeine intake in an attempt to stay alert and focused, often getting only four hours of sleep. Despite all his efforts and hard work, his work began to slip, and he was sent to see the occupational health team, who suggested he was showing signs of burnout and recommended time off work.

Grudgingly, in denial, James took a month off. He booked himself a soaring safari in South Africa, a holiday that promised to deliver his lifelong ambition to see lions and elephants in the wild, combined with his love of gliding. As the days leading up to the holidays passed, James started to look forward to it. He threw himself into researching and planning to make the most of his break. He worked hard to ensure that all his projects were safely handed over to his colleagues, his emails were completed, and clients reassured about his absence. He researched and booked the best travel insurance, researched and bought suitable clothes, got involved with online forums, and learnt some of the local language.

Eventually, the day of his flight to South Africa arrived. James had driven to Gatwick airport many times. As he drove to the airport, he caught up on his last remaining phone calls, ate a sandwich, and drank an energy drink, finishing his phone calls just as he pulled into long-term parking for Terminal 2. Only as he stepped out of the car did he realise that he was at the wrong airport. His flight was due to depart from Heathrow, yet somehow he had driven himself to Gatwick airport!

Has something like this ever happened to you? Don't worry: you're not alone. Less dramatic examples include arriving for a meeting at the wrong time or on the wrong day or forgetting appointments and things you were supposed to be doing. Luckily, it isn't a sign that you're experiencing early onset of executive dementia! This is an example of 'mindlessness' or going on 'autopilot'.

In the following sections, we explore what it means to go on autopilot, how you can recognise habitual responses, and why sometimes the mind tends to wander.

Observing autopilot in action

It's estimated that the human brain processes around 400 billion bits of information every second. The more primitive areas of the brain process the majority of this information and are highly efficient at doing this. They process incoming information speedily while expending relatively little energy. All this happens at a subconscious level. The majority of the time, this is good news because it frees up your powerful, but slower, more energy-hungry 'thinking' brain to focus on the things that require conscious processing. So far, so good?

The downside is that problems can arise if you try to process too many pieces of information simultaneously. Your working memory can usually process only four to five pieces of information at a time. Trying to handle more can create a bottleneck. In an effort to be efficient, the brain has a tendency to process as much as it can unconsciously, freeing up your limited working memory capacity to focus on other things. This strategy is both time and energy efficient.

When juggling too much information, or when under pressure, your primitive brain sometimes gets it wrong. Its autopilot subconscious responses, based on past experiences or predictions of the future, are sometimes incorrect, leading to poor decisions and missed opportunities.

Recognising habitual responses

You form habits in the brain by repeating actions or thoughts over and over again. As you do this, you form robust physical neural pathways in the brain, making it easier to repeat the thought or action in the future. Habits are stored in the more primitive areas of the brain, which means they can be repeated without conscious thought. The upside of this is that it's a tried and tested response that has worked in the past. It's also quick and energy-efficient to repeat.

James's journey to Gatwick airport is an example of operating on autopilot (see the earlier section 'Mindfulness or Mindlessness: Discovering the Difference'). With little or no conscious brain effort, he was able to drive a car, navigate to an airport, drink, eat, and have a number of phone conversations without crashing his car. Each of these activities is highly complex in nature. To drive, James's brain had stored a number of habits connected with the activity of driving, such as clutch and break control, steering, and changing gears.

In the same way, James's brain had stored habits connected with how to eat and drink while driving. Because habits extend working memory, James was able to make phone calls while driving to the airport by using these habits or autopilot responses. The problem is that as James was doing so many things simultaneously, his unconscious brain started to make some important decisions for him – in this case, driving him to an airport it was familiar with, which unfortunately wasn't the right one.

Responses that may have served you well in the past may not always be appropriate to present-moment situations. Despite this, especially when under pressure, your brain defaults to old ways of thinking and doing things long before the conscious higher brain kicks in and you have the opportunity to question their appropriateness. The good news is that practicing mindfulness enhances your awareness of your unique patterns of behaviour and habits. This awareness is the first step towards replacing unhelpful habits with more appropriate ones via the power of neuroplasticity.

Noticing the mind's tendency to wander

James story detailed in 'Mindfulness or Mindlessness: Discovering the Difference', earlier in this chapter, vividly illustrates the human tendency to work on autopilot. Now read on to find out what it can tell us about the mind's tendency to wander.

> As soon as James realised his mistake, he got straight back in the car. He had three hours before his flight departed, and Heathrow Airport was around a 50-minute drive away, so he might still make his flight – by the skin of his teeth. As he drove from Gatwick to Heathrow, James became angry with himself. How could he have ended up at Gatwick when he knew his flight was from Heathrow? What would people think of him! They would think he was losing it.

> James started to think about what the company thought of him and his career prospects, concluding that this mistake would definitely impact his promotion prospects and he'd no longer be invited to get involved in key prospects. He mentally protested that none of this was part of his plan, and maybe he had been foolish to put down a deposit for a new waterside apartment in Docklands. Now his promotion prospects were blighted, he would never be able to keep up the mortgage payments. James gripped the steering wheel tighter. His shoulders and arms tensed, and he pressed the accelerator pedal down harder.

Recent research suggests that the human mind wanders for around 47 per cent of the day. The same research concluded that when the mind wanders, people tend to feel unhappy. At a time when James should have been focusing on driving his car safely to the right airport in time to catch his flight, his mind was again elsewhere, trying to anticipate the future and making himself thoroughly stressed and miserable in the process, his body holding onto tension, ready to fight the imaginary tiger he imagined his future to be.

Spending this amount of time in mind wandering is a phenomenon unique to human beings due to our advanced brain function, but it comes at an emotional cost and has huge impacts for workplace well-being, decision-making, and productivity.

Close your eyes and try to empty your mind completely of all thoughts, just for one minute. How did you get on? When we ask people to do this activity during mindfulness introductory sessions, most people find this more difficult than they thought it would be. This is no surprise. It's estimated that your mind can generate around 50,000 individual thoughts in the course of 24 hours. Day after day and year after year, your mind is constantly churning. Thoughts come and go continuously, and few require immediate action. Despite the fact that thoughts aren't facts, people often treat them as so, triggering knee-jerk responses, including emotions and tensions in the body.

REMEMBER

Developing greater awareness of your thoughts and habitual patterns of behaviour gives you greater control over your life. It gives you choices. Many high-powered executives, like James, silently wish to stop the madness. And in an effort to cope with increasing workloads, they spend more and more of their life on autopilot. Do you, like James, ever find your thoughts spiralling away from the facts of the present moment into elaborate stories of the world, which, although not real, trigger more thoughts, emotions, sensations and tension in the body?

If you were a caveman facing mortal threats to life and limb, this would be a wholly appropriate response to keep you alive and safe from harm. The possibility of less status or a lack of promotion at work could hardly be described as life-threatening, yet people respond in much the same way – treating it as if it were a life-and-death situation. As a result, they spiral towards a 'hyper' state, wired and ready to fight for their lives, or tumble down to a 'hypo' state, where they start to shut down and are rendered inactive – a freeze response that works on the ancient principle that if you play dead, the danger will pass you by and you'll live to see another day.

Tuning in to the Present Moment

Do you remember the first time you ate your favorite food? Perhaps you paused to savour the flavour, texture and smell. Did you pause to notice the pleasure it gave you at that moment? Do you still pause to fully appreciate this pleasant experience, or do you eat it with little or no conscious attention?

For some people, food is simply a source of fuel, while others really enjoy the whole eating process. Eating is an everyday thing that all people do, often with little or no conscious attention, but it provides opportunities to tune in to the present moment and fully experience the richness of the experience.

TIP

Try this mindful eating exercise to practice tuning in to the present moment.

Select an everyday item of food you normally eat with little or no conscious attention. It could be a biscuit, a snack bar, an apple, a bag of seeds, dried fruit or nuts. Pick something that doesn't need preparation or peeling to eat. Then follow these steps:

1. **Hold the food item in your hands or between your fingers and thumb.**

Focus your full attention on it as if you've never seen it before. How heavy is it? Explore your item with a sense of openness and curiosity.

2. **Look closely at the food item.**

What can you see? What is its texture like? What do you notice about its colour? Is it hard or soft? Explore it meticulously with full attention. Is it smooth? Is it uniform in shape? Does it have any recesses or dimples?

3. **Notice the sensations you feel in your hand as you hold the food item.**

Explore the texture of the item. How does it feel to be holding it at this moment?

4. **Place the food item under your nose and smell it.**

   What do you notice? Does it have a scent? Very little scent? Does it evoke any memories? Are you aware of any impulses or urges?

5. **Place the item on your tongue (but don't chew).**

   If the item is small, like a nut or raisin or small sweet, place it on your tongue. If the item is bigger, like a biscuit, apple or sandwich, take a bite and let the bite of food sit on your tongue. Simply tune in to the experience of it resting on your tongue. If you wish to, try exploring the object with your tongue. Notice any urges, avoiding the urge to chew, and tune in to the changing sensations in the mouth right now.

6. **Chew.**

   When you're ready, bite the item and notice any flavours that emerge. Slowly and consciously chew the item but don't swallow. How do the textures and flavours change? Tune in to what's going on in your mouth at this moment in time.

7. **Swallow.**

   When ready to do so, swallow the food. See whether you can notice what your tongue and throat do in preparation for swallowing and follow the sensations of swallowing as the item moves down the throat. What do you notice now?

8. **Notice the aftereffects.**

   End this exercise by spending a short while noticing what happens after eating. How does the mouth feel in the absence of the food item? Are you aware of any thoughts, urges or emotions?

Many people eat with little conscious awareness while having a conversation, travelling, or working at their desk. How did this short exercise change the experience of eating?

Many people attending WorkplaceMT training and trying this for the first time are surprised at how the simple act of eating an everyday food whilst consciously focusing on it transforms the experience. For example:

> 'I love raisins and normally eat them a handful at a time. Eating the raisin evoked memories of childhood Christmas cooking with my mother. The raisin had a different texture than I was expecting, and the taste when I bit into it was more intense and flavor-filled than I thought it would be'.

> 'I selected an oaty biscuit I regularly eat at our weekly meetings. The same biscuit selection is provided each week along with tea, coffee and water. When I explored the texture, it felt rough and unappetizing. The smell, to my surprise, was mildly unpleasant, but I persisted. I took a bite and discovered the taste was bland and sickly sweet. I wondered why I had been eating these biscuits each week. I never want to eat that biscuit ever again!'

Stepping out of autopilot allows you to see things as they really are – and make wiser decisions based on present–moment facts rather than memories of the experience achieved by your brain. A seemingly insignificant thing like a raisin can provide a taste explosion, or a biscuit might trigger pleasure or revulsion. It also illustrates just how much of life passes by and the big impact that focusing on small things can bring. It illustrates the cost of your inattention – just think of all the pleasant experiences you could be missing out on. Also consider the habits you repeat that are no longer serving you well.

Focusing Your Attention

So far in Week 1's WorkplaceMT training you have discovered the mind's tendency to wander and to work on autopilot. James, who we met earlier in the chapter, found it difficult to focus when he returned to work.

> When James returned from his break from work, his occupational health team offered him some one-to-one mindfulness training. At first, James was cynical, "I was asked to focus on a raisin to improve my attention and awareness. I thought the

trainer was nuts, but it made me realise just how little I was aware of what was really going on around me. It was a real wake-up call for me that something needed to change." James knew that he couldn't instantly change the world and his organisation's working culture, but he realised that he could change the way he responded to it.

Mindfulness certainly isn't about switching your mind off. In fact, it's quite the opposite. Brain scans indicate that increased metabolic brain activity occurs while practicing mindfulness – in other words, you become more aware of what's going on around you. You experiment to see whether you can simply acknowledge what's going on around you rather than springing into a reactive cycle. You learn to turn towards your brain chatter – noticing patterns and chain reactions and creating a thinking gap between the stimulus and your response to it.

Simply committing to be fully aware of the present moment isn't enough. You need to train your brain to focus and maintain attention where you want it to be. You need to recognise unhelpful habits that drive your routine behaviour and replace them with new habits that serve you well. Mindfulness isn't something you can simply read about and then magically become mindful. If it was, we would instantly become a mindful nation! Mindfulness is something you need to experience for yourself. Developing mindfulness takes time and effort, but the potential gains are enormous.

WorkplaceMT mindfulness training is a combination of psychological education, combined with formal and informal everyday mindfulness practical exercises. The practice elements of WorkplaceMT help you to rewire your brain to reduce inappropriate emotion-based reactivity, increase your ability to focus your attention, and stand back to see the bigger picture of what's really going on – within yourself – and within your organisation.

Practicing mindfulness of breath

The first of the formal mindfulness exercises we would like you to practice as part of your training is mindfulness of breath. Why breath? Because everyone breathes. It's universal. Breathing is something that most people take for granted, but without it, we'd all be dead.

Focusing on the breath provides a simple and natural object to anchor your attention on. The breath can be surprisingly sensitive to how you're feeling. By progressively training your brain to notice your breathing patterns (shallow or deep, smooth or rough), you can monitor your internal weather patterns, taking skillful action when you need to take care of yourself.

Why practice mindfulness of breath?

Using your breath as an anchor for your awareness enables you to notice more easily when your mind has wandered, if you become bored or distracted, or if you experience emotions such as happiness or sadness.

The exercise takes less than ten minutes and provides an opportunity to see how things are for you in this moment. It allows you to practice the art of letting go of the doing, fixing mind and to experience simply being – allowing life to live itself – just for a short while. It provides the opportunity to observe the insights and wisdom that occur when you stand back from thinking and doing.

How do you practice mindfulness of breath?

We recommended that you practice mindfulness of breath at least once a day for the next seven days – more if time allows. In WorkplaceMT courses, we guide people through mindfulness of breath as they sit in standard office chairs in the workplace. In our experience, most people practice their formal mindfulness exercises at home because they're less likely to be disturbed. If this is the case for you, feel free to try this exercise sitting or lying down – find a posture or position that's comfortable for you. If you do decide to lie down, remember that practicing mindfulness is about falling awake, not falling asleep!

Experiment with practicing at different times of the day – first thing when you wake, after you've had breakfast, after you're dressed and ready to go to work, when you arrive home and have settled, before you start your evening social and domestic routine, after supper, or before bed. See what works for you, but make a commitment to practice daily. Doing so will get results – training the muscles of the brain in the same way that you'd train your body muscles at the gym.

If you do miss a practice session, don't make things worse by getting angry or frustrated with yourself. Simply start practicing again the next day. If you're practicing by yourself, rather than attending a six-week WorkplaceMT course, feel free to repeat a week if you managed to practice only two or three times that week. Alternatively, you may decide to move on to the next week and come back to that week at a later date.

Although relaxation is a welcome by-product for many who practice mindfulness, it's not the aim. It's about tuning in to your present-moment experience, warts and all. Sometimes this is a pleasant experience; sometimes, it's not so pleasant.

Your mind will naturally wander during this exercise. The important thing is recognising that it's wandered. Only once you notice it has wandered can you redirect your attention to where you want it to be. Repetition of this activity strengthens the neural pathways in your brain, making it easier to notice mind wandering and easier to sustain focus and attention.

Mindfulness of breath – the science

Practicing mindfulness of breath helps you to develop the ability to

>> Direct and sustain the focus of your attention

>> Notice when your mind has wandered

>> Suspend judgment and experience the present moment as it is

The simple act of your mind wandering, you recognising that it's wandered, and then bringing your attention back to where you want it to be forms new neural connections in your brain. Every time you go through this process, you reinforce these neural pathways and make it easier to do the next time.

Practicing exercises like mindfulness of breath for as little as eight weeks has been proven to thicken the parts of the brain's cerebral cortex responsible for decision-making, attention and memory.

PLAY THIS

On WorkplaceMT training courses, we recommend that you download and play the accompanying MP3s to guide you through this practice. Play Track 1A or 1B for the mindfulness of breath exercise. (*Note:* If you prefer not to use the accompanying tracks or are unable to do so, simply familiarize yourself with the instructions and set a timer for 10 minutes.)

1. **Settle yourself in a chair where you can sit in a comfortable upright position.**

2. **Plant both feet firmly on the floor, relax your shoulders with the chest open and your head facing forward with the chin dipped slightly to your chest.**

Your upper body should feel confident and self-supporting, embodying a sense of awakeness and alertness. Close your eyes.

3. **Direct your attention to the contact points between your body and the chair and floor.**

Spend a few minutes exploring how your feet, legs, bottom and any other areas in contact with the chair and floor feel in this moment in time. Briefly scan each area of your body in turn, starting at the feet and finishing at the crown of your head. If you detect any tension, experiment with breathing into the area on the in breath and imagine releasing the tension on the out breath.

4. **Focus your attention on the breath.**

Notice how the chest and abdomen feel as the breath enters and leaves the body. If this is difficult, focus first on wherever you feel the breath most vividly.

5. **Place your hand on your abdomen and focus your attention on the sensations of the abdomen rising and falling in its own natural rhythm.**

6. **Allow your hand to gently return to your side and shift the focus of your attention to the short pause that occurs naturally between the in breath and out breath.**

7. **Refocus your attention to the tip of your nostrils.**

   Observe the sensation of the breath entering and leaving the body through the nostrils. Notice any subtle differences between the temperature of the air as it enters and leaves your nostrils.

8. **Refocus your attention back to the body.**

   Tune in to your body and notice how it feels in this moment in time.

9. **At the end of the practice session, gently stretch your fingers and toes and open your eyes.**

   Now you're ready to re-engage with the rest of your day.

TIP

If at any point your mind wanders, don't beat yourself up! Simply acknowledge the fact that it wandered, make a mental note of where it wandered to (if you're aware of this) and then kindly and gently refocus your attention back to where you intend it to be. It doesn't matter if your mind wanders 100 times; the act of recognising that your mind has wandered and bringing it back is what's important.

REMEMBER

This exercise isn't about controlling your breath. Simply observe the natural rhythm and sensations of breathing, unique to this moment in time, without the need to engage in judgment.

Try your best to suspend judgments about how your practice is going. Doing so puts you under pressure and can send your thoughts spiralling. Let go of ideas of success and failure or right and wrong, and allow your practice session to unfold just as it is moment by moment.

On WorkplaceMT courses, we encourage personal reflection following mindfulness practices. Doing so helps you to learn and benefit more from your time spent practicing. After each session, reflect on the following questions:

>> How hard did you find it to remain focused on your body or your breath?

>> How many times did you notice that your attention had wandered?

>> Did you notice where your attention had wandered to or how long it had been wandering?

>> Did you find yourself at any time making judgments about your experiences or being self-critical?

>> Can you make any other observations about this experience?

When James first tried this exercise, he noticed that, in his own words, his mind was like an 'unruly monkey. It was like there was a drunken monkey, constantly popping up and down, scuttling around, screeching and endlessly chattering away'. He said it felt as if this monkey was constantly center stage, clamoring for attention. In truth, of course, the 'monkeys' in your head never fully go away. It's useless to fight them or to try to banish them from your mind because, as you're probably aware, that which you resist persists. Practicing mindfulness on a regular basis can help you befriend your inner monkey and, maybe, in time, even tame him.

James also noticed his mind's tendency to flit from thought to thought, making it hard to stay focused. This recognition is important when learning mindfulness for the first time. Your mind will wander; the important thing is recognising it has wandered and regaining your focus. How you do this is important.

REMEMBER

If you get angry and frustrated with your inability to stay focused, you'll find it even harder to focus. Kindness and gentleness are key here. Cutting-edge research suggests that it's neurologically impossible to be simultaneously kind to yourself and angry at the same time. Being kind to yourself when your mind wanders and cutting yourself some slack diffuses tension and helps you to regain your focus more quickly.

Week 1 WorkplaceMT Practice Exercises

The mindfulness techniques you're invited to practice as part of your WorkplaceMT training can help you to reduce the time that your mind wanders. By reducing the time your mind spends wandering, even by a relatively small percentage, you gain back hours of time every week. By progressively developing the ability to notice that your mind has wandered, you'll increase focus and concentration and open up a world of creative possibilities.

Your core practice activities for Week 1 consist of a formal brain-training activity and informal everyday mindfulness activities that you can easily fit into your day. In total, all we're asking you to do each week for the next six weeks is around 20 minutes of practice a day. That includes 8 to 15 minutes of formal practice each day plus a few minutes of everyday mindfulness scattered throughout your day. Research demonstrates that the more you practice, the greater the benefits you'll experience.

TIP

Before you get started, consider carefully two very important questions

>> **What difficulties do you see yourself encountering?** Difficulties often include making a time to practice, overcoming distractions, and keeping going when things aren't going to plan for you.

>> **How will you overcome these difficulties?** Planning strategies to overcome the inevitable barriers and difficulties you encounter in the next few weeks is really important. Partnering up with someone else who is working through the programme or involving a friend who already practices mindfulness can be really helpful. Some people find the act of physically diarizing an appointment with themselves to practice mindfulness does the trick. Find a strategy that woks for you, but do spend a few moments planning to help ensure that this programme will have maximum benefit.

Week 1 formal mindfulness exercises

Here is a summary of your Week 1 formal exercises.

Practice mindfulness of breath (see earlier section 'Practicing mindfulness of breath') – using MP3 track 1A or 1B to guide you each day. We have included two versions of this exercise – use the one that works best for you.

If time allows, spend a few moments afterwards reflecting on your experience.

Week 1 informal everyday mindfulness exercises

Following is a summary of your Week 1 informal exercises.

Mindful eating

Try eating a few bites of your lunch mindfully or taking a few mindful sips of tea or coffee. Use snacking as an opportunity to practice a little mindfulness. Try to fully tune in to the experience of eating and drinking, which changes moment by moment. See what you notice.

Reconnecting with the present moment

Although you're always physically in the present moment, your mind may be frequently elsewhere, trawling through memories of the past and trying to predict the future. Twice a day, try to use an everyday experience to bring your mind back to the present moment.

For example, when sitting in a chair, ask yourself how you feel in this moment in time. Be specific. The following questions may help you to reflect:

>> How do your feet feel in contact with the floor?

>> What other parts of your body are in contact with the chair? What sensations can you notice at the contact points?

>> Are you experiencing any positive or negative emotions? If so, what are they?

Releasing habits

Try to do one or two things differently this week. Try out a different coffee bar, drive a different route if you can, sit in a different chair, or park in a different area of the car park.

You may also try to do a routine activity mindfully, such as washing up, showering, getting dressed, walking up or down stairs. As you do, consider what thoughts arise. Are you aware of any urges, impulses or emotions? Observe what arises with a sense of gentle playfulness, fun and curiosity.

Chapter 9

Week 2: Observing the Mind-Body Connection

D o you spend long hours working on the computer? Many people now do. Although working at the computer may not be a physically demanding job, it can be tough on your body.

This chapter is all about reconnecting with your body at work. Traditional theories in psychology state that the brain generates behaviour. Most recent developments in neuroscience are now rewriting the brain's job description with studies that show that people's thoughts also have a foundation in their bodies.

Although the brain is important, it isn't the only resource you have for problem solving and managing your behaviour. Reconnecting with your body is proven to improve health, well-being and productivity. It can even make you happier.

Exploring the Impact of Work on Your Body

Your body is sensitive to even the tiniest hint of emotions. Working under pressure can lead your body into a high state of alert. Your body doesn't differentiate between a life-and-death threat and a stroppy boss or overdemanding client. It treats them in the same way. It prepares itself to fight or run away fast. In this aroused state, the body can lock in tension and hold onto it for very long periods of time.

In the next few pages, you will find a number of examples of how your body and emotions have a greater impact on your work than you might imagine.

Working as a board member

When Alvin was first introduced to the WorkplaceMT programme, he was a senior board member who was experiencing some problems working due to board room politics. At times, his frustration with board room game playing would spill over, and he would have an angry outburst. He realised that not only was this response unhelpful, but it was also limiting his career.

REMEMBER

To have emotions is to be human. For the most part, emotions serve you well – faithfully working in the background to help you respond appropriately to both the joys and challenges of everyday life. Emotions are psychological events, and as such, with practice, you can raise your awareness of their presence and impact. This awareness will help you take steps to manage them when needed.

As a young man, Alvin had enjoyed a successful career in the United States as an athlete. Being in his mid-50s, he retained a powerful and striking physique. In Week 2 of his mindfulness training, he practiced the body scan exercise. Reflecting on the experience afterwards, he said it was hard and he disliked it. Upon further reflection, he realised that as an athlete, he had trained his brain to tune out the messages that his body sent him. If he felt pain or discomfort, he ignored it, focusing instead on his end goal.

During the next week of his mindfulness training, he injured his leg. His mind-body disconnect was so great that during his spinning fitness class he had pedalled so hard that he physically sheared off one of the pedals and injured his leg in the process, leading to missed meetings and time off work.

Over the weeks as his WorkplaceMT training progressed, Alvin learned how to use his body as an early warning system. By learning how to tune back into the messages his body was sending him, he was better able to manage himself. He started to notice the sensations in his body that indicated his emotions were rising and was able to take the necessary steps to calm himself. By avoiding an emotional outburst, he was able to steer work meetings back to a more productive direction.

Of course not all emotions need to be managed. It's critical for modern leaders to show their authentic human side – that you care, that you are happy, excited, or sad – but to do so wisely in a way that supports respectful communication. This is a valuable lesson that Alvin took on board.

WARNING

If you do start experiencing very strong emotions that persist and you can't shake off, consider talking to your doctor.

Working in IT

When Lin started WorkplaceMT training, she worked as a senior programming analyst for a well-known software company. She had seven years of technical experience in the design, development and deployment of complex business applications. She was responsible for engineering and developing highly complex projects as well as maintaining and supporting existing software applications. Some of her time was taken up with translating business requirements into effective and efficient IT systems. She spent many hours of her day designing coding, undertaking system testing, and documenting software applications. She also managed a team of five programmers and provided training on the software applications she developed.

Lin's company provided an excellent working environment. An amazing subsidized restaurant served a wide range of food, from super healthy vitamin-packed salads to comfort food. Sweets, drinks and snacks were freely available for staff to dip into when the need or urge arose. The staff restrooms were luxurious, with expensive soaps and lotions, fluffy towels and powerful showers. Employees had access to a lounge area full of comfortable colourful chairs, bean bags and stools, with free Wi-Fi and access to gaming systems. All human needs were catered for, and there was little need to leave the building. Some staff enjoyed the working environment so much that they sometimes felt no need to go home and would end up working day and night for several days before leaving the building for a short break. Lin loved working for her company and felt highly privileged to be there.

The nature of Lin's job meant that she spent many hours in front of a computer screen. She was often so absorbed by her work that she could go from breakfast (eaten in the staff restaurant) to a late lunch without moving from her desk. Lin complained that at times she felt like 'a brain on a stick'. Her body was simply there to transport her brain from job to job.

Do you sometimes feel like 'a brain on a stick'? Sitting for long periods can cause back pain, negatively influence circulation, and increase your risk of cardiovascular disease. Intensive use of the keyboard and mouse can lead to stiffening of the muscles in your hands, arms, and neck, as well as inflammation and injuries. Staring at a bright screen for too long can cause dry eyes and headaches. As if that weren't enough, computer work can be stressful, isolating, and lead to depression and anxiety. Working on the computer can be seriously unhealthy.

When Lin arrived home (often late), she liked to watch TV on her iPad in bed. Just before switching off to sleep, she would have one last scan of her emails, answering any that she saw as urgent. Some nights she went to sleep and dreamt about work, her mind rehearsing the next day or taking up the sword on epic quests to find solutions to technical issues in a matrixlike world.

Does this sound familiar? It's all too common. And instead of being efficient, as many people think it is, it's bad for your productivity.

A recent study published in the journal of *Organizational Behaviour and Human Decision Processes* involved 82 senior managers. Researchers found that smartphone use after 9 p.m. was associated with decreased sleep quantity at night. That decreased sleep quantity was associated with morning depletion the next day, and morning depletion was associated with decreased work engagement for that day.

Lin was working on a project for a demanding US client. She found herself endlessly on Skype calls at all hours of the day and night. One morning, a member of her team came to her desk to ask her opinion on a technical workaround, and she ended up yelling at him aggressively.

Lin's company decided to offer staff access to mindfulness training during work time. Although it was advertised as an employee benefit, it was also offered because the company was experiencing a drop in productivity and an increase in burnout. Lin decided to attend training because she had heard that mindfulness could help with sleep problems and help her to manage strong emotions better.

Lin started to recognise that she was not a brain on a stick and realised the extent to which she had been ignoring and mistreating her body. She started making time for a 15-minute walk at lunch time and a weekly Pilates session. She managed her iPad habit more wisely, using it after supper and leaving it on the kitchen table when she went to bed rather than on her bedside table. She started to regain a sense of control and perspective, and she started to sleep better.

Exploring Mind-Body Science

Your body communicates with your brain every second of every day – both when you're awake and when you're asleep. If your body senses that anything is wrong, it messages the brain to alert it. For example, did you know that your stomach is controlled by a network of neurons that line your stomach and your gut? This network, sometimes called 'the little brain', contains 100 million neurons – as many as there are in the head of a cat. The neurons of the little brain keep in close contact with the brain via the vagus nerves, which influence your emotional state.

When your body is tense or uncomfortable, it sends alert messages to the brain. It tells your brain that something isn't right and you need to prepare for action. In this state, the body can activate a default operating system that puts you into safety mode. When operating in safety mode, your choices are restricted, and you'll tend to opt for safe, tried and tested solutions rather than seek out new, creative or innovative ways of working. In addition, your ability to effectively engage and influence others is diminished.

The cumulative impact of a day of emails, phone calls, meetings, deadlines, and computer-based work result in a roller coaster of emotions, triggering reactions in the body, which send signals to the brain to watch out for danger or impending harm. Similarly, hours spent huddled over a computer can lead to stiffness due to lack of movement, which also signals to the brain that a problem needs to be addressed and to operate in safety mode until things are rectified.

In the next few pages, we explore how your mind and body connections interact, learning how your posture and body tissue can influence your decisions and judgments, actions and confidence.

Influencing your decisions and judgment

Did you know that feeling hungry or tired impacts your decision-making? A University of Amsterdam study in 2007 concluded that feeling tired, hungry or thirsty can lead to you choosing much higher-risk strategies. Conversely, when your body is out of this 'state of urgency', you're more likely to make a more balanced and reasoned decision.

In another experiment conducted by Mirjam Tuk, of the University of Twente in the Netherlands, participants were asked to either drink five cups of water (about 750 millilitres) or take small sips of water from five separate cups. After about 40 minutes, the researchers assessed participants' self-control (they waited 40 minutes because that's about how long it takes for water to reach the bladder). Participants were asked to make eight choices; each was between receiving a small but immediate reward or a larger but delayed reward.

The researchers found that the people with full bladders were better at holding out for the larger reward later. They concluded that having a full bladder and resisting the urge to go to the toilet is an act of self-control. And while having to control themselves physically, people are more likely to choose low-risk options and to avoid impulse decisions.

Altering your relationship with your body can have a dramatic impact on your work. According to Antonio Damasio, a professor of neuroscience at the University of Southern California, your body and emotions play a key role in the way you make decisions. In his book *Descartes' Error: Emotion, Reason, and the Human Brain* (Penguin), he argues that the body is a major contributor to the workings of the mind. He says that 'the mind is embodied, in the full sense of the term, not just embrained'. He goes on to emphasise 'the crucial role of feelings in navigating the endless stream of life's personal decisions. . . . The intuitive signals that guide us in these moments come in the form of limbic-driven surges from the viscera' (your gut instinct).

Discovering the link between your tissue and your brain

Fascia tissue is a sheet or band of fibrous connective tissue enveloping, separating, or binding together muscles, organs, and other soft structures of the body. It can contract independently from muscle movement and can relay signals to the brain faster than nerve impulses.

Eighty per cent of back pain can't be explained by damage to bones or cartilage, and it's now thought that much of the back pain people experience may be due to matted fascia. Stress hormones have a direct impact on fascia. In a laboratory setting, fascia tissue removed from the body contracts when introduced to the stress hormone cortisol. In the body, fascia tissue may become knotted and rigid when exposed to stress. This can lead to back problems and even depression.

Matted tissue is a sign of stress or bodily trauma – it sends signals to your brain that all is not well and to be alert and ready for danger. When primed for danger (fight or flight), creativity diminishes and your choices become restricted. Even when the supply of stress hormone is switched off by the brain, fascia may remain matted and tense for long periods and continue to send signals to the brain that all is not well. Movement and stretching can reduce fascia matting and thus reduce pain. Reduced pain signals to the brain that all is well, enabling you to consider a wider range of options and be more creative in finding solutions.

Mindfulness exercises, such as the body scan, help you to tune back into the messages your body is sending you, enabling you to maintain high performance for longer.

Two-way communication systems link the body with the brain. How your body feels has a direct impact on your work.

Assessing the impact of posture on performance

Your body posture also plays a surprising role in your interactions with others and your creativity. In groups of primates, dominant members strike power poses – making themselves look big and in control. They expand out to take up as much space as possible. Submissive members of the group make themselves look small, adopting a 'low pose' by huddling up and tucking in their limbs, averting their gaze downwards. It's the same in humans. Confident individuals often take up a lot of space, while those lacking in confidence close themselves down in a subconscious effort not to be seen and not enter into unnecessary conflict.

You may be one of the millions of people who have watched Harvard researcher Amy Cuddy's famous TED Talk on the impact of posture on hormone levels and performance. If you haven't seen it, it's well worth a look. In the talk, Amy shares her research findings on the link between posture and performance.

Volunteers were asked to adopt either high-power poses or low-power poses. Without telling them what the poses signified, volunteers were asked to maintain these poses for two minutes and then take part in an unnerving job interview where the interviewer didn't display any sign of emotion. After this, the volunteers were given a creativity task to complete. When asked who they'd pick, the interviewers all selected volunteers who (unbeknown to them) had been power posing for two minutes before the interview. What's more, the volunteers who power posed were much more creative in the creativity task than those who had practiced the low poses.

Just two minutes of holding a confident 'everything's okay, I'm in control' pose makes a big difference to both your performance and others' perceptions of you.

TIP

Periodically tuning in to your body posture and correcting it if necessary can have a surprisingly positive impact on your work. Figure 9-1 can help you check your posture and see if it needs adjusting.

CHECK YOUR POSTURE

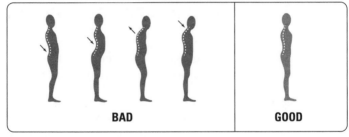

BAD   GOOD

© John Wiley & Sons, Inc.

FIGURE 9-1: Check your posture.

Tuning in to Your Body

In Week 1 of your WorkplaceMT training (see Chapter 8), you start to develop focused awareness, placing the spotlight of your attention where you want it to be. You also observe your mind's tendency to chatter away endlessly. You can't stop these thoughts from arising – it's part of being human! What you can do is control what happens next.

The next step in your WorkplaceMT training is to deepen your ability to observe your mind's reactivity cycles by training your brain to pay mindful attention to the body. The next few pages tell you how and why.

Tuning in to your early warning system

When your body detects even the slightest emotion, it triggers a chain reaction, which can often make things worse. Your body can respond by acting as an accelerator, generating a reactive spiral of thoughts, emotions, and sensations. This week's training helps you to stand back and observe what's going on, observing patterns and trends and surveying your inner landscape.

Gaining a clearer picture of what's going on enables you to make wiser decisions about what happens next. You can use your body as an early warning system to alert you to the first signs that your thoughts and emotions are starting to spiral so you can decelerate, take stock and regain control.

Pausing to appreciate the moment

As you discover in Chapter 3, an inbuilt evolutionary bias means that people tend to pay more attention to things that are potentially harmful or threatening than to the good things in life.

The good news is that you can correct this bias. Doing so gives you a more balanced perspective. In the Week 2 WorkplaceMT practice section of this chapter, you find a short informal exercise that you can experiment with.

Pausing for just a few seconds to bring conscious awareness to the good things in life when they arise helps you to create new neural pathways in your brain, making pleasant things more noticeable in the future and improving your mood and outlook on life. In addition, it helps you to engage your approach mode of mind circuitry, opening up new creative possibilities. You discover more about approach versus avoidance mode in Week 3 (see Chapter 10).

Observing your reactivity cycles

The simple body scan exercise we invite you to try in this chapter is designed to help you to re-integrate your mind and body back into one powerful whole.

The body scan exercise involves settling yourself into a comfortable position and spending a short period of time focusing on your breath, just as you do in Week 1. Following this, you redirect the spotlight of your attention onto your feet and slowly move up the body, focusing on one body area at a time until you reach the crown of your head. If you practice yoga, you may have encountered a similar exercise aimed at relaxing your body (called yoga Nidra). However, this exercise isn't about relaxing – it's about exploring what's going on in the present moment with openness and curiosity. It's like going on a safari in your own body – you never know what you'll find. Simply let the experience unfold moment by moment.

On a safari, you may be rewarded by seeing a magnificent wild animal; in the case of the body scan, your reward may be a strong or noticeable sensation in the body. On safari, you may spend long periods of time observing the landscape, concentrating hard but noticing very little. As you go on more safari expeditions, you start to tune in to the landscape more and notice more and more of what's happening around you. It's much the same with this body scan exercise – your time and effort will be rewarded.

REMEMBER

As you move through the body, you may encounter boredom or frustration. If you do, just acknowledge them and let them go. Doing so will help you to regain your focus more quickly. You may also find that you mysteriously miss whole areas of your body, or even fall asleep! Try to persist as best as you can, even when you feel tired or in a bad frame of mind – this is often when you need it most.

Scanning Your Body

Consider your time spent on training as an investment in you and your future. In a few weeks' time (or even immediately), you'll start to reap the benefits. You may find that things start to become easier both at home and at work as you start the process of dissolving away old habits that are no longer serving you well.

As with all mindfulness practices, be kind to yourself! If you start to beat yourself up because your mind keeps wandering or you fail to detect any sensations in a particular area of your body, all you're doing is making things more difficult for yourself. Simply accept how things are in this moment and try to focus your attention back on the exercise. The body scan isn't a competition – there are no rights and wrongs – simply your experience unfolding moment by moment.

It's recommended that you practice the body scan at least once a day for the next week – more if you can. If you're feeling pressured for time, remember that your mind may be wandering for a high percentage of the day. Taking just 15 minutes to practice a little mindfulness will improve your focus and attention, saving you time in the long run.

Body scan exercise

This section details the body scan exercise step by step. It's recommended that you practice the body scan somewhere you won't be disturbed for around 15 minutes.

PLAY THIS

Use the MP3 recording track 2A or 2B to guide you through the exercise. We have included two versions of this exercise – use the one that works best for you.

Most people practice at home, so you may like to try this lying on a bed, but beware – doing so may put you to sleep! If it does, no problem – you probably needed the sleep – just try it in a chair the next day.

TIP

If at any point during the exercise you feel any discomfort, treat it as an opportunity to explore what's going on. What is your reaction to the discomfort? What stories do you tell yourself about the discomfort? Approach the discomfort with kindness and curiosity. What does it feel like? What sensations arise? What thoughts enter your mind? What emotions are you experiencing? Then try letting go of the discomfort as you breathe out.

1. Sit on a comfortable chair with your feet firmly on the floor.

Sit with your back upright, your knees slightly lower than your hips, and your arms supported and resting comfortably. Make sure your whole body feels balanced and supported. Close your eyes, and try to remain aware of your posture throughout the exercise, and realign yourself if you notice that you're slouching.

2. **Focus your attention on your breath.**

Feel the sensations of your breath coming in and your breath going out. Do so for approximately ten breaths.

3. **Focus your attention on your toes.**

Start with your right foot, and identify whether you can feel any sensations in your toes, such as hot, cold or tingling. See whether you can feel your toes in contact with your socks or shoes. Spend a few moments exploring your toes, and then repeat the process with your left foot. Don't try to create any sensations or make it be any different from how it is; just notice what is there in that moment. If you can't feel any sensation at all, just notice the lack of sensation – that's absolutely fine.

Compare your right and left toes. Do they feel any different?

4. **Focus your attention on the soles of your feet.**

Start with your right sole, and identify what you feel. Repeat the process with your left sole, and then compare the sensations you experienced with your right and left soles.

5. **Focus on your lower legs.**

Spend time exploring the right lower leg then the left, and then compare the two.

6. **Focus on your knees.**

Examine the sensations in your right knee then your left knee, and then compare the two.

7. **Focus on your thighs and bottom.**

Explore how they feel when in contact with the chair.

8. **Explore the sensations in your internal organs.**

Focus on your liver, kidneys, stomach, lungs and heart. You may not notice any sensation at all, and that's okay – just see what you can notice.

9. **Focus on your spine.**

Move up your spine slowly, focusing briefly on one vertebrae at a time, noticing any or no sensations.

10. Focus on your arms.

Identify the sensations in your right arm then your left arm, and then compare the two.

11. Focus on your neck and shoulders.

If you experience any tension or discomfort, try letting it go as you breathe out.

12. Focus on your head

Notice any feelings and sensations in your jaw and facial muscles. Notice how your nose feels? How your eyes feel? How your scalp feels?

13. Expand your attention to gain a sense of how your whole body feels at this moment in time.

14. Open your eyes and return to your day.

Body scan – the science

People commonly carry around pain or tension in their body for long periods. Your body's fascia tissue is like a 3-D woolly jumper covering your muscles and bones. Fascia tissue tenses independently of muscle movement when introduced to the stress hormone cortisol and can hold onto this tension for long periods of time. This tension is quickly communicated to the brain, which registers that something is amiss or needs attention. The body scan achieves three things:

>> It helps you to tune in to and directly explore how your body is feeling in this moment in time.

>> It helps you to further embed and develop the skill of directing attention to where you want it to be, notice when the mind wanders, and gently direct it back

>> It cultivates an open approach mode of mind, which can increase your parasympathetic nervous system activation, resulting in a greater sense of relaxation and mindful awareness.

Awareness of tension, sensations, or other bodily needs enables you to take steps to address them, resulting in an enhanced ability to maintain focus and productivity for longer. This is often as simple as taking a stretch, letting go of tension, or stopping for a drink.

Reflecting on the body scan

Reflect on your learning from the body scan by answering the following questions.

>> What did you notice (try to be as specific as possible)?

>> Did you manage to keep your attention focused throughout, or did your mind wander?

>> Did you find this exercise harder or easier than the mindful breathing exercise in Week 1?

>> Did you notice any marked differences between sensations in different parts of your body or on different sides of your body?

>> Did you encounter any discomfort in your body? If you did, what was the impact of approaching the discomfort, examining it with openness and letting go of it?

>> Can you make any other observations about this experience?

Managing Expectations

On Week 2 of WorkplaceMT courses, we frequently hear comments like these:

'I was expecting to feel more calm and relaxed by now, but instead all I'm noticing is how much my mind wanders'.

'I had thought after practicing for seven days my mind would be a little clearer and I would be sleeping better'.

'I found the body scan so relaxing that I kept on falling asleep. I just could not stay awake!'

Brain scans taken of people before and during mindfulness practice demonstrate that when practicing mindfulness, people often become more aware rather than less. This awareness can create some tension for learners. It takes a lifetime to create habitual patterns of thought and behaviour, and people still think that they can miraculously change things in one week.

In Week 2, it's important that you try to let go of expectations and ideas about what success and failure look like. Your newly acquired awareness of thoughts, emotions and sensations may at times be annoying, but awareness gives you choices. Conversely, if you're unaware that you're doing something, it's impossible to change it.

On this basis, you are invited to view the distractions you encounter when practicing the formal elements of your WorkplaceMT training as a good thing. Congratulations! You're now noticing just how much your mind is wandering. You're noticing your patterns of worry and rumination. The act of noticing and acknowledging these things means they have less power over you. It's a bit like having a tug of war with a strapping rugby player – the harder you pull, the harder he pulls. If you just say to yourself, 'I'm not going to play this game anymore', and let go of the rope, the rugby player no longer has any power over you in that moment. The simple act of acknowledgment is like letting go of the rope that pulls you, making it easier to refocus your attention.

If you fall asleep during this exercise (as many do), don't waste time and emotion by getting frustrated – simply accept it. Working long hours or working in a stressful job takes its toll. Maybe you just needed sleep. A 2008 study of 75,000 US adults jointly conducted with the National Centre on Sleep Disorders identified that 37.9 per cent reported unintentionally falling asleep during the day at least once in the preceding month. So if you do fall asleep during body scan, treat it as a power nap, not a failure.

REMEMBER

Self-kindness is a key element of WorkplaceMT training. Getting angry or frustrated just makes it even harder to concentrate. Remember: It's only a tug of war if you continue to hang onto the rope! it's impossible to fail when practicing mindfulness – every experience is an opportunity for cultivating greater awareness. The simple act of becoming aware of the interplay between your thoughts puts you back in control.

Lin (who we introduced earlier in this chapter in the section 'Working in IT') was offered mindfulness training as a personal well-being and productivity tool. She attended a WorkplaceMT60 course (60 minutes a week for 6 weeks). During Week 2's training session, just after trying out the body scan exercise for the first time, she was given the opportunity to reflect on the exercise with a colleague. Lin confessed that she had found the body scan to be boring. She said, 'It was too slow. I just could not wait for the teacher to bring it to an end!'

Lin's response is common. Not so many years ago, the body scan exercise was around 40 minutes long, but even the shortened WorkplaceMT 15-minute version seemed 'too long' to Lin. She was unaccustomed to focusing on one thing at a time. She craved constant stimulation and novelty. She was also mildly alarmed at how little she could notice about how her body was feeling, feeling the need to wiggle her toes just to check that they were still there!

In the digital age we live in, many people are constantly bombarded with data all day long. In the not-so-distant past, people were proud to say that they multitasked. It was seen as a sign of personal productivity. Of course, we now know that multitasking makes you less productive than focusing on one task at a time. Some multitasking is unavoidable, of course, but it's more productive to single task whenever possible. Despite this, some people still wear multitasking as a badge of honour – it's become a habitual pattern of behaviour. No wonder it can feel difficult when asked to single task when conducing a body scan! What once came naturally now takes time and effort to cultivate.

The more you live your life in your head, the more likely you'll get a sense of disconnection with your body. This was the case for Lin. Lin was able to notice the main contact points of her body, such as her feet in contact with the ground, her bottom in contact with the seat, and the weight of her hands resting in her lap, but very little more than that.

During the week, Lin made time at home to practice the body scan lying down on her bed. Upon the advice of her trainer, she resisted the urge to wiggle her toes or move her body to trigger a sensation. Instead, she tried really hard to simply focus on one bit of the body at a time to see what she noticed. By the middle of the week, she started to tune in to some sensations she hadn't noticed in the past. She noticed mild sensations in her ankles, shoulders, and arms. The bit in the middle still evaded her, but she progressively started to notice more. By the end of the week, much to her surprise, she was starting to notice sensations around her mouth and her eyes.

The foundation work of starting to reconnect with your body is built on further in future weeks of WorkplaceMT training, providing you with the tools to progressively help you to reconnect with and work more effectively with your body.

Week 2 WorkplaceMT Practice Exercises

This week's brain training is designed to help you to tune in to your body and start to hear the messages it's sending you. Doing this will enable you to look after yourself better and ensure that primitive body-based brain circuitry doesn't hijack your attention or limit your thinking.

Week 2 formal mindfulness exercise: Body scan

Your formal practice for this week is the body scan (see the earlier section 'Body scan exercise'). It's a great way to reconnect with the messages your body is sending you.

Practice at least once a day in a location where you won't be disturbed. Use MP3 track 2A or 2B to guide you and keep you on track.

Week 2 informal everyday mindfulness

During Week 2, your informal everyday mindfulness practice includes bringing mindfulness to a routine activity, taking a mindful walk, watching the Amy Cuddy TED talk, and appreciating the moment. How to do each of these is detailed in the following pages.

Mindfulness of a routine activity

Try to pay some mindful attention this week to simple activities that you routinely do without notice. Try being fully mindful when exercising, cycling, or even cooking or washing the dishes. Doing so is another opportunity to increase your awareness of bodily sensations, break out of habitual patterns, and improve your ability to focus.

Observe what arises with a sense of gentle playfulness, fun, and curiosity.

Taking a mindful walk

This week, see if it's possible to do some walking. Walking is great exercise, but it's also a great opportunity to tune in to bodily sensations. If you have a walk on your way to or from work – however short – see if it's possible to fully focus on the sensations of walking. Notice the sights, sounds, and smells surrounding you. Do they evoke any memories? If there's a breeze during your walk, how does it feel against your face? Against your body? If it rains during your walk, focus on how the rain feels as it hits your face and clothes

One mindfulness student tried this on her way back from work each day. She said, 'I started to notice all sorts of architecture that I hadn't noticed before – despite walking this route hundreds of times, I noticed all sorts of things. I walk past a war memorial each day. I stopped to look at the names carved into the stone and the faded poppy wreath by its base. I also witnessed a couple of amazing sunsets, with vivid orange and pinks illuminating the sky'. When asked how much longer her walk home had taken, she commented, 'a few minutes maybe, but it was worth it as I entered the house in a much better mood!'

However desk-bound you may be, at some point in the day, you need to walk somewhere, even if it's simply to the toilet or to and from work. Use some of these moments as an opportunity for a few minutes of mindfulness practice. When walking, really tune in to the sensations of walking. How does it feel as you lift one leg and place the foot down? How does it feel as your body weight shifts from side to side when you lift the other leg and place the foot down? How does it feel to walk on different surfaces (for example carpet versus tarmac)? Can you feel the sensations of muscles contracting and extending?

Experiment with letting go of ideas of 'right' or 'wrong' and just be fully aware with the present-moment raw sensations of walking.

Watching the Amy Cuddy TED talk

This exercise is optional, but it may help to enhance your understanding of the mind-body connection. Search the Internet for 'Amy Cuddy TED Talk how your body language shapes who you are'.

Pausing to appreciate the moment

Try this simple technique to correct your inbuilt negativity bias and give you a more balanced perspective.

When you next encounter something you appreciate or find pleasurable or beautiful, purposefully pause to appreciate it. Spend 10 or 20 seconds to notice the impact it has on you. It doesn't have to be something big; it could be something simple you see every day, such as a beautiful sky, natural landscape or cityscape, or stroking a family pet. It could be pleasant cooking smells, such as baking bread, or someone smiling at you, or a 'thank you' from colleagues or clients at work. As you pause to appreciate these things, consider the following questions:

>> What can you notice about its impact on your body? (Maybe you're smiling or your body has relaxed?)

>> What can you notice about its impact on your mood?

>> Does it trigger any thoughts or memories? Make a mental note of them.

Chapter 10

Week 3: Minding the Gap

I n this chapter, Week 3 of your WorkplaceMT training, we recap learning to date, explore how to work smarter, not harder, and show you how to 'mind the gap'.

In Week 1 of your WorkplaceMT training, you consider how your brain's drive for efficiency can cause problems. It can lead you to live much of your life on autopilot and respond to life challenges with restrictive thinking and behaviour that can inhibit creative opportunities. Over the last two weeks, via your formal and informal WorkplaceMT exercises, you've discovered just how much of the time your attention isn't where you want it to be. You'll hopefully have started to observe that although thoughts aren't facts, they nevertheless can have a powerful influence on your life. You should also be noticing the stories your brain constructs and practicing separating these stories (mental constructs) from present-moment facts.

If you've followed the suggestions in the last few chapters, you're experimenting with suspending judgment and the urge to instantly jump into doing mode. You may have started to pause, stand back, and decide how to deploy your limited attention resources more wisely. You may be accepting and parking things that can't be changed (or are in truth not worth the effort) and making wiser decisions about which things are worthy of your full attention.

You should also be starting to notice the mind-body connection, and tuning into the messages your body is sending you. You will hopefully now be starting to notice the impact that (often hidden) emotions are having on your ability to lead. By acknowledging the presence of these, you may have noticed that their impact is lessened or even eliminated.

Working Smarter, Not Harder

Between 1983 and 1986, Commodore Computers was a market leader. Its sales of the Commodore 64 computer were over 2 million units a year, which equated to a staggering 50 per cent of the market. The Commodore 64 outsold both Apple and IBM.

To extend its market reach further still, it attempted to innovate by releasing the Commodore plus/4. The new unit was faster and smarter, boasting a state-of-the-art colour screen. The new model was incompatible with the old, much cherished, Commodore 64. Commodore Computers tried to discontinue its old model but only succeeded in alienating its original customer base. It announced that it would stop selling the 64 in 1985, but this tactic also failed. Customers all over Europe continued to buy the old model until eventually it became impossible for the company to manufacture them at a reasonable cost. The company went bankrupt in 1994.

When you find that things aren't working, what do you do? Do you continue to push and work harder and harder in an effort to make it work? Sometimes stubbornly pushing at things achieves little. In many cases, it simply makes things worse, as in the case of Commodore Computers. It can close down creativity and send you running in ever-decreasing circles. If something isn't working, it's often better to stop and try something different.

Perhaps if Commodore had stopped and taken stock, asking questions like, 'Why do our customers love the Commodore 64?' 'What makes our customers so loyal?' 'Why do customers want to stick with the 64 when the new plus/4 offers more features?' If it stopped stubbornly trying to force its customers to change and had listened instead, it would quite possibly still be in business today.

Minding the Gap

In the next few pages, we explore the 'gap' between how we think things are, or how we think things should be, and how they actually are in this moment in time. In WorkplaceMT training, we call this 'minding the gap'.

Like all animals that roam the earth, people are products of their thoughts and experiences. This is, for the most part, a good thing. If you accidently burn yourself by getting too close to a fire, you remember not to do so again in the future, thus keeping yourself safe from harm. Over time, your brain stores a number of hidden rules for life. These rules for the most part probably serve you well and have almost certainly contributed to your career success to date.

The problem with hidden rules is that they're hidden! Cultivating mindfulness will help you to progressively notice these hidden rules. In WorkplaceMT training, we humorously refer to this as 'mind the gap'. We teach people to progressively observe their ways of thinking and patterns of thought. As you discover in Chapter 2, your mental construct is how you'd like things to be, how you think things are or how you think things should be. Your mental construct may be at odds with present-moment reality.

Only when you're consciously aware of your mental construct can you decide whether your thoughts are facts or fiction.

Consider this example: Thomas, a UK Army major, had finished 25 years' service in the Army and was entitled to leave with a decent pension. As he was still relatively young (in his late 40s), he decided to embark on a second career. Thomas secured a new job working in a leadership role on the risk management side of a multinational company. Despite having years of experience in man management, he found himself struggling to engage staff and gain support for his proposals.

In his Army career, Thomas's leadership was built on a number of key leadership principles. Thomas diligently applied these to his new role. He encouraged his team to seek responsibility and take responsibility for their actions. Unfortunately, his new organisation seemed to have a blame culture, and few people wanted to seek new responsibilities.

Thomas tried hard to develop a sense of responsibility in his followers, to engender a sense of pride and ownership when they successfully accomplished a new task given them. He reasoned that by delegating responsibility to his followers he was indicating that he trusted them. He tried hard to deploy his team, according to their capabilities. He reasoned that as their leader it was his job to use his judgment to deploy staff where they would best serve the company. In his mind, failure was not an option. Experience had taught him that only by deploying the team properly would he ensure mission accomplishment.

Unfortunately, his new team didn't see it quite that way. In their eyes, everything had been fine before Thomas arrived. They always received their bonuses, they knew what they were doing, and they liked the way that they had always worked.

Thomas couldn't understand why his new team was failing to get behind his plans to make the department more efficient. Thinking back to the 11 principles of Army leadership he had been taught at Sandhurst, which had always served him well in the past, he couldn't comprehend why they were failing him now. Didn't his team want to grow and develop? Didn't they want to improve their technical capability? Didn't they want to set an example to other departments?

Thomas was no fool – in fact, he was highly intelligent. Although he was making a conscious effort to do things differently, he still defaulted back to old patterns of thoughts and behaviour. This can be explained by the brain's innate drive to maximise reward while at the same time keeping you safe. In Thomas's case, leading people in a certain way had been both financially and practically rewarding. It got him to the rank of major and helped him to successfully lead his teams over the years and safeguard the communities he served.

What Thomas was experiencing was a classic 'mind the gap' moment. In his mind, he thought his staff should be thinking and behaving in a certain way. His mental construct was that they should all want to grow and develop, to improve their technical capabilities, and to set an example to other departments. The present-moment reality or facts were that his team's desire for growth and development was limited, and they had no desire to stand out from the crowd or be different in any way.

Recognising 'mind the gap' in action helped Thomas to start to rewrite his rule book, replacing old ways of leading with new ones.

TIP

When you find yourself getting tense or frustrated that things aren't as you'd like them to be or thought they would be, smile and think to yourself 'mind the gap!' Take stock of the present-moment reality. What are the facts? What's going on? See whether you can simply acknowledge and accept present-moment reality. Doing so will prevent you from spiralling into unhelpful cycles of negative thoughts and emotions and make wiser decisions about what to do next.

Remember that you are the author of your brain! You create your unique neural circuitry that governs how you live your life. Mindfulness helps you to develop awareness of your mental processes. You can use this awareness to help you to rewrite your rule book periodically.

Noticing Patterns of Thought

In Week 1 of the mindfulness training (see Chapter 8), you consider that thoughts are not facts. In the same way, mental programming is simply mental programming. It may take time and effort to replace faulty or out-of-date mental programming, but it can be done. Over the next week, try to notice patterns of thinking and thoughts that restrict. Avoid the judgment trap, and observe them just as they are – not good or bad, efficient or inefficient – and without wasting any emotions on them. They are as they are!

As you notice more and more of your hidden rules, you may spot trends or patterns of thinking or behaving. If these aren't serving you well, you can make a conscious decision to try to replace them with new ways of thinking and responding.

Applying Kindness to Your Work

The benefits of mindfulness can't be fully appreciated without a foundation of empathy and self-kindness. These are concepts that have not, until fairly recently, formed part of management and executive education. In business circles, some people view empathy and kindness as a sign of weakness – the preserve of tree-hugging hippies. Nowadays, more people realise that kindness, empathy and self-care make good business sense.

For example, many people report feeling overwhelmed by a growing number of meetings and conference calls that drain the life out of them. Even worse, many of the hours spent in meetings can be unproductive. In a global productivity survey by Microsoft, 70 per cent of the 38,000 survey participants felt that their meetings were a waste of time.

Imagine yourself in a meeting where politics and games are at play, and attendees are jockeying for airtime. Imagine having your contribution shot down in flames or not being able to get a word in edgeways about something you care passionately about. How do you feel just thinking about that now? What are your thoughts? How does your body feel? Are you experiencing any emotions? Try to be as specific as possible.

The simple act of thinking about something you find unpleasant can evoke really strong reactions. Even though it's only a thought, it can feel as if it's really happening. It can trigger your threat response and tip you into avoidance mode, which can be bad news for work from a creativity, cooperation, and innovation perspective.

The good news is that research now indicates that kindness and empathy can reduce self-criticism and act as an effective 'off switch' for the threat system. Even the act of wishing yourself or others well in your head can do this. This may be explained by Polyvagal theory. You respond to the world via your nervous system. Polyvagal theory proposes that you have three key nervous system responses – life threat, danger and safety. You can be in only one of these states at once.

In a hostile meeting, you may be operating in danger mode. You're ready to fight your corner or retreat to safety when needed. In this state, you're operating in avoidance mode – you're likely to make safe decisions based on things that have worked in the past. Creativity and innovation are off the agenda.

If you recognise this and decide you want to switch to a more productive working mode, simply be kind. You don't need to go out and physically hug someone or give away your life savings to a random stranger; simply wish yourself or others well in your head. Try to be genuine. If that is difficult, then imagine that you really mean it. Visualise the interaction as vividly as you can. Doing so will help you transition towards a safety state, from which it's easier to socially engage with others and come up with new and creative solutions. Transitioning from danger mode to safety mode is likely to have a positive impact on others around you who may also start operating from a position of trust and social engagement.

Being kind and empathetic is good for you, your employees and your company as a whole.

TIP

When you next start a meeting, take a second to wish that everyone attending the meeting should have a successful meeting and the opportunity to express his point of view. Observe the impact that this has on your experience of the meeting.

Adopting an Approach Mode of Mind

In simple terms, when in 'approach mode' your motivation for acting is to make something 'good' to happen. When in 'avoidance mode' your motivation for action is to avoid something 'bad' from happening.

In a well-known study published in 2001, Ronald Friedman and Jens Forster examined how the approach and avoidance systems impact task performance. In this study, college students were given a simple task to undertake: to find a way through a maze printed on a sheet of paper. One group was told that it needed to find a way through the maze to help a mouse towards a tasty lump of cheese. The other group was told that it needed to help the mouse through the maze to avoid it being eaten by a hungry owl that was chasing it. Both groups completed the task in relatively little time, after which they were asked to complete a simple task. The group who'd been helping the mouse towards the cheese was 50 per cent more creative than the group who had helped their mouse to avoid the owl.

The action of helping the mouse to seek security by fleeing away from the owl, even though it was imaginary, put the student's minds into *avoidance mode.* This mode of mind is concerned with survival and, as a result, closes down options and increases caution. The act of helping the mouse towards the cheese put the group's minds into *approach mode,* which reduces stress and increases curiosity and creativity. The following explore these two modes in further detail.

Adopting an approach mode of mind at work

When under pressure or when times are hard, it's easy to slip into avoidance mode of mind, which narrows your outlook and reduces your effectiveness. Practicing mindfulness helps you to cultivate an approach mode, which increases your creativity and improves your negotiation skills.

To adopt an approach mode of mind at work, try the following:

>> If you hear someone talking about what he doesn't want, ask him what he would like instead.

>> If someone is fixated on a problem, ask her what an ideal solution would look like.

>> If negotiations or discussions have stalled, invite people to describe a similar situation in the past and what worked then.

Understanding the science of approach and avoidance

Neuroimaging studies, using fMRI or PET, have shown that approach mode activates the left prefrontal cortex. It also activates the medial prefrontal cortex (associated with decision-making and perspective taking) as well as the nucleus accumbens (associated with our reward circuitry). Avoidance mode activates the right prefrontal cortex. It also activates the amygdala (often described as our fear center) and anterior cingulate cortex (which helps regulate blood pressure and heart rate).

Taking Stock of Your Progress

In Week 3, you should be beginning to notice the power of mindfulness to enhance many aspects of your life. The changes you're experiencing may be subtle, but they're nevertheless starting to make an impact.

Maybe you're sleeping better and trying new things. You may be getting less wound up with little things. You may be smiling a little more, possibly noticing and appreciating the architecture and landscapes surrounding you, when someone smiles, or when someone says thank you.

Consider this example of Lin, an IT worker (described in Chapter 9), who was noticing a subtle shift:

> Each month, Lin had administrative tasks to complete, including overtime claims and expenses authorization for her team and project reporting. She normally procrastinated and avoided these tasks until the last minute, leading to her ploughing through, late into the night, working through gritted teeth, harbouring a deep sense of resentment. After all, she reasoned, it wasn't 'real work' and certainly wasn't a productive use of her time.
>
> After noticing the patterns of her thoughts around administrative work, Lin recognised that she was working in avoidance mode of mind. On top of this, she noticed just how tense her body became just thinking about completing her monthly

tasks. Instead of leaving it to the end of the month, she experimented with staggering her administrative work over the month. Whenever she noticed signs of tension in her body, she made an effort to observe any thoughts or emotions associated, take a stretch or move round, and then refocus on the task in hand.

Lin experimented with simply accepting that the tasks needed doing, without attaching judgments such as 'a good use of my time' or 'a bad use of my time'. Her sense of the burden of the administrative aspects of her work reduced. Towards the end of the month, she was out one evening with some friends from work. One of her friends started to moan about work, saying, 'Authorising expenses involves duplicating the same information into three different systems. What are they thinking of? Anyone would think I have nothing better to do with my time, and don't get me started on the version control and flagging system for project reporting!' Lin noticed how her friend's shoulders were hunched and tense. She found herself smiling as she remembered how stressed she used to feel and realised that she no longer felt that way.

REMEMBER

Mindfulness is about recognising your patterns of thought and behaviour and using this knowledge to manage yourself better. It's about changing how you live your life so it becomes more enjoyable. Mindfulness certainly doesn't turn your life into a bed of roses. Anger, sadness and frustrations will still occur, but they should become easier to deal with and be significantly less debilitating.

Stretching without Striving

This week's formal exercise builds on last week's (see Chapter 9), helping you to increasingly reconnect and befriend your body. This week's exercise takes it a step further, showing you how to stretch without striving. Mindful movement involves anchoring your present-moment awareness in the moving body. It has the added benefit that it can help you to realign your body, muscles and joints.

You should plan to do this at least once a day for the next week.

You may feel a little stiff or uncomfortable, especially if you've been sitting still for long periods of time. If this is the case, simply explore these sensations, but don't push your body beyond its limits. Let your body decide what's okay for you. If you're at all concerned about your health, consult a medical practitioner for advice. Try to avoid being overly competitive. This exercise is not about how far or high you can stretch; it's about reconnecting with the experience of moving.

Pay particular attention when working with areas of your body that have been injured in the past or are hurting. Tune in to your experience of stretching and stop if you need to.

Stretching without striving exercise

This week's mindful movement exercise consists of three chair-based stretches. In each of the stretching exercises, you're guided to do the exercise yourself, fully experiencing its impacts, before pushing the stretch a little further and experiencing the impact of the deeper stretch.

Be sure to start each exercise in approach mode, with openness and curiosity, suspending judgment and experiencing sensations and thought as they arise in the present moment.

Stretch 1: Elbow and arm stretch

This exercise involves a simple elbow and arm stretch as illustrated in Figure 10-1.

1. **Sit comfortably in your chair in an upright position with both feet on the floor.**

2. **Gently raise your right arm above your head. Bend your right arm at the elbow 90 degrees. Rotate your right arm down so that it's touching your left shoulder blade. Gently pull your right elbow slightly to the left until you feel a comfortable stretch.**

   Hold the stretch for a few moments, noticing the sensations of the stretch, any thoughts, emotions or impulses.

© John Wiley & Sons, Inc.

FIGURE 10-1: Elbow and arm stretch.

3. **Extend the stretch a little further, using your left hand to pull your right elbow a little further to the left.**

   Once again, pause to notice your physical and cognitive response to the exercise.

4. **Let go of your right elbow, extend your right arm back up towards the sky, and then gently lower it back to your side.**

5. **Repeat with the other arm, observing the interplay of thoughts, sensations, and emotions as they arise while suspending judgment.**

Stretch 2: The shrug

This exercise involves a simple shoulder stretch as illustrated in Figure 10-2.

© John Wiley & Sons, Inc.

FIGURE 10-2: The shrug.

1. **Place both feet firmly on the floor with your buttocks firmly on the chair base and your knees bent at 90 degrees.**

   Allow your hands to hang loosely from your sholders.

2. **Shrug both sholders upwards.**

   Tune in to the sensations, thoughts, or emotions that arise with a sense of oppeness and exploration.

3. **Relase the shrug and let your sholders fall back to their natural resting position.**

4. **Repeat slowly several times and see what you observe.**

5. **Shrug your sholders up as far as it's comfortable to do so, and hold as long as it's comfortable to do so.**

   Again, observe the interplay of sensations and thoughts. Release when ready, observing the aftereffects.

Stretch 3: Head rolls

This exercise involves a gentle neck stretch as illustrated in Figure 10-3.

© John Wiley & Sons, Inc.

FIGURE 10-3: Head rolls.

1. **Place both feet on the floor and sit in a comfortable upright position.**

2. **Lean your head forward and slowly and gently roll it to the right.**

   Hold this pose for a few moments, placing your attention on any sensations, thoughts or impulses you experience.

3. **Gently roll your head back to the centre.**

   Notice the aftereffects of the exercise.

4. **Repeat on the other side.**

5. **Being careful not to stretch your neck muscles too far, repeat Steps 1 and 2, stretching your neck to the right, but this time stretch your neck a little further.**

Hold and observe.

6. **Repeat on the other side.**

Reflecting on mindful movement

How did you get on with the three mindful movement exercises? What did you notice? Did you notice any aversion or even mild fear creeping in when you pushed the stretch a little further or held the stretch a little longer?

Here are some examples of other WorkplaceMT participants' experiences of the exercises.

>> Jim, an HR Partner, attended a WorkplaceMT course recently. His competitive nature led him to try to outstretch everyone else in the session. As he pushed each stretch further and further, his body started to tense. He was striving too hard, and this started to tip him into avoidance mode. During reflection time after the exercise, he started to recognise for himself how his competitive nature had impacted his experience during the exercise, and he started to consider whether this was benefitting him at work or achieving little and making life harder than it needed to be.

>> Margo, a health and safety specialist experienced an ongoing right shoulder rotator cuff problem. During the exercise, she experienced a fear response. Her fear of pain was restricting her movement. She noticed that she began to tense each time she moved her right arm. She took a deep breath, relaxed her muscles and tried the stretch again, progressively stretching a little further each time while tuning in to the experience and observing her responses. She discovered that she had a much greater range of mobility in her right shoulder before discomfort arose than she had thought possible. She was tensing *in anticipation* of the pain, not because of the pain. She smiled to herself as she recognised a 'mind the gap' moment in action.

The science behind stretching without striving

REMEMBER

Mindful movement helps you to further reconnect with your body and tune in to the messages it's sending you. You welcome messages of feeling good and messages of feeling fearful. Intentionally embracing and approaching mild discomfort can be a valuable skill for life. Often the act of avoidance (as in Margo's example in the previous section) triggers a disproportionate response. It often takes more effort to avoid discomfort than approach it and learn to accept and live with it. The simple act of approach and exploration of things you normally avoid in life can be truly liberating.

In addition to this, stretching at your desk improves well-being while releasing stress and tension. Research indicates that periodic workplace stretching may reduce pain by up to 72 per cent. Some studies show that a bit of exercise in the workday can relieve both physical and mental stress. Physical activity – even for short periods of time – can improve your mood, making you more agreeable to work with and more likely to work in approach mode.

TIP

Experiment with stretching without striving while doing exercises such as cycling, swimming, running or using the cross trainer at the gym. You can try pushing yourself a little harder and observing the impacts this has on your thoughts and the messages your body sends you back in response.

Mindfulness of Breath and Body

In Week 1 (see Chapter 8), you experience mindfulness of breath. Repeating this mindfulness exercise just after physical exercise can help you tune in to the subtle changes that arise in your body following exertion. Maintaining an open monitoring state – observing sensations as they arise, change, and get stronger or softer – helps to deepen your connection with your body. Doing so helps you tune in to the messages your body is sending you more and more quickly, improving your ability to manage yourself.

PLAY THIS

Try this exercise (Track 3) immediately after exercising to help you tune in to the subtle changes that arise in your body following exertion:

1. **Settle yourself into a chair and sit in an upright posture that is both comfortable and confident.**

   Place both feet firmly on the floor, your knees slightly lower than your hips, your spine upright with a natural curve, and your shoulders and arms relaxed.

2. Close your eyes or hold them in soft focus gazing downwards.

3. **Focus your attention on your breath.**

   Explore the sensations of the breath coming in and the breath coming out. Remember that you don't need to change or control your breathing in any way – how you're breathing right now is just fine. Spend a few minutes resting your full attention on the rich tapestry that forms the sensations of breathing.

4. **Move your attention to your body.**

   What sensations can you notice? What are the qualities of these sensations – soft, hard, tingling, hot or cold? Where do you feel them? Try to be as precise as you can.

5. **Continue to maintain a broad awareness of your whole body for a few minutes.**

   Allow sensations to enter your awareness as they arise without the need to change them or make them go away – simply notice that they're there. Notice any thoughts that arise, acknowledging them and then letting them go, like clouds drifting past on a windy day.

TIP

   If you notice your mind wandering, inwardly smile and then kindly and gently escort your attention back to monitoring how your whole body feels.

   If intense sensations arise, observe if possible any chain reactions they trigger. Observe how or if they draw your attention away from focusing on the body as a whole. In time, the sensation may change or dissipate.

If the intense sensation does not dissipate and it proves to be really distracting, move your body gently. As you do so, tune in to how it feels to move and the aftereffects of moving. Pay attention to the precise qualities of sensations.

6. **Open your eyes, stand up and stretch, if you wish, in preparation to reconnect with your day.**

The Three-Step Breathing Space

In Weeks 1 and 2 (see Chapters 8 and 9, respectively), you start to observe the wandering mind. The object of the exercise isn't to control or clear your mind but rather to hold a magnifying glass to your patterns of mind. By now, you have likely started to develop the ability to observe your mind in action and have begun to notice when your thoughts start to wander. With practice, you'll begin to notice this at an earlier stage and will benefit from improved focus and attention and increased positivity.

You may have also noticed that when you experience unpleasantness, you don't automatically fall into a state of anger, despair, fear or distraction. You can start to simply observe intense sensations as they arise, accept their presence, and then watch them gently shift, dissipate or remain. By stopping striving and simply letting them be, they often resolve themselves or shift into something more manageable.

The next exercise brings together a number of the things you've practiced in the last few weeks into a neat compact model that you can use anywhere, anytime. The exercise is very short (three minutes or less) and involves both fixed concentration (as you experience in Week 1's mindfulness of breath) and open monitoring (as you experience in mindfulness of breath and body).

While you've probably been practicing your formal exercises in the peace of your own home, this exercise is commonly practiced on the job in the workplace. But you can practice it anywhere, anytime. You can use it to punctuate your day, or when you feel under pressure or when you're switching activities and want to start afresh. The whole exercise should not take longer than three minutes but can be practiced in less time, or extended to take longer. It's your choice.

In Step 1, you move from your busy work-life doing mode into being mode. You observe what's going on for you at this moment. In Step 2, you anchor your attention on the sensations of breathing. In Step 3, you return to an open monitoring state, aware of everything that's going on around you, ready for the rest of your day. (Figure 10-4 provides an illustration to help you visualize these steps.)

Observing and accepting thoughts, emotions and bodily sensations in the present moment

Narrowing the focus of your attention Present moment sensations of breathing (interrupting the brain's narrative)

Open, relaxed awareness, ready to refocus on the task in hand

© John Wiley & Sons, Inc.

FIGURE 10-4: The three-step breathing space.

PLAY THIS

Track 4 guides you through this exercise, and you can also consult the following steps to work through the three-step breathing space exercise:

1. **Start with a wide focus on what's going on for you now:**

- Settle yourself into your chair in a comfortable upright posture and close your eyes, or hold them in soft focus.

- Direct your attention to your thoughts. Observe them simply as mental processes that come and go, without the need to get involved, judge or fix.

- Notice any emotions you're experiencing and how your body is feeling.

2. **Narrow your focus to fixed concentration:**

- Direct your attention to your breath.

- Using the breath as an anchor, tune in to the sensations of the breath coming in and the breath coming out.

  You don't need to change anything or do anything different; simply use the breath as an anchor or magnet for your attention.

3. **Expand your awareness, ready to focus on the rest of your day:**

- Expand your awareness to notice any sounds that may be surrounding you, the temperature of the room, and the sounds in the room and outside, perhaps any smells if present. How does your whole body feel as you're sitting in this moment in time?

- Open your eyes, if closed, ready to reconnect and focus on the rest of the day.

Week 3 WorkplaceMT Practice Exercises

This week's formal mindfulness exercise builds on last week's, helping you to increasingly reconnect and befriend your body. Mindful movement takes this a step further by showing you how to stretch without striving. Mindful movement involves anchoring your present-moment awareness in the moving body. It has the added benefit that it can help you to realign your body, muscles and joints.

Your informal everyday mindfulness exercises this week include cultivating an approach mode of mind and practicing the three-step breathing space while at work.

Week 3 formal mindfulness exercise

Your formal practice for this week is mindful movement followed by mindfulness of breath and body, as detailed earlier in this chapter.

The mindful movement exercise consists of three chair-based stretches In each of the stretching exercises, you're guided to do the exercise yourself, fully experiencing its impacts, before pushing the stretch a little further and experiencing the impact of the deeper stretch. Notice what happens when you stretch further. Observe your tendency:

>> Do you push beyond your limit and strive to go as deep as possible even if it's uncomfortable?

>> Do you pull away, in aversion to the discomfort?

Your tendency to relentlessly strive or to pull away when under pressure may mirror your autopilot approach to life in general when faced with a difficulty.

Practice at least once a day in a location where you won't be disturbed. Use the MP3 recording Track 3 (mindfulness of breath and body) after your mindful movement.

Week 3 informal everyday mindfulness

During Week 3, your informal everyday mindfulness practices are as follows:

>> Practicing the three-step breathing space twice a day or whenever you can fit it in. Use MP3 Track 4 to guide you initially when practicing at home, but try to practice without it when at work.

>> Experimenting with cultivating an approach mode of mind when you procrastinate or go to lengths to avoid doing something

>> Doing an everyday activity mindfully, as detailed in Chapter 10's informal home practice

Chapter 11

Week 4: Recognising That Thoughts Are Not Facts

R ead the following story one line at a time. After reading each line, pause for a moment. Noticing the thoughts, images, emotions and sensations that emerge as the story unfolds line by line.

Reggie entered the bank.

He drew a gun.

He pointed it at the cashier, looked her in the eye, and uttered the words 'bang, bang'.

He left the bank holding his mother's hand.

What did you notice? Who was Reggie? Was he a gangster? A bank customer? A bank employee? Or was he a little boy? What stories were you making up as you read each line?

This story illustrates how your brain works tirelessly in the background to try to make sense of the world around you. We call it 'the guessing game'. Your mind continuously tries to fill in the gaps it encounters, using all available information, including your past experiences. It elaborates and embellishes the information, it judges, and it tries to fit what you're seeing or experiencing with past experience. Furthermore, the negativity bias means that the mind has a bias towards applying negative interpretations to fill the gaps when seeking to make the uncertain more certain.

The focus of Week 4's exercise is to help make you more aware of self-attacking and unhelpful thoughts that restrict your choices in life. It provides the tools to help you stand back and gain perspective instead of being pulled down or derailed.

In this chapter, you explore further your brain's 'guessing game' and the impact it can have on your work. You examine common causes of mental pain, and develop strategies to help reduce them. You are also introduced to your mindfulness activities for this week, which includes continuing on with the three-step breathing space from Chapter 10 and mindfulness of sounds and thoughts.

Observing the Guessing Game

The guessing game illustrated by Reggie's story in the chapter intro repeats itself all day every day People see things differently. What one person may view in his mind's eye can differ wildly from what someone else sees. Consider this example:

> Gerald was a 15-year-old boy with severe autism. One of his greatest pleasures in life was travelling up and down the local shopping centre's escalators. Each week on Sunday morning, his mother took him to the shopping centre where he would travel up and down, giggling and smiling. One Sunday, he arrived at the escalators and froze on the spot. His face fell, his body tensed, and he burst into tears. He was inconsolable, and

his mother could get no sense out of him. He stood glued to the spot wailing inconsolably. It was only then that his mother noticed that something had changed. A new sign had been added to the escalator that read 'dogs must be carried'. She realised that due to his autism, Gerald had taken this literally, and because he had no dog to carry, he believed that he was no longer allowed to ride the escalator!

The way you interpret the world has a major impact on how you respond to it. Consider the story of Jim, a 56-year-old HR director, who was suddenly faced with redundancy. Just thinking about the possibility of redundancy evoked strong emotions. His heart pounded, and his body tensed. One thought triggered another and another, sending him into a negative thought spiral.

Being concerned when your job security is threatened is natural, because losing a job can impact so many areas of your life. However, overthinking or excessive worry is rarely helpful. As you can see from Jim's example, just the *thought* of being made redundant was causing immense mental pain.

Although Jim had no control over the *situation* he found himself in (being at risk of redundancy), he did have control of his *interpretation* of the situation and thus his *response or reactions* to what was going on.

Separating the facts from your interpretation

Discovering how to separate the situation you're facing from what comes next (see Figure 11-1 for a visual) is an important skill for life and a skill we try to get participants to develop on WorkplaceMT courses. Although mindfulness can't possibly shield you from the challenges you'll face in life, it can help you to pause and take a few moments to interpret the situation more fully, which may help you to choose a more skilful response.

Whilst you may not be able to control what life throws at you (the facts), you do have control over your interpretation and what happens next.

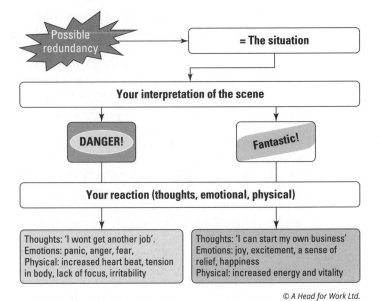

FIGURE 11-1: Separating the facts from your interpretation and response.

Try following these steps to help you separate the facts in any given situation from what comes next:

1. **Think of a mildly challenging situation you encountered at work recently. Describe the situation in as much detail as possible.**

2. **Ask yourself these questions about the situation:**

- What were the facts?

- What was your initial interpretation of what was going on? Did you judge it as good or bad, as a threat or an opportunity?

- How did you react as a result (behaviours, emotions, actions)?

3. **Consider the situation and ask yourself these questions:**

- Looking back on it now, are there any different interpretations that you could have drawn?

- Could your response have been different?

Surviving adversity

Viktor Frankl was an Austrian neurologist and psychiatrist as well as a Holocaust survivor. He was born in Vienna in 1905 to a Jewish family of civil servants. As a medical student, he organised and offered a special programme to counsel high-school students free of charge to reduce risk of suicide. As a result, in 1931, not a single Viennese student at his campus had committed suicide.

From 1933 to 1937, Viktor Frankl studied neurology and psychiatry at the Steinhof Psychiatric Hospital in Vienna. He was responsible for the 'suicide pavilion', where he treated more than 30,000 people who had suicidal tendencies. At the beginning of the Nazi takeover of Austria in 1938 until the early 1940s, he worked at the Rothschild Hospital, where he headed its neurological department.

In December 1941, Frankl married. On 25 September 1942, Frankl, his wife, and his parents were deported to the Nazi Ghetto. There, Frankl worked as a general practitioner in a clinic. On 19 October 1944, Frankl and his wife, Tilly, were transported to the Auschwitz concentration camp before moving to the Kaufering concentration camp, where he arrived on 25 October 1944. There, he spent five months working as a slave labourer.

Frankl's experiences as a concentration camp inmate drove him to write the book *Man's Search for Meaning*, where he discusses the importance of finding meaning in all forms of existence, even the most brutal ones, and thus a reason to continue living. The following quotes from his book powerfully illustrate why separating the situations or challenges you face from what comes next is a vital self-management tool.

> 'Everything can be taken from a man but one thing: the last of the human freedoms — to choose one's attitude in any given set of circumstances, to choose one's own way'.

> 'Between stimulus and response, there is a space. In that space is our power to choose our response. In our response lies our growth and our freedom'.

> 'When we are no longer able to change a situation, we are challenged to change ourselves'.

The mental attitude of those living in concentration camps could literally mean the difference between life and death. Frankl watched as some inmates were able to pick up their weary, malnourished bodies and trudge on, while others simply mentally gave up and died.

Luckily for us, few people reading this book live in daily fear of death. What we share with them is the human search for certainty. Humans hate uncertainty and go to great lengths to create certainty when it's absent. As a result, your mind is constantly making guesses to bridge the gaps in your knowledge. It regularly creates elaborate works of fiction that it uses as the foundations for your decisions and actions.

For example, consider the following list. Which of these are facts?

>> Christopher Columbus discovered America.

>> Bats are blind.

>> The Great Wall of China is the only man-made structure that can be seen from outer space.

>> People thought the world was flat before Christopher Columbus.

>> Mars is red.

>> The pyramids in Egypt were built by slaves.

All the above are untrue. They are myths that persist. The human mind often finds it very difficult to differentiate between fact and fiction. The stories that our minds construct can have a powerful impact on our lives, decisions and actions.

Acting on assumptions

In October 2008, CNN's iReport website posted that Apple founder and CEO Steve Jobs had suffered a heart attack. Apple shares fell dramatically as a result. The report was later removed after a Silicon Valley insider and others confirmed with Apple that Jobs did not have a heart attack. Stock jumped back up to its opening levels again later that day.

Although CNN's iReport website clearly stated that 'the views and content on this site are solely those of the iReport.com contributors. CNN makes no guarantees about the content or the coverage on iReport.com', people interpreted the post as a fact, and it temporarily wiped around 5 per cent off Apple's share value.

TIP

We encourage you to try a little experiment. Over the next week, pay special attention to the assumptions (rumours of the mind) that you make. Carefully separate fact from assumption, and label them as such. Avoid falling into the trap that assumptions are bad – they can be very valuable, and they may even be correct. The simple act of acknowledging them as assumptions saves you from the compulsion to embellish them further. Facts are facts; assumptions are assumptions – treat them as such. Do so with good humour and a gentle sprinkling of self-kindness. It's not your fault that your brain makes assumptions – it's only doing so to try to help you.

Reducing Mental Pain

Are you your own worst enemy? As the saying goes, we are usually our harshest critics! We don't always have control over the challenges that life throws in our path, but we do have control over how we respond. Unfortunately, as humans, we have a tendency to make life harder than it needs to be. Although some level of difficulty and some unpleasant events are inevitable, self-induced suffering and metaphorical self-beatings are entirely optional.

If you consider the difficulties you may encounter in life – physical pain, insults from others, rejections at work or home, loss (financial or personal), problems associated with aging, or sickness – you will probably observe that although these quickly lead to uncomfortable physical symptoms, in time they pass. And they often pass quickly.

Self-induced pain arises through your thoughts, which are based on your interpretation of the event, and not the event itself. If someone gave you a wooden baseball bat and asked you to beat him with it, you'd probably conclude that he was mentally ill or a masochist. Yet many people routinely cause themselves unnecessary avoidable pain every single day.

Mental pain is self-induced pain, which is non-physical in origin. All humans suffer mental pain, with some suffering more than others. Most of the time, people are unaware that they're causing themselves pain as their mind spirals away from the present moment and into a fantasy world of assumptions and predictions of the future.

As we describe in Chapter 3, just imagining things can lead to changes in the brain that are very similar to actually experiencing them in real life. Practicing mindfulness increases your awareness of the interplay between your thoughts, emotions and physiology. This awareness coupled with self-kindness is vital for effective self-management, helping you to maintain peak performance, resilience and well-being.

Think about an event that happened recently that caused you mild anxiety, fear or pain, and then follow these steps:

1. Define the event objectively, noticing and labelling any emotions that arise.

2. Describe your immediate thoughts and responses to the event.

3. Describe your thoughts, emotions and actions following on from this event as if you were observing this chain of events from an outsider's perspective:

    - How helpful or unhelpful were your thoughts and emotions following on from the event?

    - Was the 'pain' caused by the event itself more or less than the 'pain' induced by your thoughts about it?

    - See if you can rate the 'pain' caused by the event itself versus the pain caused by fretting or overthinking (for example, 40/60 or 50/50).

How did you get on? Was the self-induced pain equal to, less than or more than the pain generated by the event itself? What do you take from this exercise?

Thoughts and the stories your mind constructs can be the cause of much suffering. Dismissing thoughts as nonsense or telling yourself to 'get a grip' often does little more than simply make you feel worse. The more stressed you become, the more self-criticism and mental pain you're likely to experience.

Becoming aware that thoughts are not facts enables you to stand back and gain perspective then decide whether to take them seriously or not.

This exercise is not about *fixing* things and *avoiding* unpleasantness – it's about experiencing life as it is, accepting it, and making the effort to stop it escalating further.

Recognising your inner bully

Within most people dwells something quite unpleasant – something everyone would rather keep secret – a unique inner bully.

The taunts and abuse people receive from their inner bully vary from person to person but may include fear of criticism, fears that you're not good enough, or fear that if you relax and let go, everything will fall apart. One doctor I worked with had a fear of being 'found out' – that although she was a qualified doctor with many years' experience, she was somehow not up to the job and at any moment she might be discovered for the imposer she was. In my experience, *imposter syndrome* is common amongst leaders, and it's certainly something the inner bully likes to play upon.

People often try to drown the inner bully with alcohol, or tranquilize it with drugs, or forget about it by indulging in online shopping. A number of women I know have tried to 'eat it into submission' with chocolate or ice cream. Unfortunately, none of these strategies work.

No matter how in control or successful people seem to be, most have an inner bully. The difference is that some are better at managing it than others. The fastest way to make an inner bully retreat is a healthy dose of acceptance and self-kindness.

As with all bullies, the first thing to do is to expose them. You can do this by calmly and kindly acknowledging that you're bullying yourself. Some inner bullies are clever, flying under the radar to avoid detection, making you feel stressed, useless or miserable. Noticing your inner bully at work and shining a spotlight on it starts the process of putting you back in control. Admitting that you have an inner bully is an act of radical self-kindness, a sign of true inner strength and authenticity as a leader.

Observing your inner bully at play

In the next few pages, we take a look at an example of an inner bully at play.

Catriona was a veterinary surgeon working in a busy veterinary practice in Scotland. Her father had been a vet, and as a child, she had accompanied him on some of his visits to local farms. She also assisted her father with some of his veterinary work on their family farm.

Catriona loved all animals large and small. She often said that she found animals much easier than humans. At school, her subject choices were selected on the basis that she wished to study to be a vet. She studied hard, and after six years of study, she qualified as a vet. She specialised in small animals.

Catriona worked long hours with sick and suffering animals. She treated a wide range of health conditions and saved many animals' lives. She treated some family pets from early life to old age. Unfortunately, she often had to put pets to sleep, which she found distressing, and struggled at times to retain a professional facade when witnessing the suffering of their distraught owners. The pressure of long hours and emotional trauma led her to start feeling a little depressed and stressed. She started thinking thoughts like these:

>> My family sacrificed so much for me to study to become a vet. I'm such a loser.

>> Everyone sees that I'm failing.

>> My clients will never forgive me if I let their pets die.

>> Expressing emotions is a sign of weakness.

>> I caused their pet to suffer because I'm hopeless at diagnosing.

>> The practice is struggling because it has to carry me.

>> I'm not cut out to be a vet.

>> I have no life and no future.

Catriona's veterinary practice was part of a nation-wide chain of veterinary surgeries. After a health and safety audit flagged the need to reduce risk of suicide in staff (vets have a much higher than average suicide rate), they decided they needed to act. After a successful mindfulness pilot, they decided to roll out training on an optional basis across the whole country.

TIP

Catriona signed up for a course and found the following exercise very helpful when her inner bully came out to play. Give this exercise a try yourself and see if you find it helpful as well.

1. **Accept that you have an inner bully. Notice the messages your inner bully is broadcasting.**

   Try to observe the dialogue with openness and a sense of detachment – not getting involved, reacting, or getting drawn in further.

2. **Make a mental note of the patterns or themes that are emerging.**

   Knowledge is power!

3. **Remember that 'thoughts are not facts'.**

   The voice of the inner bully is just a mental construct, and you don't have to listen to, try to fix or otherwise engage with the messages of the inner bully.

   Kindly acknowledge these thoughts, after which you can choose to shift your attention elsewhere. If you wish to, you can visualise them scrolling away like the credits at the end of a film or clouds passing by in the sky.

4. **Try to observe each time your inner bully starts to nag you or poke at you, recognising that taking notice or believing them is entirely optional.**

Identifying Sounds and Thoughts

Author Sara Maitland spent many years trying to understand more about silence. She spent silent time in silent places – on Skye in the Hebrides, in the Sinai Desert, in forests and mountains, in a flotation tank, and in monasteries and libraries. Her conclusion after many years of travel was that nowhere is truly silent.

In the following pages, we explore the impacts of sounds on your work and introduce a new formal exercise – mindfulness of sounds and thoughts.

Observing the impact of sounds

You are always surrounded by sound. Sounds surround you, wherever you are. They are a part of the environment that surrounds you each and every day. Certain sounds can evoke memories and trigger behaviour or strong emotions that can have an impact on your work at a conscious or unconscious level.

Cultivating awareness of the impacts of sounds can help you become conscious of their impact on you. Observe your subtle responses to different sorts of sounds.

>> **Background sounds:** These may include traffic noise, the whirring of a fan, and voices in the hallway.

>> **Melodic sounds:** These sounds form a melody, such as a chorus of birds or the pitter-patter softly hitting your windowpane. If something melodious moves you, stay with it for a short while, noticing how it affects your body.

>> **Abrupt sounds:** These sudden, shocking sounds may momentarily interrupt you, but they can also serve to bring you back to awareness. The sudden arising of a sound can wake you up to the present moment if you've been lulled into habitual thought patterns.

Sounds are like thoughts in that they both occur randomly. They both come and go. You have no control over the majority of sounds that surround you, and they can trigger strong emotions.

Mindfulness of sounds and thoughts exercise

Your formal WorkplaceMT exercise for this week is mindfulness of sounds and thoughts. It will help you to discover that relating to difficult or unsettling thoughts in the same way that you deal with sounds is possible. During this exercise, you practice approaching and observing sounds simply as sounds, without attaching meaning or judgment to them. You'll also be invited to treat thoughts simply as thoughts – mental events that come and go.

In this week's exercise, you observe the impact of sounds before letting go of them. You discover how to simply allow sounds to come and go as they please, tuning in to the qualities of the sound – the pitch, volume and tone – along with any emotions or impulses they evoke, noticing how you label them and any layers of meaning you attach to them before switching back to receiving mode.

PLAY THIS

To practice mindfulness of sounds and thoughts, listen to Track 5 and follow these steps:

1. **Settle yourself into a chair, sitting in a comfortable upright position that embodies the intention to practice mindfulness.**

2. **Close your eyes, or hold them in soft focus gazing downwards.**

3. **Gently direct your attention inward towards your breath.**

   Tune in to the sensations of your breath entering and leaving your body. Allow your breathing to fall into its own natural rhythm.

   You don't need to change your breathing in any way – your body knows exactly how to breath. Focus on the sensations of breath for around two minutes.

4. **Shift your attention to the sounds that surround you.**

   As you notice each sound, let go of the habit of naming and judging it. Treat everything you hear as equal – beyond being pleasant or unpleasant. See whether you can notice more subtle sounds or sounds within sounds.

TIP

   If your mind wanders, kindly guide it back to focusing your full attention on the sounds that surround you. Simply allow sounds to enter and exit your conscious awareness.

   Practice focusing on sounds for around five minutes.

5. **Gently move your attention back to your breath.**

   Remember: you don't need to change your breathing in any way. Focus on the sensations of breathing for around two minutes.

6. **Shift your attention to any thoughts that may or may not be entering your conscious awareness.**

   Try to simply view them as mental processes that come and go. You may observe them like credits scrolling past at the end of a film, like clouds passing by in the sky, or like leaves floating past you as they drift downstream in a river. If you have no thoughts, gently smile and simply sit with an absence of thoughts, resisting the temptation to fill the space with something else.

TIP

   Notice that thoughts, like sounds, may arrive randomly. There is no need to control them, fix them or try to change them. If you notice that the thoughts are generating any feelings or sensations, tune in to them, and then see if you can let them go. Maintain thoughts as the anchor for your present-moment awareness for around five minutes. If your thoughts become too scattered, simply return to focusing on your breath.

7. **Refocus your attention back to your breath, focusing on the sensations it generates, for around a minute.**

8. **Shift your attention back to your body, spending the last two minutes observing how it feels in this moment (and if you wish, releasing tension), working from the tips of your toes to the crown of your head.**

9. **When you're ready to do so, open your eyes. Have a stretch if you wish to, ready to reconnect with your day.**

What did you notice? Did you hear any sounds you hadn't noticed before? Did you notice any different qualities to the sounds? When you invited in thoughts, did the floodgates open, or did you experience a lack of thoughts?

When Catriona (see earlier section 'Observing your inner bully at play') tried this exercise for the first time, she was at home, sitting in her garden. It was a lovely summer evening, and the birds were singing and the bees humming. She realised how much she enjoyed the sounds of nature and how pleased she was to live in the countryside. She concluded after the exercise that sounds were something she found really easy to focus on and looked forward to the next time she practiced.

The next time Catriona tried the exercise, she was at work. She had a cancellation, which allowed her just enough time to do some practice. This time, focusing on sounds, Catriona noticed some very different sounds. She noticed the sounds of the air-conditioning unit and of people and animals outside her room. She noticed that her shoulders and jaw were starting to tense. She heard a slightly distressed meow from the hospital area of the surgery and noticed her mind wandering to the operation she had carried out on another cat that morning. She noticed that her mind had wandered, took a slow deep breath, and refocused her attention on observing thoughts.

Catriona became increasingly aware of the way that certain sounds triggered thoughts and, at times, anxiety and tension in the body. She dragged her attention back again and again to sounds, but the thoughts continued to roll in randomly. With a mental sigh of resignation, she decided that the best thing to do was simply accept that they were there and accept the fact that she found sitting with them unpleasant. The sounds remained in her conscious awareness, but Catriona noticed that the less she fought with them, the easier it was to remain focused. Catriona noticed her body starting to relax. When invited to focus on thoughts, she discovered to her irritation that 'she had none to work with'.

Catriona's experience isn't uncommon. Thoughts are generated by a split second of brain activity. What follows next (and is often more noticeable) is a chain reaction of emotions, sensations, more thoughts, more emotions and so on. Often, when you direct your full attention to the process of thinking, it dissolves the chain that follows. Focusing on thoughts is like taking your foot off the accelerator pedal – that is, the thoughts lose momentum – it can be an interesting process to observe.

Another interesting thing about this exercise is that the patterns of your mind can change rapidly from feeling fine to feeling down. At times like this, it's worth remembering that mindfulness exercises are not about relaxation; they are a form of brain training and can be tough at times. If you notice a change in your internal weather pattern when practicing (and you will), simply celebrate the fact that you have noticed and welcome in your uninvited guest.

Even those who have been practicing for many years will find their mind wandering. The only difference is that they have become highly proficient in starting again! Some thoughts require lots of kindly patience to be around. It's often the times that life is most difficult that you learn from and benefit from most. As with all forms of mindfulness practice, repetition is key. It helps you to develop neural pathways. It helps you to become more aware of unhelpful repetitious patterns of mind – the human tendency to endlessly repeat things that don't work. You start to notice subtle differences that occur moment by moment.

Developing mindfulness is like planting a seed – it takes time, patience and nurturing.

REMEMBER

Living with Frustration

There will be times in your life when you encounter things that frustrate you. Maybe you have just run for a bus and missed it. Maybe you have 30 minutes for lunch and you end up queuing for 10 minutes.

When you next find yourself getting frustrated, notice how you're responding to the situation. Does your response achieve much? Little? Or make you feel even worse?

For example, if you've just missed a bus or train, maybe you're fretting about how long before the next one comes, how long this will delay you, the knock-on effect of the delay, or berating yourself for the choices that led you to this missed transport moment. If you're in a queue, try to notice thoughts about being in the wrong queue, the wrong sandwich or coffee shop, the alternative uses of your time, or why the person at the front of the queue is being so selfish by taking up so much time!

Try to take a step back and ask what's going through your mind and what sensations you notice in your body. Try to simply accept that some things are unpleasant or frustrating. Accept what's happening – warts and all. Try to separate, if you can, the initial stressor (missing a train or getting stuck in a queue) from the emotionally laden turbulence that follows. Simply accept that you're experiencing frustration. Doing so prevents it from escalating further. The act of accepting the frustration as 'simply a moment in time that will pass' can be highly liberating.

TIP

If you feel able, you may also wish to experiment with a little self-kindness. In your head, simply wish the people ahead of you in the queue (or waiting for the next bus or train) well. Research shows that kindness (real or imagined) to others can rapidly switch you into a more positive state of mind.

Mastering the Three-Step Breathing Space

In Chapter 10, you were introduced to the three-step breathing space. The three-step breathing space is a quick exercise that you can practice anywhere, anytime. Due to its flexibility and short duration, it's one that often proves popular amongst WorkplaceMT participants. It's often used at work between meetings, when transitioning from one task to another, after difficult encounters, or at moments when people simply can't see the wood for the trees.

REMEMBER

The three-step breathing space is not about fixing things – it's about stepping back and gaining perspective, interrupting your brain's internal narrative.

This exercise incorporates techniques that you've been practicing over the last three weeks – observing without fixing, allowing things to come and go, and focused concentration. The exercise normally takes around a minute for each step, so three minutes in total. Timing isn't critical – it can take you more or less time depending on how you feel, what you need, or how much time you have available. What is important is that you follow all three steps.

Try to fit in this exercise at least three times a day as you practice this week. Play MP3 track 4 if you need a reminder.

Week 4 WorkplaceMT Practice Exercises

This week's brain training is designed to help you develop the skill of standing back and gaining perspective. It's about learning how to suspend judgment appropriately and accept things as they are. We're not suggesting that you should become weak and ineffectual – just letting things wash over you and shrugging your shoulders in resignation – quite the opposite actually. It's more about expending your limited resources (attention and energy) wisely. While some things can be changed, others simply are as they are, and it's wiser to accept them, park them, and spend your time and energy on something more worthwhile.

Week 4 formal mindfulness exercise

Your formal practice for this week is mindfulness of sound and thoughts (covered earlier in this chapter). Practicing sounds and thoughts helps you to cultivate an open monitoring state, allowing things to come in and out of your conscious awareness without knee-jerk autopilot responses that may be unhelpful or a waste of energy. Cultivating this ability is very useful for meetings or times when emotions are high and you need to gain perspective.

Practice mindfulness of sounds and thoughts at least once a day in a location where you won't be disturbed. Use the MP3 Track 5 to guide you and keep you on track.

If time allows, we recommend that you practice a little longer this week. Practice mindfulness of breath and body (MP3 Track 3; see Chapter 10) and then continue by playing mindfulness of sounds and thoughts (MP3 Track 5).

Week 4 informal everyday mindfulness

During Week 4, your informal everyday mindfulness practices are as follows:

» **Three-step breathing space:** Practice twice a day or whenever you can fit it in.

» **Approaching frustration (optional):** The next time you find yourself stuck in a queue, or having just missed a bus or train, or even stuck in traffic, try this exercise. There is no need to shut your eyes, and no one needs to know you're doing it. Observe how or if your thoughts, sensations or emotions shift.

» **Observing your inner bully (optional):** Again, this is optional but can be highly beneficial. Keep a note of the messages your inner bully is whispering in your ear. Notice each time your inner bully comes out to play, recognising that no matter how hard it shouts, getting drawn in or taking notice is entirely optional.

Chapter 12

Week 5: Turning Towards Difficulties

A ll your WorkplaceMT training to date has been leading you to this point. We certainly wouldn't invite you to try out this week's formal mindfulness exercise any earlier in the programme. As you work through this chapter, try to treat your-self kindly, and cut yourself some slack. Approaching difficulty can be difficult, but the rewards you'll gain could literally change your life. This chapter starts with a true story:

At 8:50 a.m. on 7 July 2005, 37-year-old Australian Dr Gill Hicks was travelling on the London Underground on her way to work. Seated close by in the tightly packed Tube carriage was 19-year-old terrorist Jermaine Lindsay. He detonated a suicide bomb, killing 26 people and injuring hundreds more.

Gill was the last person to be pulled alive from the train wreckage. She lost both legs below the knee and 75 per cent of her blood. Her injuries were so severe that she was initially not expected to live. To this day, she still feels discomfort and pain every day at the point where her legs now end. It would be easy for her to feel bitter, angry, and to give up on life. Instead, she has become a major force for good in society.

Gill is the founder of the London-based not-for-profit M.A.D. for Peace organisation and is also a motivational speaker and author. She is determined to do all she can to deter anyone from following a path of violent action and believes everyone can make a personal difference to create a confident global community and a sustainable peace.

This chapter is all about facing difficulties and responding to them in a different manner.

Facing Up to Difficulties

When faced with difficulty, a common response is to throw more and more resources (physical or emotional) at it, in an attempt to fix it or change it. Dr Gill Hicks recognised that this practice was pointless. She says that she's 'had to readjust my thinking to not expect recovery because my legs aren't going to grow back . . . I just have to learn how to adapt; otherwise, I'll be stuck in a bitter mess'.

Instead of being stuck in 'a bitter mess', Gill decided to set herself ten extreme physical challenges to force her to face her fears. She has taken her anger and channelled it in a way she hopes will make the world a better place. She has managed to create a 'constructive anger', she says, and feels 'so fortunate to have this second chance'. She doesn't 'want to spend a second of that time in bitterness'.

Gill Hicks was selected to carry the 2008 Olympic Torch in Canberra, Australia, being recognised with an MBE in the Queen's New Year's Honours List (2008–2009) for her services to charity. In 2013, Gill gave birth to a little girl, describing that experience as her finest achievement and greatest acknowledgment of the brilliance and resilience of the human body.

After her horrific injuries, Gill naturally faced many 'mind the gap' moments where she thought about how things should have been, how she would like them to be, or how they ought to be (for details about minding the gap, see Chapter 10). Her decision to accept what happened helped her to park her bitterness and inner torment and move forward, becoming a force for good in the world.

The following pages explore new strategies for relating to difficulties.

Accepting difficulty

When people encounter difficulties, the natural response is to want to push them away. You may try to push them away by attempting to solve them, by ignoring them, or by trying to distract yourself. Unfortunately, this approach often doesn't work. Your difficulty simply shouts louder to make itself heard.

TIP

When you encounter difficulties, you can either continue to suffer by pretending that everything's okay or embrace a new way of looking at things – simply accepting yourself, accepting what's troubling you, and turning towards it, befriending it. You can do this even if it scares you or you don't like it.

REMEMBER

Acceptance isn't a sign of weakness or defeat, as is clearly illustrated by Gill's story (see earlier sections). It's not about detaching from the difficulty; it's about embracing it and getting acquainted with it at a deeper level, accepting it as it is. You pause, you allow the difficulty to step onto your field of awareness, you let it be, you gain a clear picture of how it is, and then, when you're ready, you calmly decide what happens next. Doing so provides you with the time and space to respond. Mindful acceptance gives you choices.

Consider this Jamaican poet Barbara Dixion's poem 'Acceptance'. Barbara was involved in a serious car accident that killed two of her relatives. Doctors told her that due to the injuries she sustained she should give up the idea of an academic career. She ignored their advice, studied and worked hard, and is now a celebrated poet.

Dear self,
This is who I am
This is all I've got
These are my mistakes
And everything I'm not
I'm not asking for your love
I want you to accept me
Let go of these chains
Set me free

Yes I mess up
And I'm nowhere near perfect
But are the bruises and scars
Really worth it?

Barbara Dixion (Used with permission)

What do you take from this poem? Do you accept your mistakes and deficiencies as they are? Are the bruises and scars you inflict upon yourself for your perceived failures and inabilities really worth it?

Try to accept and value yourself for who you are. Yes, acceptance can be difficult. It's a common stumbling point on WorkplaceMT courses. Some participants find it difficult to accept themselves just as they are. They may have experienced years of parents, teachers, friends and work colleagues trying to force them to change into something that they're simply not. Other participants view acceptance as a sign of weakness – of giving up – which, of course, is not the case.

Approaching difficulty

In Mark Williams's and Danny Penman's best-selling book *Mindfulness: A Practical Guide to Finding Peace in a Frantic World*, they tell a story of a king who had three sons. The first two were handsome, clever and popular. The third son was a bit of a liability, so the king pushed him further and further away – both literally and metaphorically. He threw more and more financial and physical resources at trying to keep his problem son at arm's-length. Eventually, the king realised that the sheer effort involved in keeping his son away was disproportionate to the actual difficulty that would arise if he simply learned to live with him.

When you encounter a difficulty in life, what do you do? Do you, like the king, expend time, energy and resources trying to make it go away or hold it at arm's-length? Alternatively, do you (like Gill Hicks earlier in this chapter,) embrace the difficulty and find a way to live with it?

As we discuss in Week 4 (Chapter 11), some things are worth the time and energy to fight for, while fighting other things simply drains you of energy and achieves little or nothing. Acceptance is a matter of choosing your battles wisely. It's the sign of a strong and pragmatic leader rather than an act of weakness.

REMEMBER

Acceptance has two key steps:

1. Notice

Simply notice and acknowledge the thing you're seeking to accept. Try to avoid the urge to push it away or suppress it in any way. Simply accept it as it is.

2. Approach.

Approach the difficulty with an open mind. Try to see it as it is without attaching any further meaning or inferences to it.

Noticing, approaching and accepting in a calm and open manner prevents rumination and, as a result, stops things from escalating further in your mind. By following these steps, you're able to meet the things you find difficult and simply park them, allowing you to focus on something more productive. Approaching and accepting difficulties can be tough, but doing so is worthwhile and prevents your life from being further blighted by mental suffering.

Approaching difficulty exercise

Spend a few moments selecting a difficulty you want to work with today. Try to select an ice-cube-sized difficulty rather than an entire iceberg!

TIP

When approaching difficulties, practicing a familiar mindfulness exercise before you start is a good idea. Doing so will help you to settle a little and be in a more receptive mind state to actively approach and explore your chosen difficulty. If you do as we recommend, you can skip Step 1 from the following list because you should already be sitting in an appropriate posture.

PLAY THIS

You can also play MP3 Track 6 for guidance.

1. Settle yourself into your chair, with both feet firmly planted on the floor.

Settle yourself into a comfortable, upright dignified position.

2. Focus your attention on your breathing, exploring the sensations of the breath coming in and the breath going out.

TIP

If your mind wanders, don't worry. Just congratulate yourself on recognising that your mind has wandered, and refocus on the current sensations of breathing.

3. **Bring to mind the difficulty you have chosen to work with and explore today.**

If you're a visual person, place it on an imaginary workbench so you can explore it in more detail. If you're not a visual person, simply get a sense of how it feels to be sharing your space with it.

4. **Starting at some distance away from your difficulty, explore it from the top, bottom and sides.**

Does it take on a visual appearance? If so, what does it look like? Is it solid? Is it still or in motion? Like a movie? Does it evoke any feelings or emotions? If so, what are they? Can you detect any sensations in the body? If so, explore them and notice where they're manifesting in the body. Do you feel any aversion or discomfort? Is it possible to accept it and stay with it?

5. **Approach and explore your chosen difficulty with kindness and curiosity.**

TIP

Stay in *being mode* – that is, being with the experience of the difficult encounter. If you find yourself trying to find solutions to problems or alternative ways to behave, you've slipped into *doing mode.* Kindly escort yourself back to the present-moment experience of observing what's going on. If things feel too difficult, remember that you can let it go, and return back to your breathing at any time.

6. **Try to move a little closer to the difficulty that is sitting on the workbench of your mind.**

Again, explore its visual form if you can see one. Is it the same, or has it changed? If it has changed, what has changed? Notice any feelings, sensations or thoughts that being in this proximity to the difficulty evokes. Has anything changed? If so, what? Things may remain the same or may change – simply accept your experience as it is in this moment.

7. **Try to move as close as you can to the difficulty.**

Again, explore its visual representation, thoughts, feelings, and sensations (if any). Notice what remains the same and what, if anything, has changed. Remember to be kind to yourself throughout this exercise; doing so will help you to get the most from it and hopefully help you to release any tension that may have arisen.

8. Let the difficulty go, and once it has vanished away out of sight, shift your attention back to your breath for a couple of minutes.

9. When you're ready to do so, open your eyes, ready to return to your day.

Reflecting on your experiences

Before reflecting on your own experience on the approaching difficulty exercise, consider the experience Dan had. Dan is an events coordinator who decided to try the approaching difficulty exercise on a difficulty he was experiencing with a 'demanding' client. When told to 'place the difficulty on the workbench of the mind', he said, 'It was just like watching a movie. I could see [the client] walking round the venue, tutting and criticising. I felt my muscles contract and tighten. Quite frankly, it was really unpleasant'.

Dan tried to relax his muscles, but the minute he returned himself to the movie playing out in his head, he found himself tensing again. He decided to return his focus back to his breath again. He decided to give the exercise another try. Again, the movie in his head started to play in glorious Technicolor. This time, he decided to stick with it a little longer. He told himself, 'It's okay to feel like this. This isn't forever – it's only a moment in time. It will pass'.

Dan reflected afterwards that he had noticed some interesting things. He had noticed how quickly and impulsively he sprang to try to fix the difficulty, despite knowing that this wasn't what he should be doing. He noticed the amount of aversion he had to even thinking about the client and started to question whether the client was the whole problem. He wondered whether maybe some of the problem was being caused by his aversion to the client. He also noticed during the exercise that the more he wrestled with the difficulty, the worse it got. At moments, he was able to just sit back and observe with an open mind, and when he did, things seemed to change subtly. The difficulty didn't go away, but somehow it seemed easier to live with.

Was your experience the same or different from Dan's? Although Dan's difficulty was very visual (a person), not everyone's is. Some people can't visualise difficulties like a movie. Some people simply get a sense of a random shape, even moving or stationary.

Others get no sense of visual representation, simply a sense of how the difficulty feels to be close to.

Even if you can't visualise the difficulty, sensing it and sitting with the sense of being close to something you find difficult is equally powerful. The more senses you can tune into, the better.

What did you notice? Reflecting on your own experience, answer these questions:

>> Were there any patterns or themes that emerged in your thoughts about the difficulty?

>> Do you recall any specific thoughts or impulses as you progressively approached the difficulty?

>> Did the difficulty remain the same or change as you got closer to it?

>> Did you notice any specific sensations in your body? If so, what were they and where were they? Did they change or shift as you approached the difficulty more closely?

When approaching difficulty in this way, sometimes something happens. At other times, you experience very little. Sometimes when you approach and explore a difficulty, it subtly changes or shifts. Sometimes it remains the same or even feels like it's increasing in size. Remember that the object of the exercise isn't about fixing the problem or making it go away – it's about seeing it as it really is. Doing so often provides insights or fresh perspectives. It goes without saying that approaching difficulties can be really difficult, so try to be kind to yourself and don't push it too hard.

Take a look at another example. Sarah, an HR manager, experienced intense sensations in her body when sitting with her chosen difficulty of a difficult team member. She felt her neck and shoulders tense the moment she 'invited in' her difficulty. Sarah was not (by her own admission) a very visual person. She gained no visual representation of the encounter in her head but did sense heaviness in its presence. Initially, she said, it 'felt very heavy' to approach the difficulty, but as she progressively got closer, she felt things lightening a little. Eventually, it felt very small indeed, and she felt herself relaxing a little. To her surprise, she suddenly felt herself feeling a little sorry for the 'difficult' staff member.

When Sarah and Dan finished the exercise, their difficulties didn't magically vanish, but they somehow felt less urgent and not as raw.

Approaching difficulty works by helping you to break down the sequence of mental events that may otherwise thrust you into a negative spiral of thoughts and rumination. The simple act of noticing and accepting negative thoughts, emotions, and sensations prevent aversion kicking in. By choosing not to engage in a downward spiral, you can reduce or eliminate its forward momentum.

FALLING INTO THE HAPPINESS TRAP

One of the wealthiest men in the Southwest of America was recently interviewed on television. He had money, freedom, friends, and family but somehow lacked happiness. He had a preoccupation with, in his own words, 'keeping what I've got'. It transpired that far from his life being perfect, he had alienated kids, a wife who bitterly resented his obsession with work, and no time to simply relax and feel good. He had fallen out of love with life.

Despite the media image of contented wealthy billionaires, wealthy people are unhappy just as often as people without much money. Money, unfortunately, doesn't bring happiness. Pursuit of it can lead to stress and burnout. Despite the increasing wealth of society, social scientists say that people aren't happier – in fact, they're becoming unhappier.

People often fall into a number of 'happiness traps'. These might include

- **Trying to buy happiness:** This mindset tells you that if/when you can earn or acquire sufficient money, then you'll be happy. Unfortunately, for many, the more they possess, the more things they think they 'need' to maintain their chosen lifestyle.

- **Seeking pleasure:** This mindset is when you think that doing pleasurable things will lead to happiness. Attending festivals, drinking, shopping, buying/having designer goods, and eating in expensive restaurants can, of course, make you feel happy. The problem is that when you become too accustomed to these pleasures, they often lose their power to make your happy.

(continued)

(continued)

- **Trying to resolve the past:** This mindset tells you that if you can only resolve things that happened in the past, you'll feel happy. Unfortunately, the subconscious can't be emptied of its dark and dreadful contents merely by bringing them to the light of day. Whether memories are good or bad, they remain a part of you for as long as you live.

What are your 'happiness traps'? In the pursuit of happiness, are you simply making yourself unhappy?

You can't just decide to be happy any more than you can decide to be taller. Happiness isn't a finite entity but the sum of a number of lived qualities. It isn't about being in a good mood and feeling full of joy; it's a way of life. It's a mental attitude. The good news is that anyone can cultivate it.

In the past, it was thought that some people were simply born happy or that happiness or unhappiness was determined by people's genes. Research in recent years has demonstrated that mindfulness practice can help you to alter your underlying level of happiness for the better.

Brain scans reveal that when people are upset or unhappy, their right prefrontal cortex becomes more active than their left prefrontal cortex. In a research study, workers at a high stress biotech start-up company were taught mindfulness for eight weeks. Their brains were scanned before and after training. At the start, their emotional set point was tilted toward the right. This is no surprise because many were working a hectic, 24/7 schedule. After just eight weeks, they showed, on average, a greater tilt toward the left. They also reported feeling happier, less anxious and more engaged with their work.

Picking Your Battles Wisely

As you discover throughout this book, acceptance is a key element of mindfulness and a useful leadership skill that needs conscious cultivation. The act of accepting things as they are, in this moment, takes the heat out of the situation. It stops emotions from rising, situations from escalating, or rash actions from occurring.

Don't sweat the small stuff

A project deadline, presentation you need to make, a meeting with a new client, finding time to mentor or support a team member or to develop yourself are probably all things that are worthy of your time and attention. However, someone driving inconsiderately, a boss with no manners, or an overdemanding client are all things that, although annoying, in most cases, you can do little to change. If you can't change it, a wiser course of action is to accept it – that is, accept your current thoughts, emotions, and bodily sensations – and then let it go, avoiding further wasted time and energy.

Accepting something just as it is in the present moment, without the need to mentally engage with it further, is a highly effective self-management tool for the following reasons:

>> It prevents you from falling into a thought spiral.

>> It saves you time and money by not expending unnecessary time and emotion dealing with it.

>> It helps you to stay alert and focused, which enhances your productivity.

REMEMBER

Acceptance isn't about becoming a human sponge, accepting everything that life throws at you. Acceptance is simply choosing your battles and using your resources more wisely. It's about stopping yourself from expending unnecessary time and mental energy on things that, upon closer inspection, aren't really a big deal. Learning to choose your battles wisely will help you win the really important battles in life.

Practicing acceptance will help take the weight off, allowing you to create momentum by doing nothing. Try it. It can be very liberating.

Practice mindful acceptance

When you encounter difficulties in life, the brain has a tendency to tip you over into a safety operating mode. In an attempt to safeguard you from the perceived risk, your brain may adopt a defensive avoidance mode of mind, shutting down creativity and restricting your thinking.

Mindful acceptance allows you to evaluate the accuracy of your thoughts. Imagine if you had been trapped in the carnage of the London Underground bombing in 2005. What might you have been thinking as you lay trapped in the train wreckage? Maybe you would have been questioning whether you would live or die. Maybe you'd be asking yourself 'why me?' Maybe you'd be berating yourself for not having taken an alternative route to work that day.

Obviously, this example is extreme, but it demonstrates a valuable point. Just the act of imagining yourself in this situation may have caused you to tense your muscles, or your smile to fade from your face, or possibly your stomach to feel knotted.

REMEMBER

When dealing with things that are difficult, you need to make objective decisions. By acknowledging and accepting fear as an emotion, physical sensations often fade, and you regain the ability to see things more clearly and make more rational decisions.

When practicing approaching difficulties, as we outline earlier in this chapter, remember that it all starts with acceptance. You need to accept that you're finding something difficult and want to explore it – warts and all! You do this against a backdrop of self-acceptance (you are human, not Superman or Wonder Woman), and self-kindness. Remember that you are still learning and will continue to learn for the rest of your life. Difficulties don't instantly become less difficult; you just cultivate the ability to reduce their negative impact.

When learning how to swim, people commonly wear a floating device, like a life jacket. Doing so helps you to float and increases your confidence in the water. In the same way, acceptance and self-kindness help you to maintain a positive state of mind, allowing you to remain focused and deal with life's challenges in a calmer, more effective manner.

TIP

When practicing mindfulness this week, don't try to be macho and dive straight into the deep end, but rather be kind to yourself. Take it steady by picking an ice-cube-sized difficulty, not an iceberg. Remind yourself that it's not about dealing with or fixing things, problem solving, or analysing.

Using the Breathing Space to Deal with Daily Challenges

When you encounter minor irritations this week (such as missing the bus, encountering someone who is rude or off hand, or dealing with your broadband playing up), try this adaptation of the three-step breathing space.

1. **Settle yourself into your chair.**

Sit in a comfortable upright position with both feet firmly planted on the floor. Close your eyes or hold them in soft focus gazing downwards.

Acknowledge and observe any thoughts, bodily sensations or emotions that may have been generated by the irritation or minor challenge.

Approach with an open mind and explore.

2. **Narrow your attention onto your breath.**

Focus on the sensations of breathing for around a minute – timing isn't critical here.

3. **Widen your awareness, tuning in to any sounds that may be surrounding you.**

If you're still experiencing the impact of the irritation, simply accept its presence without trying to change it. Acknowledge how you're feeling and any associated bodily sensations, consciously acknowledging that 'it's okay to feel like this'.

When you're ready to do so, open your eyes, ready for the rest of your day.

TIP

This exercise takes three minutes or less but can have a major positive impact on your day.

Week 5 WorkplaceMT Practice Exercises

This week's brain training is designed to help you to approach, explore and relate to life challenges in a different way.

Week 5 formal mindfulness exercise

Your formal practice for this week is approaching difficulty (see the earlier section 'Approaching difficulty exercise'). Practice approaching difficulty at least once a day in a location where you won't be disturbed. Use the MP3 recording to guide you and keep you on track.

REMEMBER

Approaching difficulty is by its very nature difficult. It's recommended that you allow some time to settle before approaching difficulty.

Practice mindfulness of breath and body (MP3 Track 3; Chapter 10) or mindfulness of sounds and thoughts (MP3 Track 5; Chapter 11), and then continue straight onto approaching difficulty (MP3 Track 6; as described earlier in this chapter).

Week 5 informal everyday mindfulness

During Week 5, your informal everyday mindfulness practices are

>> **Three-step breathing space when you encounter a difficulty:** Practice twice a day or whenever you can fit it in.

>> **Habit releaser:** Pay mindful attention to something you normally do on autopilot (see Chapter 8 for details).

>> **Stop procrastinating:** If you find yourself procrastinating or putting off something you'd rather not do, change your approach: first, explore and acknowledge the emotions and sensations generated when you think about doing it, and then try to accept that this is how you feel – then get on with it.

Chapter 13

Week 6: Developing Intention

Week 6 is the final week of your WorkplaceMT training. It begins by focusing on consolidating learning before moving on to evaluating how you live and work and developing an intention to live your life in a way that's happier, healthier, more productive and better for those around you. It's also a reminder that however driven and outcome-focused you may be, self-kindness coupled with improved self-management are key.

Over the last six weeks you have been invited to explore and apply a number of mindfulness principles.

Week 1 helped you to recognize just how much of your life is spent on autopilot. Over the weeks via your formal and informal mindfulness exercises, you have started to observe your habitual thinking patterns and have possibly taken action to change some that are not serving you well.

Week 2 invited you to start observing the mind-body connection, with an emphasis on its impacts on your work. You may have seen patterns emerging, such as your tendency to hold tension in certain areas of your body when you are under excessive pressure. You may have started to tune into your body, listening to the messages it's sending you to take better care of yourself, allowing you to maintain peak performance for longer.

We playfully invited you to 'mind the gap' between your expectations and present-moment reality, reducing the impact of self-induced mental pain when things are not as you think they should be.

You have been encouraged to appreciate the nice things in life that often pass you by unnoticed. As you have learnt, doing so helps you to correct the human negativity bias, gaining a more balanced perspective on life. You have also been encouraged to operate in approach mode of mind, tapping into your higher brain's creativity to produce the best outcomes possible.

As your skills in observing your mental processes have developed you may have smiled as you witnessed how you constantly tell yourself stories. Your newly acquired ability to separate present-moment facts from these mental constructs or stories will be helping you to accept the things you can't change, whilst taking ownership and responsibility for your interpretation and response to life's challenges.

Your formal and informal mindfulness 'brain training' each week has helped you to improve your focus and attention, reducing the time that your mind wanders. In addition, you have started to cultivate the ability to stand back and simply observe what is happening around you objectively without reactivity.

In Week 5, we invited you to try out some techniques for relating differently to difficult situations – approaching and exploring them with openness and curiosity. You may have noticed that at times, when approached and explored, 'difficulties' in life are not as you perceive them to be, and the act of approaching them can sometimes lead to new perspectives or solutions.

We hope that over the last few weeks that you've noticed some positive improvements in your work and home life. By reflecting what you've practiced in the last five weeks through the exercises in Chapters 8 through 12, we hope that you've identified lots of good reasons to continue to develop mindfulness and integrate these mental hygiene principles into your life – now and in the future.

Accepting Your True Self

Self-knowledge is one of the most powerful things you can possess. It allows you to monitor yourself and take responsibility for your actions. It's the key to self-transformation.

Take a moment to reflect on the last five weeks of your WorkplaceMT training (from Chapters 8 through 12). Here are a few things to consider:

>> Have you noticed any habitual patterns of thought and behaviour that are unhelpful? What actions have you taken?

>> Has your increased knowledge of the mind-body connection benefitted you? If so, how?

>> Have you managed to find time to pause and soak in the benefits of the good things (however small) that punctuate your day? What impact has this had?

>> When working towards a desired goal, have you been able to identify whether you're working in approach or avoidance mode? Have you been able to switch modes?

>> What have you noticed about your storytelling mind? Are you becoming more adept at separating present-moment facts from your stories (mental constructs)? What impact is this having?

>> Have you become more aware of the voice of your inner bully or critic? If so, how do you now respond when you notice you inner bully at play?

>> What have you learned about approaching and exploring things you find difficult?

>> Have you started to notice when your mind wanders? Are you noticing more quickly than before? Are you able to refocus your mind again more quickly?

>> Are you starting to be able to suspend judgment and reactivity long enough to gather evidence objectively?

>> Are you starting to understand yourself better and manage yourself more skilfully as a result?

>> Do you feel that your WorkplaceMT training has helped you to take better care of yourself at work? If so, how? What impact has this had?

REMEMBER

The impact of WorkplaceMT training varies from person to person because no two people's brains are wired identically. The positive outcomes of mindfulness increase in direct correlation with the amount of time people spend actually practicing. So make mindfulness practice a part of your daily routine, and you'll notice the long-term benefits.

Knowing When It's Time to Do Things Differently

One of the most valuable things that mindfulness offers is the ability to observe and break free from fixed patterns of thought and behaviour that are holding you back. Inability to break free from fixed thinking can be disastrous. History is littered with companies that went bust because their leaders failed to change thinking and behaviour that no longer served them well.

Eastman Kodak was founded in 1880 and for much of the 20th century was the gold standard of the film and camera industries. By 1963, the company was number 44 on the Fortune 500 with sales of more than $1 billion. In 1984, Fuji began selling film similar to Kodak's for 20 per cent less than Kodak's price. Kodak continued to charge premium rates for its film. Kodak scientists invented the first digital camera and first megapixel camera, but their leadership team remained focused on selling film. Kodak filed for bankruptcy in 2012.

Maybe they were experiencing 'sunk cost bias': the tendency to stick with a less-than-optimal strategy merely because a lot of money, time or effort has been sunk into it. In 2013, Andrew Hafenbrack, of INSEAD business school in France, conducted research into the impact of mindfulness on sunk cost bias. He found that research participants who had spent just 15 minutes practicing mindfulness were 77 per cent more likely than others to resist sunk-cost bias when making decisions.

Have you ever experienced sunk cost bias? Most of us have at some time or another. It's a very human trait. The trick is to notice when sunk cost bias, or other fixed patterns of thought and behaviour are at play. Mindfulness is a highly effective way to cultivate this ability.

Balancing Your Life and Work

Andrew was a young ambitious consultant working for a well-known consultancy firm. Prior to qualifying, he enjoyed a wide variety of social activities, which he fitted in around his demanding work life. Andrew got a huge buzz from his work and didn't resent working long hours because he was constantly learning and making new contacts and derived energy from getting results for his clients.

Andrew's work made him feel good about himself. He also felt energised when spending time out with friends and family at pubs, clubs and festivals. He chatted with friends all over the world on Skype, sometimes finding time to visit them when travelling abroad for business. Once a month, Andrew found time to go gliding. Being above the clouds gave him a sense of peace and serenity. Despite Andrew often devoting around 70 per cent of his waking hours to work, his life felt rich and full.

When Andrew passed his exams, he secured a great new job working for another top consultancy firm. As time went on, work demands increased. Andrew wasn't someone who liked to say no, so he decided that he simply needed to work a little harder to get through his workload.

Slowly over time, Andrew started to find his work less energising. As the demands placed on him increased, he found less and less time for his social life, and somehow the time was never right to go gliding any more. Every week, he thought that the next week would allow him time to go out gliding, but when the weekend arrived, there always seemed to be a pressing deadline for Monday that had to be met. One Monday morning, Andrew's alarm went off, and he couldn't motivate himself to get out of bed, despite client meetings being booked back to back that day. Andrew had reached burnout. His energy tanks were empty.

Do you identify in any way with Andrew's story? The good news is, your work doesn't have to be depleting. It can be nourishing, too, as it was for Andrew at the start of his story. For some people, spending 80 per cent on work and 20 per cent on home and social activities can work really well – but only if the work is meaningful and nourishing at a deeper level.

In the following pages, we explore ways you can balance work and home life and then walk you through steps to fill your energy tanks.

Striking a balance that's right for you

Barack Obama, President of the United States, is reported to regularly go to bed at about 1 a.m. and get up at 7 a.m. Margaret Thatcher is famously said to have slept for only four hours a night. The ideal work-life balance has no magic formula; it's more a matter of finding the correct balance between activities that nourish you (fill your energy tanks) and activities that deplete you (empty your energy tanks) – and sleep, of course!

If you really enjoy your work, the barriers between work time and home time can become blurred, and this isn't necessarily a bad thing. Sometimes, just the effort involved in trying to live up to an idealized, compartmentalised view of work-life balance is depleting in itself! Sometimes it's better to just consider your life as a whole without compartmentalising it into 'work' and 'home' life. However, if work is less nourishing and meaningful than you'd like it to be and it drains you of energy, make sure that you balance it with activities that you do find nourishing at a deeper level – be that painting historic sets of model soldiers, socialising, volunteering, spending time with your family, or even gliding.

If you discover that your work is hugely depleting, maybe it's time to find something more rewarding to do with your life. If, like many others, your work is part nourishing, part depleting, be sure you prioritise some quality activities outside work that refill your energy tanks and make you feel good. Instead of obsessing about work-life balance, simply focus on balancing activities that nourish you with those that are wholly necessary but depleting. Give nourishing activities (whatever they may be for you) equal importance in your diary to stay healthy, well and fit for work.

Filling your energy tanks

Energising activities uplift you and fill your energy tank, while depleting activities leave you feeling low and empty your tank. To ensure an adequate balance between nourishing activities and those that, although necessary, tend to deplete you, take a moment to assess where you are now. Follow these steps:

1. **Think of a typical week. List the activities that make up your week.**

These activities may include getting up and dressed in the morning, eating meals, commuting or travelling, spending time with clients, attending meetings, doing admin work, having drinks with work colleagues, participating in social activities with friends and family, doing DIY projects, shopping or whatever fills the hours of your day.

2. **Decide which activities energise you – fill your mental energy tanks and make you feel good – and which tend to deplete you and make you feel empty or bad. Mark the activities as either 'E' for energising or 'D' for depleting.**

Some activities may leave you physically tired but mentally energised – mark these as 'E'. Other activities are sometimes energising and other times depleting – decide on balance if at present they're more energising or depleting, and mark them down as such.

3. Review your list.

Do you feel like you have the right balance of energising activities? Are there any depleting activities you can drop or do less of? Are there any energising activities that you can do more of? If some depleting activities are an inevitable and unavoidable part of your day, could you approach them differently? Might it be possible to accept that they need doing, and let go of any resentment or bad feelings you are harbouring towards them?

TIP

Use this activity as a starting point for striking the right balance for you and your life. Remember: everyone is different. What works for you may not work for others, and there's no textbook right or wrong answer. If you derive energy and nourishment from your work, and this makes you genuinely feel fantastic, great! Just remember that your idea of happiness and balance may be someone else's idea of hell. Others you work with may work best by working standard or part-time hours and prioritising social activities that recharge their batteries for the next working day. Respect and accept others' working preferences. And simply focus on finding the balance that works best for you.

Managing Yourself for Resilience

WorkplaceMT training equips you with powerful tools to understand and manage yourself better. The six-week training programme puts an emphasis on self-kindness, and for good reason.

Not so long ago, the notion for kindness as an effective leadership skill would have been an alien concept for many. It would have been unusual to find it in a practical leadership book, but now we know that being kind to yourself and others is a central tenant of authentic leadership, resonant leadership and mindful leadership. Knowing when and how to be kind to yourself and others is the sign of an effective leader. It's an effective way to achieve maximum engagement, productivity and creativity while improving well-being.

In the next few pages, we explore how Andrew (see the earlier section 'Balancing Your Life and Work') could have used mindfulness to make meetings more effective and work better when under pressure.

Getting the most out of meetings

Many people hate meetings because they go on for too long or end with no decisions being made. For example, when Andrew entered meetings, his primary focus was on ensuring his message was heard, gaining the information needed for his projects, getting his own way, and making himself look good. He had adopted this approach after watching senior colleagues in meetings and reasoned that if it worked for them, it would work for him, too.

Recent UK Management School research concluded that people need to be mindful so they can see things more clearly, set aside personal agendas, and make more inclusive decisions. By focusing on observing what's actually happening in the meeting in the present moment 'in a non-judgmental and purposeful way', better decisions are made, and more is achieved.

REMEMBER

People aren't machines. Providing a meeting environment that is kinder and less adversarial and caters for people's needs (providing refreshments, breaks when needed and the opportunity for everyone's voice to be heard) pays big dividends. It triggers a neurological shift in the brain that encourages collaboration and creativity. Shifting from fight-or-flight mode and into a state of social cohesion fosters engagement and trust, which results in more beneficial outcomes for all concerned.

Dealing with pressure

When Andrew was faced with multiple deadlines that couldn't be realistically met, his response was to work harder. He feared for his future, his reputation, his boss's response, and clients' future success.

Andrew was operating in avoidance mode. His primary driver was to avoid something bad from happening. In this state, his outlook, perspective and creativity were limited. Andrews's brain believed that he was under threat and needed to be protected, so it increased his heart rate and primed his muscles to sprint away from the imminent danger it thought he was facing. In this survival mode, his ability for higher-brain big-picture thinking was severely restricted.

When under pressure of this sort, what Andrew really needed to do was to switch his neurological operating mode from fight or flight to a state of safety and social cohesion. This, of course, is much easier said than done. When you're under pressure, simply telling yourself to relax and think rationally is usually doomed to failure. The more pressure you pile on yourself to relax, think creatively, and refocus your attention, the less likely you are to achieve it.

Emerging research suggests that it's neurologically impossible to be in a state of safety, trust and social cohesion while at the same time being in fight-or-flight mode. Surprisingly, the simple act of wishing yourself or others well (even if it's just imagining doing so in your head) is a rapid way of switching your fight-or-flight threat response down and shifting into a more productive neurological state that allows you to focus better and approach work in a more open-minded and creative manner.

Cultivating Kindness

The final formal mindfulness exercise in your WorkplaceMT training is optional but highly recommended.

When I first encountered this exercise on an MBSR mindfulness course, it simply didn't resonate for me, despite the fact that it improved my mood following practice. Why, I reasoned, should I be spending my time wishing myself, others and random strangers well? It felt a little bit hippy to me, and far too 'pink and fluffy' for my taste For several years after this, I dismissed the exercise. It was only when I discovered some research on the topic that I re-evaluated it.

This is what changed my mind: researchers were exploring the areas of the brain that become more active when a person is in fight-or-flight mode. A volunteer with a severe pigeon phobia was placed into an MRI brain scanner. When the researchers showed her pigeon pictures, all the areas of her brain that the researchers expected to be activated were activated.

Suddenly and unexpectedly, the areas of the brain being monitored became dramatically less active. When they removed the volunteer from the scanner, the researchers asked what had happened. The volunteer replied that eventually the pigeon pictures had become overwhelming and she couldn't cope, so she practiced a self-kindness exercise she had learned in a mindfulness course. The brain scanning technology clearly demonstrated that this simple exercise had literally acted as an off switch for her threat response.

More recent research placed volunteers with high levels of self-criticism in a virtual reality suit. Volunteers were confronted with a person who was in distress and allowed to interact with the person as they chose. Many felt compelled to comfort the virtual person. This simple act reduced their levels of self-criticism. The profound thing here is that being kind to others has a positive impact on the person providing the care. Even imagining being kind or sending kind thoughts to others has a profoundly positive impact on your mental state.

Time and cultural constraints mean that we don't always teach cultivating kindness exercises in our courses. When we do teach this, we suggest that participants think of it as a highly effective off switch for their threat system, but really it's much more than that. It's a way of making friends with yourself. It's a profound act of kindness to yourself at the times you need it most. With a little practice and perseverance, it can also help you learn how to relate differently to those you find difficult and challenging, reducing unnecessary mental pain and suffering for all concerned.

Cultivating kindness exercise

Before you start this exercise, think of a number of people who you'll call to mind during the exercise. These may include

>> A friend or loved one who cares about you deeply. You can use a pet if you want.

>> A person you know vaguely – maybe a neighbour you pass and nod to, someone who works in a local shop, or someone you often see commuting.

>> A person you find mildly challenging or difficult (but not too difficult).

>> A group of people – maybe your fellow workers, the inhabitants of your local town or village, or even people you see on TV who are having a tough time.

PLAY THIS

Next, follow these steps. MP3 Track 7 guides you through this exercise.

1. **Settle yourself into your chair, sitting in a comfortable, open, upright position. Close your eyes or hold them in soft focus gazing downwards.**

2. **Focus for a few minutes on the present-moment sensations of breathing.**

   Fully experience the sensations of the breath entering and leaving your body.

3. **See how it feels to be kind to yourself by using phrases such as these:**

   - 'Wishing you health and happiness'

   - 'Wishing you peace of mind'

   - 'Wishing you ease of being'

   Feel free to adapt the words so they have meaning and resonance for you. You want the kind wishes you select to feel realistic for you and not simply empty words. You need to be able to genuinely mean what you say. Pause briefly after each well wish to notice any impact it may have on you. There are no rights or wrongs here – simply observe the impact or lack of impact.

4. **Bring to mind your friend or loved one. Imagine this person wishing you well, using the phrases you've chosen.**

   Observe the impact of receiving these words and wishes of kindness.

5. **Wish your friend or loved one well.**

   Pause to observe any impacts that each good wish has on you, the well-wisher.

6. **Let go of the image of your friend. Bring to mind the person you know vaguely. Wish this person well.**

Pause to observe any impacts that each good wish has on you, the well-wisher.

7. **Let go of the image of your acquaintance. Bring to mind the person you find a little difficult or challenging. Wish this person well.**

Pause to observe any impacts that each good wish has on you, the well-wisher.

8. **Let go of the image of your selected 'difficult' person. Bring to mind the group of people you want to wish well. Wish them well.**

Pause to observe any impacts that each good wish has on you, the well-wisher.

9. **Refocus your attention to your body.**

Spend the last few minutes checking in with how your body feels. Notice any specific sensations as you work from the tip of your toes to the crown of your head.

10. **End with a sense of how your whole body feels as you sit in your chair at this moment in time.**

When you're ready, open your eyes.

What did you notice when practicing this exercise? Here are some questions to use as you reflect on this experience:

» How did it feel to wish yourself well? Was it easy or challenging?

» How did it feel to wish others well?

» Was it easier to wish certain people well than others?

» Was it easier to receive good wishes from a friend than wish yourself well?

» Were you able to genuinely wish your selected 'difficult' person well?

» Do you feel the same or different from when you started the exercise? If you feel different in any way, try to be specific about what has changed.

Cultivating kindness short exercises

In WorkplaceMT courses, we often include shortened informal everyday variations of this practice. Here are two of our favourites.

Cultivating kindness in meetings

At the start of a meeting, pause to wish everyone attending the meeting well in your head. You can do this shortly before the meeting starts in a place you won't be disturbed or just as you enter the meeting.

A course participant once said that when he enters a meeting, he pretends to be reading the agenda and meeting papers when really he's secretly conducting this exercise in his head.

Experiment to find the right words that resonate for you. Here are some suggestions:

>> Wishing you all a successful meeting

>> Wishing you all achieve your aims

>> Wishing you all the opportunity to get your point across

Cultivating kindness when delayed

When you're stuck in traffic, delayed on a train or bus, or stuck in a queue that is moving too slowly, wish those in front of or behind you well in your head. Find words that resonate for you. You may try the following:

>> Wishing you a happy life

>> Wishing you health and ease of being

TIP

If any of the cultivating kindness exercises in this section are too challenging at first, try experimenting with simply remembering that the person you're irritated by, that has insulted you, made you late or has 'stolen' your business is still a human being with the same hopes for success, security and recognition that you have.

Setting an Intent to Make Mindfulness Part of Each Day

Within your WorkplaceMT training (refer to Chapters 8 through 12), we have tried to include lots of practical examples of how to use mindfulness in your everyday life. You can think of your daily formal sit-down practice as brain training and everyday mindfulness as a means to maintain your mental hygiene, in the same way as you brush your teeth to ensure good oral hygiene.

TIP

Find ways to punctuate your day with a few moments of informal mindfulness. Here are some suggestions:

>> **Start your day with a mindful shower.** Tune in to the sensations, sounds and fragrances as fully as you can

>> **If you commute to work in a car, pause to appreciate the good for a moment.** Your car has started – yes! You don't need to walk to work – yes! You're sitting in a nice warm car and not outside in the cold and wet – yes! You can listen to the radio or your favourite music – yes! You're driving through country or city scapes – yes!

>> **If you have a moment to grab a drink in the morning, try to be fully in this moment.** If you drink, just drink. Don't allow work to hijack this precious experience that refocuses you in the present moment.

>> **If you're desk-bound for most of the day, set up a simple mindfulness bell on your PC or mobile phone.** You can set this bell to remind you to pause and be mindful periodically throughout your day.

>> **Check in with your body periodically throughout the day.** How your body feels has an impact on your work. Use your body as an early warning system – detecting and releasing tension at an early stage.

>> **When experiencing difficulties with colleagues, clients or customers, don't get angry.** Doing so hurts you more than it hurts them. Alternatively, try to see the person as simply a

human being with needs and hopes, and extend her a little sympathy or wish her well. If nothing else, this act may make you feel a little better.

» **When things aren't going to plan, mind the gap.** Explore the gap between how you think things should be or ought to be, and then accept the present-moment reality, stopping your self-induced mental pain from escalating.

» **When walking between meetings or appointments at work, take the opportunity to focus your attention on the sensations and full experience of walking.** No need to slow down unless you want to, but focusing on the everyday act of walking can steady a busy mind and reconnect you with the present moment.

» **Use the three-step breathing space to help you transition between tasks and cleanse your mind between difficult meetings – or whenever you feel the need.** For details on the three-step breathing space exercise, see Chapter 10.

» **When eating a snack, biscuit or lunch, enjoy a few mouthfuls mindfully.** Doing so can add pleasure and novelty to something you normally do on autopilot. It can also help to re-engage your rest and relaxation circuitry, improving your state of mind for what the rest of the day holds.

» **Carry out random acts of kindness.** You don't need to do anything dramatic here. Your acts of kindness could simply be opening a door for someone whose hands are full, helping a young mum onto a train with her buggy, or giving a seat to a person who needs it more than you. Research shows that doing acts of kindness benefits the giver of the kindness just as much as the person who receives it.

» **Use the time between getting home from work and starting your evening at home to practice mindfulness formally.** WorkplaceMT formal exercises are short and should easily fit into even the busiest person's schedule. Practicing mindfulness will benefit you in both the long and short term.

There are hundreds of ways to fit a little mindfulness into your day. Experiment, have fun, and find things that work for you.

TIP

Week 6 WorkplaceMT Practice Exercises

This week's brain training is designed to help you to consolidate learning and cultivate some kindness in your life.

Week 6 formal mindfulness exercise

Your formal practice for this week is cultivating kindness (see the earlier section 'Cultivating Kindness exercise'). Practice at least once a day in a location where you won't be disturbed. Use the MP3 Track 7 to guide you.

Week 6 informal everyday mindfulness

Pick one or more of the informal everyday acts of mindfulness each day (detailed in the section 'Setting an Intent to Make Mindfulness Part of Each Day') and observe the impact.

4

Applying Mindful Leadership

Use mindfulness to enhance your personal presence and influence.

Navigate the impact and demands of leading in a digital age.

Discover mindful strategies for leading change and become a leader who others want to follow.

Chapter 14

Enhancing Your Personal Presence and Influence

C an you command the room? Do people stop and listen when you speak? If the answer is yes, you have *executive presence*. A recent survey of New York recruiters found that 'executive presence' accounts for 26 per cent of what it takes to get promoted. At the heart of mindfulness is self-awareness. Self-awareness and the ability to manage your emotions are vital if you want to enhance your personal presence and influence. Mindful leaders have a clear idea of who they are, what they value and what they stand for. Remaining authentic to yourself helps you build your presence and influence in a way that is sustainable and powerful.

But what if who you are and what you stand for don't resonate with your organisation? You have three choices:

>> You can leave the organisation and try to find one that is a better fit for your values and outlook on life.

>> You can simply be yourself, leading by example and, by doing so, try to change the organisation from the inside. This can be a long-term project, which may or may not be worth the effort.

>> You can put up and shut up.

The latter may be an option for some, but research shows that trying to behave in a way that is contrary to your preferred way of being and doing for extended periods is unsustainable. In the end, something will give – either your physical health or your mental well-being.

If you already work for an organisation that's a good fit for your authentic self or are happy to just be yourself and encourage the organisation to change, this is the chapter for you. This chapter is all about being true to yourself and harnessing your values in a way that will positively improve your profile and influence both internally within your organisation and externally to your customers and peers.

Establishing Your Personal Brand

If you wish to be a more authentic leader, you need to have a clear idea of the values that drive your behaviour.

Discovering your values and personal drivers

Identifying your values helps improve your focus and clarity and enables you to make more consistent decisions and take more committed action. A set of values can be viewed as a set of priorities that help you decide how to best use the precious resource that is time.

After time is gone, it's gone forever. If time was irrelevant, values and priorities would be irrelevant. Living as humans with finite life spans, we need to plan in order to make the best use of the time we do have.

You may find yourself becoming inconsistent in how you invest your time and energy. Getting distracted and drifting off course is easy to do. Imagine if you were on an aeroplane that went wherever the wind took it. Your destination would be undefined, and the flight itself would be stressful and uncertain.

Limited time and distraction makes living by your values extremely important. Values are your compass, which helps you keep on track each and every day and live the best life you can. The closer you get to this ideal, the more enjoyable and easy life becomes.

Identifying your personal values

Have you ever taken the time to identify the values and beliefs that underpin your life? Doing so is a valuable exercise.

TIP

You can find a simple tool to help you do this on the Resources page of www.aheadforwork.com.

Once you have identified the key values that underpin your life, its worth spending some time to assess to what extent you're currently living your life to achieve the things that are most important to you. want. Before you do, think back to our aeroplane analogy in the previous section. Your list tells you where your plane is currently heading. So looking at your list, ask yourself, 'Is this the direction I want my plane to continue to go?'

Spend a little time re-examining your values. Your values are your current compass, but they aren't necessarily always the real you.

REMEMBER

You're not stuck with these values, which may or may not be right for you. You can consciously change them – even radically if desired. You can go from a person who values success most highly to one whose top priority is calm and serenity, or vice versa. You are not your values. You are the thinker of your thoughts, but you are not the thoughts themselves.

Seeing yourself through the eyes of others

Equipped with your list of values that represent the real you, a good starting point for improving your personal presence is to try to see yourself through the eyes of others. Your peers and your team members may have different values from you. They may not view your drive for consistency and discipline in the same way you do. A work colleague who values expressiveness, non-conformity and outrageousness may find himself at odds with another who values conformity, accountability, and carefulness.

Achieving greater presence at work isn't about being all things to all people. It's about being consistent and true to your values while respecting the values of others. You can think about your 'presence' as being your 'personal brand'.

Think about your personal brand as what people say about you when you're not in the room. Although this can be a scary exercise, knowing what others think of you from the way you look, speak and behave is critical to building your presence and impact.

You can start determining your personal brand in two ways.

>> You can ask your peers and team members to give you some candid feedback on the qualities and behaviours that uniquely make you, you.

>> You can also make a concise list of the ways you *want* to be perceived by others and the behaviours that would model this. Then do a quick sanity check. If you can't model it authentically, ask yourself if it's really realistic, and don't be afraid to ditch it if it doesn't represent the real you.

Review both your lists. Do others' observations of you match your own observations of yourself? On the second list, are there more 'could do' behaviours than 'already do'? After you've identified where gaps exist between your behaviours and your desired behaviours, which will shift others' perceptions of you, you can work out a strategy for moving forward with a strong, authentic personal brand that will resonate with your key stakeholders.

BEING TRUE TO YOURSELF

A number of years ago, I (Juliet) worked with personal brand expert Jennifer Holloway. Jennifer (author of *Personal Branding for Brits*) taught me some very important lessons about myself. Those who run their own businesses will appreciate the sheer time and effort it can take to convert an enquiry into paid work. Jennifer made me realise that, like many in my situation, I was trying too hard to be all things to all people. Jennifer told me candidly, 'You are like a wonderful robust cup of espresso, but some people may prefer Earl Grey tea'. Espresso, delicate teas, and hot chocolate shouldn't try to be other than they are. Instead, accept and rejoice in it. Can you imagine what an Earl Grey espresso would taste like?

This advice has served me well over the years. I accept who I am, my values, and my preferred ways of working. I accept that I, and my way of doing things, may not be for everyone. This acceptance has helped me to better target my efforts on those around me who value what I bring to the party – my drive, enthusiasm, tenacity, pragmatism, warmth, and independence – instead of twisting myself inside out to work with people who value other things.

Remember that your personal brand – what makes you, you – may not always be to everyone's taste, and this is fine. You're much more likely to succeed in life if you're true to yourself. Being true to yourself and comfortable in your own skin means that you're much more likely to attract people who resonate with your values, and people will find you easier to work with, as they know exactly what you stand for and what you value.

Don't be afraid to seek feedback from colleagues you trust to measure the impact of your efforts.

TIP

Harnessing the Power of Influence

Gaining influence, like learning any skill, takes time and effort. You can find a lot of books on how to influence others at work, but few focus on how to influence with honesty and integrity – key attributes of mindful leadership.

Influence is important in this busy world that demands results fast, but it's not a Machiavellian power trip. Gaining influence takes time and effort. Being true to yourself, listening and valuing others, and being consistent in your leadership will help you earn the respect and influence you need.

Promoting trust

Influence is most easily gained though trust. Wise leaders always invest time and conscious effort in building trust with those they work with. Only when your co-workers trust you will they be open to your influence. When you hold a position of power, you can demand that tasks be carried out by employees, but true influence involves free will. If you want an effective and influential working relationship, you must work to cultivate trust. The easiest way to do this is to be open, honest and consistent no matter what.

Being consistent

Inconsistency can quickly ruin your reputation. For example, consistently always delivering on your promises will encourage people to rely on you and know what to expect from you. Consistency is vital for building influence. An air of unpredictability in a leader can be stressful for others and reduce the effectiveness of those around you.

Showing assertiveness without aggression

When building your influence, it's important to be assertive, not aggressive. Being assertive is important when working to get your ideas noticed, especially if you're in a meeting competing with others for visibility.

There's a big difference between being assertive and being aggressive. Present your thoughts and ideas with confidence, but don't overdo it. Excessive confidence could be misconstrued for arrogance and may compromise your perceived authority. Being assertive and sure of yourself is a way to cultivate a reputation of authority and earn the ability to influence your peers and employees. Who wants to follow someone who hasn't got a clue where he's going or how to get there?

Being flexible, not rigid

Be flexible whenever you can. Life happens, so flexibility is important. Let go of decisions or plans that no longer serve you or your organisation well. At times, being inflexible can work against you, and people may see you as stubborn and rigid. This can decrease the respect people have for you and compromise your overall influence.

TIP

Work actively to demonstrate your flexibility while remaining true to your values and beliefs. If people believe that you're flexible, they'll be more open to listening to you even if they disagree with your viewpoint or are inflexible themselves.

Being personable

Be yourself. A little personality displayed appropriately can go a long way, especially when building influence in the workplace. Try to go out of your way to have personal interactions with your colleagues at work. Personal working relationships cultivate team spirit and a sense of belonging. If people see you as part of their group, they'll be more open and receptive when you share your ideas or opinions.

REMEMBER

Be yourself, accept your imperfections, and be as approachable and human as you can. Distancing yourself too much from others can lead to alienation and distrust.

Walking the talk

Actions speak louder than words – however eloquent you are! You can't hope to influence by speeches and arguments alone. Working hard, being consistent and getting good results shows people that you're able to walk the walk. Show instead of tell.

Listening

Last, but by no means least, you gain influence by listening to others. You have two ears and one mouth – use them in that proportion! Influence is a two-way street. The more you listen to the people around you and incorporate their ideas, the more they'll believe in your ideas and incorporate them into their work.

Building relationships with others at work starts with listening. Encourage people to speak up and share their ideas and opinions – creating the space for them to think. Take the time to respect, value and acknowledge others' opinions, creating an atmosphere of mutual trust, mutual respect, and teamwork.

Becoming a 3-D Negotiator

Not everything goes to plan. Just because you're a leader doesn't mean that others will agree with everything you say or propose. Compromise and negotiation are part of everyday leadership life. Negotiations can range from the simple, such as agreeing to holiday plans or negotiating a pay raise, to the complex, such as negotiating contracts, acquisitions or mergers.

At a complex level, negotiation is a method by which people settle differences. It's a process by which compromise or agreement is reached while avoiding argument and dispute. In any negotiation, it's natural for the individuals involved to wish to achieve the best possible outcome for their position (or organisation that they represent). However, the principles of fairness, seeking mutual benefit and maintaining a relationship are the keys to a successful outcome.

A logical negotiation process may include the following stages:

>> **Preparation:** Where and when a meeting will take place – gathering of facts.

>> **Discussion:** When individuals from each side put forward the case as they see it and their understanding of the situation.

>> **Clarification of goals:** When both sides list key factors in order of importance to establish common ground.

>> **Negotiating towards a win-win outcome:** Where both sides feel their point of view has been taken into consideration. If impossible, alternative strategies and compromises are considered.

>> **Agreement:** When understanding of both sides' viewpoints and interests have been considered, agreement needs to be made perfectly clear so that both sides understand what has been decided.

Cognitive limitations and biases – common human flaws – can affect your ability to negotiate effectively. These flaws can impact your ability to question, listen, clarify, and keep an open mind – all key skills for effective negotiation.

In the following sections, we explore some ways to negotiate mindfully and become a better negotiator in the process.

Practicing mindful negotiation

Mindful leaders are attentive to and aware of their feelings, thoughts and motives, as well as their external environment. They're able to take in information without judgment (as detailed in Chapter 8). They're also able to focus attention and awareness for longer periods of time – this skill is developed by regular practice of mindfulness ('brain training', as we call it in this book).

Consider these findings from research done on mindful negotiation:

>> Researchers including Darshan Brach and Leonard Riskin from Northwestern University School of Law have concluded that mindfulness can increase a negotiator's attention and awareness, thus improving negotiation effectiveness.

>> Jochen Reb and Jayanth Narayanan from Singapore Management University have provided empirical evidence that mindfulness improves negotiation. According to their research conducted in 2014, mindfulness improves one's ability to make high-quality judgments and decisions.

Their research found that mindfulness can help individuals at each stage of decision-making. At the stage of decision framing, mindfulness is likely to increase people's awareness of the possibility (or the necessity) to make a decision and mitigate the sunk cost bias. It may also increase goal awareness, thereby enhancing decision consistency with objectives and reducing post-decision regret. Greater goal clarity, in turn, facilitates option generation, which is further enhanced by creativity that mindfulness is likely to spark.

Becoming a better negotiator

Setting aside negotiation models, which you're no doubt familiar with, this section focuses on the skills you need to become a 3-D negotiator:

>> Adopting an approach mode of mind

>> Developing the ability to sustain your attention and focus

>> Increasing your self-awareness and self-regulation

Adopting an approach mode of mind

As you discover in Chapter 10 avoidance mode – doing something to stop something bad from happening – is concerned with survival, and as a result closes down options and increases caution. Approach mode – doing something to make something good happen - reduces stress and increases curiosity and creativity.

The relevance of this for leaders is that when facing difficult situations, it's natural to feel challenged and easy to slip into avoidance mode, which will restrict your effectiveness.

REMEMBER

Practicing mindfulness helps you to cultivate an approach mode, which increases your creativity and improves your negotiation skills.

To encourage an approach mode of mind in negotiations, try the following:

>> If you hear someone talking about what he doesn't want, ask him what he'd like instead.

>> If someone is fixated on a problem, ask her what an ideal solution would look like.

>> If negotiations have stalled, invite people to describe similar situations in the past and what worked then.

Questions like these help people shift themselves away from the defensiveness of the avoidance mode and into the creativity of the approach mode.

Being fully present

To improve attention and focus during negotiations and be fully present, try the following in your own daily activities and while leading meetings:

>> **Commit to practicing mindfulness daily for at least six weeks** (follow the six-week course in Chapters 8 through 13).

>> **Ban laptops, mobile phones and other devices during meetings.** Many Silicon Valley workplaces already do this.

>> **Embrace single tasking.** Stanford researcher Clifford Nass discovered that multitaskers get much less done because they use their brains less effectively.

>> **Apply the 20-minute rule.** Instead of switching tasks from minute to minute, dedicate a 20-minute chunk of time to a single task, and then switch to the next one.

>> **Take breaks!** You can't (and shouldn't) work all the time. Taking breaks is good for you, not to mention essential to rebuilding your attention span.

Increasing your self-awareness and regulation

Mindfulness brain–training techniques, such as mindfulness of breath (see Chapter 8), body scan (see Chapter 9) and mindfulness of sounds and thoughts (Chapter 11) help you to use all your senses to progressively step out of autopilot. This is achieved by noticing when your mind wanders and observing without judgment your unique patterns of thought and behaviour. This knowledge helps you to manage yourself better.

Mindfulness isn't a quick fix, but by practicing daily and using techniques such as those detailed in Chapters 8 through 13, your self-awareness and thus ability to regulate yourself will improve. You may also consider the following:

>> Regularly monitor your emotions, and use this information to help you to manage your emotions better when under pressure (see Chapter 11 for more information).

>> Get enough sleep. Good negotiators need to sustain their attention and actively manage themselves for long periods of time. To do so, your brain requires a huge amount of energy. If you're tired, your brain is much more likely to default back to more energy-efficient ways of working, repeating past behaviours, which may be inappropriate to the situation in hand.

>> Check in with yourself on a regular basis. See how your body is feeling in this moment and what your emotional state and thoughts are in this moment. Are you fully engaged, or do you need to make a fresh effort to re-engage?

>> Be kind to yourself. Negotiation can be a tough job. Getting frustrated or annoyed with yourself, others, or a lack of progress will make it even harder to remain focused. Telling yourself 'I'm human, and I'm doing the best I can' or acknowl-edging in your head how others are feeling switches down your threat response, helping to you sustain your attention. You can read more about this in Chapter 13.

Chapter 15

Leading in a Digital Age

S ociety today is experiencing significant changes with the transition from an industrial-based society to a digital society. As we move closer to becoming a digital society, new social structures are generating new leadership styles and different patterns of hierarchy, skills, and attitudes.

The new digital age is characterised by four elements that are reshaping leadership:

>> Rapid, far-reaching technological changes

>> Accelerated globalisation

>> A shift from brawn to brains

>> More distributed, less hierarchical organisational forms

In this highly dynamic environment, leadership innovation and adaptability are critical, especially the leader's capacity to channel the right knowledge to the right people at the right time in the right place.

Of course, some elements of leadership remain the same. Commitment, focus, discipline, communication skills, and the ability to engage others with your vision are still vital. Emotional intelligence, authenticity and mindfulness – the ability to be fully present – are becoming the new leadership essentials.

In this chapter, you explore the challenges of leading in a digital age, including information overload and executive attention deficit disorder. You discover how to work more effectively in the digital world we live in by taking control of your digital devices and being more mindful of how you use your digital technology.

Defining Digital Leadership

Digital leaders have a subtly different combination of skills, attitudes, knowledge, and experience that equips them to lead well in the digital age. Digital leaders must be adaptable, flexible, and curious about the world they lead in and have a thirst for new knowledge. They need to suspend judgment, observing the usefulness in different perspectives, and be comfortable leading in uncertainty. Digital leaders look globally for solutions and challenges and have a keenness for constant learning. They adopt a more egalitarian outlook and are firmly focused on results.

The core skills of a digital leader include the ability to

>> Build coalitions and forge communities of interest

>> Engage with people from different professional and demographic backgrounds

>> Switch more effectively between tasks

>> Remain focused on their own priorities even while seeking common ground with others

>> Assimilate knowledge quickly

>> Understand and embrace new technologies

>> Know what they don't know, and know how to get that missing knowledge

Successful leaders are able to develop and sustain a moral compass to guide their behaviour. Skills, attitudes, knowledge, experiences and ethics fit together in a mutually reinforcing 'package' for successful digital leaders.

David Segal, author of *Futurising Your Organisation,* once famously said, 'I've found that 90 per cent of problems companies have online are created by management, not technology'.

While technology is advancing rapidly, people are struggling to keep up and need to re-learn how to learn. To integrate leadership and technology, you need to un-learn past leadership theories and practices that are no longer appropriate and may even be destructive to organisations.

Many leadership practices that are still taught in many management schools persist today but evolved from business principles from the eighties or earlier. They're based on the assumption that it's up to organisations to decide what customers need. The digital age has changed this, and there is now an emphasis that moves away from the organisation calling the shots to the customer calling the shots, by demanding what they want rather than what is offered.

Identifying the role of social media

Social media used to be the preserve of marketing and PR staff. As its importance increases, it is becoming a core component of a digital leader's role. This is driven by the increase of ownership and use of mobile devices, which are driving the diverse use of social media. The role of social media for business is rapidly evolving. Not so long ago, most companies used social media purely for marketing. It was used as a form of social customer response, with businesses identifying customer complaints and requests via Twitter, Facebook and other social platforms.

Customers became dissatisfied with this form of social customer response, which often forced them back to traditional offline interactions to seek resolutions. To remain competitive, businesses now need to engage in resolving social inquiries, without resorting to offline channels or further delay. In some recent customer surveys, as many as half of customers preferred to interact with companies entirely online. This number is likely to continue to increase each year for the majority of customer groups. Some customer care specialists predict that phone and email-based contact will eventually become obsolete.

It's easy to see why more and more customers are engaging with online social customer care. They're increasingly unwilling to wait for lengthy times on hold for a customer representative to be available to take their call. Online resolutions are often quicker and more time efficient. Consider this story of a man who got caught short in a toilet cubicle of a train with no toilet roll. He turned to Twitter to express his predicament. His tweet was picked up by a customer service representative from the train operating company who contacted staff on the train. A few minutes later, there was a knock on the door, and a member of train staff handed the man a roll of toilet paper!

Not so long ago, it was acceptable to wait a week or more for a response by post from a company. The instant nature of social media has raised the bar in resolution of customer issues. In recent years, many were pleased with a response in 4 to 24 hours. For some, this time frame is now unacceptable. Top performers in the industry aim for consumers to receive initial responses to threaded social media interactions in less than 15 minutes. If your company's goal is to make customer resolutions more efficient and effective, management and use of social channels is vital.

As the frequency and use of mobile devices continue to increase and websites become increasingly mobile-friendly, there is likely to be an even greater role for digital customer care. A new generation of consumers is emerging that prefer to conduct all online interactions through mobile devices and have a preference for self-service whenever possible. To respond to this shift in customer preference, companies will need to work even harder to meet the demands and immediacy afforded by social media resolution on mobile. They will need to find ways to seamlessly escalate some interactions to human assistance when self-service applications prove inadequate.

The future also offers companies many opportunities to use social media not only for customer services and marketing purposes but also as a means to detect new trends, customer needs and demands.

Identifying the digital implications for leaders

Shortcomings in Information Technology (IT) development are becoming a major leadership challenge as more and more customers interact with organisations through IT.

As a leader, you need to recognise the importance of integrating the new digital world into your organisation as a whole. Customers, more than ever before, are leading organisations' direction of travel. The Internet has enabled them to input into and shape organisational decision-making in a way that was previously undreamt of.

Leaders need to recognise that the borderless global force of the Internet creates global customers in a truly globalised marketplace. The leadership challenge is finding ways to work creatively with the human lag, created by the inability to process and function as fast as technology can.

The fundamental shift towards digital leadership requires leaders to answer questions such as the following:

» What are the implications of the digital age for your current leadership structure and organisational culture?

» How can you further integrate your leadership methods with your technology systems?

» Is your leadership style currently an enabler or a constraint to technology?

» How are your leadership methods and technology system likely to co-evolve in the future?

Exploring the Impact of Leading in a Digital Age

Although modern technologies offer leaders many benefits and exciting new possibilities, they can also be a major source of stress and burnout, as we explore in the following sections.

Recognising signs of information overload

Information overload can be a huge contributory factor to workplace-induced stress and burnout. So what is information overload? Imagine receiving in one day 27 instant messages, 4 text messages, 17 phone calls, 98 work emails, 52 personal emails, 14 social network messages, 127 social network status updates, 5 letters, and 6 pieces of junk mail and then listening to 3 hours of radio in the car and when home watching 2 hours of television. This is a prime example of information overload that many leaders encounter every day.

Information flows towards most leaders from the multitude of devices that can distract, exert pressure, and stress them. Despite this, they continue to produce information for both themselves and others.

Every time you send out information, information flows back to you and often increases in volume. When you're constantly interrupted, you lack time to think, plan and prioritise. As a result, your ability to lead well and push your organisation forward diminishes.

Recognising executive attention deficit disorder

Information overload can have a significant impact on your brain. It can trigger a form of attention deficit disorder (ADD). Although not in the strictest sense an illness, ADD is a response to the hyper-connectivity with the environment you live in. If as a leader you're desperately trying to deal with more information than you possibly can, your ability for higher brain processing is reduced. Under pressure, you default to habitual thinking. Perspective and shades of grey disappear. You may struggle to stay organised, set priorities, or manage time and may experience a constant low level of panic.

Executive ADD is more common than you might think. A 2005 Basex survey showed that 28 per cent (2.1 hours) of a knowledge worker's day is consumed by interruptions. In the United States alone, this translates to 28 billion lost working hours and

$588 million in lost profits every year. University of London research in 2005 found that people taking an IQ test while being interrupted by emails and phone calls performed an average of 10 points lower than the baseline group without those interruptions. This is more than a control group who had been tested after smoking marijuana – they performed an average of 4 points lower than the baseline group.

A number of years ago, I worked with an enthusiastic, hardworking committed leader who wanted to take her leadership to the next level. Holly was generally well liked by her team but was easily distracted during meetings and one-to-ones by phone calls, emails and other digital distractions. Holly realised she had a problem only when she noticed some of her team members were distancing themselves from her. She asked them straight out what the issue was, and she was shocked to discover that her attempts to multitask were making them feel that she viewed their issues and concerns as unimportant.

Although Holly identified that she had an executive ADD problem, she still felt under pressure to be constantly available to senior managers and was unsure how to manage the competing demands for her attention. Holly had in the past tried out all sorts of ways to better manage her time, but none of them had produced the desired results. I suggested an alternative to Holly – to instead focus on managing her attention, which we discuss in the next section.

Managing your attention

Attention is a finite resource. How you use this valuable resource is increasingly important. Programmes like WorkplaceMT, as described in Chapters 8 through 13, are designed to help you improve your focus and attention. If this isn't for you, try something – anything – but do something instead of procrastinating or carrying on as you are. Experiment, adapt, and find something that works for you.

Jeremy Hunter created the Executive Mind Leadership Institute at the Peter F. Drucker Graduate School of Management at Claremont Graduate University. Peter F. Drucker is famously quoted as saying 'You cannot manage other people unless you manage yourself first'.

Jeremy believes that attention management 'may be the most critical management skill of the 21st century'. He proposes that practicing mindfulness can be an antidote to Executive ADD and proposes a useful model:

Intention » Attention » Awareness » Choice » Action » Result

The process starts with clearly defining your intentions – that is, what you want to be different – or your goals. Setting clear intention influences how you use your attention. The things you pay attention to impact your awareness and thus influence your interpretation of what is happening around you.

Your interpretation influences the choices you make and the actions you take, leading to an end result. If the end result isn't what you want, revisit the model of five elements outlined above to see what could have been different. The more mindful you are of each of the elements, the better able you'll be to ensure that they're aligned. The more aligned they are, the more likelihood you have of turning your intentions into the results you desire.

The next time you need to get something done but can't see the wood for the trees, try this exercise:

1. **Define your intention as clearly as possible.**

2. **Focus your attention on things that will help you deliver on your intention.**

3. **Become aware of the things that hijack your attention.**

   Suspend judgment as much as you can while you assimilate information to avoid getting sidetracked.

4. **After you have all the information you need, make a choice (decision) about what to do next based on facts rather than the stories your mind has a tendency to generate.**

5. **Act on your decision in a timely manner.**

6. **Objectively evaluate the results.**

   If they're not as expected, re-evaluate starting at Step 1.

TIP

To find out more about this, you might like to read Jeremy's chapter on 'Teaching Managers to Manage Themselves' in the excellent textbook *Mindfulness in Organizations* (see Chapter 22 for more information).

Coping with the Demands of Digital Leadership

Many people blame technology for their inability to focus their attention and curse it as a modern epidemic. A recent study identified that the average smartphone user checks his device 221 times a day. Here are a few more statistics:

>> Ninety-five per cent of people use their electronics in bed.

>> Sixty per cent read email while on vacation.

>> Sixty-one per cent admit to being 'addicted' to their technology.

REMEMBER

But technology isn't really the enemy – it's your response to it that is. Your mobile phone doesn't force you to take work calls at 11 p.m., answer emails at 2 a.m., or engage with friends on social media. It's a choice. Even if you work for a tyrannical boss or in a working culture that insists on constant connectivity, you *still* have a choice.

You can explore this choice by using a model we touch on in Chapter 11. Although you may not always have control of the information and communication that flows towards you from your digital device, you do have control of how you interpret it and respond to it.

So are you controlling the technology, or is the technology ruling you? Here are some steps you can take to find out:

1. **Analyse the volume of information you're receiving each day over a seven-day period.**

Which digital devices is it coming from? How much time is it taking? What, if any, control do you have over it?

2. Note how you manage and respond to the information and communication that flows from your mobile devices.

3. Assess whether there's a better way to manage and respond to this information flow.

Although you may have little or no control over the information you receive, you do have control over how you interpret and deal with it and exploring new ways to work with available technology. Changing the way you think about information overload, and proactively investigating new technologies and ways of interacting with it more positively, can make the difference between being an effective digital leader and one at serious risk of stress and burnout.

Working More Effectively in a Digital Age

The digital age isn't all bad. It offers many new and exciting ways to work and new opportunities for businesses. Digitalisation has increased the speed and efficiency of many things people do. It also offers amazing new opportunities to engage with your customers, quickly assessing and responding to market needs. It offers the opportunity to operate and collaborate globally in a way that would have been impossible only 20 years ago.

TIP

Here are some tips about how to harness the opportunities the digital age offers you as a leader:

>> **Take control of your digital devices.** Manage them firmly as you would an unruly animal. Set clear parameters for your use of digital devices and put yourself back in control.

>> **Be mindful of how you use your digital technology.** Monitor its usage and manage it appropriately.

>> **Fight against modern digital habits by living a proportion of your life in the real world.** Modern digital habits can lead people to be less patient, less empathetic, less productive, less able to hold conversations, less focused, and

ultimately less happy. Combat this with intention. Set aside time for genuine face-to-face social interaction.

>> **Use your mobile phone's on and off switch wisely.** Create mobile-free times of day at work and at home.

>> **Ban mobile devices from the bedroom.** Resist the urge to interact on social media late at night or answer emails. Doing so can suck you into a downward thought spiral that makes you feel stressed and stops you from sleeping. A good night's sleep helps you to be more productive at work – so prioritise sleep over digital interactions that may seem important at the time but in reality rarely are.

>> **Let your customers take the lead.** The new digital age provides opportunities to engage your customers as collaborators. If you ever feel lost as a leader, why not simply ask your customers?

>> **Choose technology for your company that makes it easier for your customers to interact with your organisation.** The more easily they can engage with you, the more likely they are to gain a sense of ownership of your brand and share their requirements with you.

>> **Use technology to help you and your company build equitable and mutually rewarding relationships with your customers.** Engaging customers who are loyal and committed are no longer just nice to have – they're must-haves.

>> **Don't fall into the trap of pushing for less technology.** Use your technology more smartly. Neuroscientists have observed how easily the brain rewires itself as a result of technological development.

TECHNICAL STUFF

A London-based company Vinaya has just launched a range of discrete hi-tech, high-fashion jewellery. The connected rings, bracelets and necklaces pair with an app on users' phones, allowing them to prioritise which notifications are important enough to filter through and make their jewellery vibrate. The smart jewellery aims to improve attention by reducing distraction, providing a much-needed break from your screens, and breaking down unhelpful habits. The jewellery is designed to help people better focus on the task at hand and maintain a state of creative flow.

>> **Add a 'mindfulness bell' to your computer to remind you periodically to take a break from your technology.** There are lots that are freely available to download from the Internet.

>> **Use a mindfulness app, such as Headspace, to keep your mindfulness practice on track.** Apps are great to use when travelling and can help you embed the habit of mindfulness.

>> **Investigate new software from Psychological Technologies (PsyT) that provides real-time feedback on the engagement, well-being and culture of an organisation.** The users gain invaluable insights into themselves creating greater self-awareness. Employees provide anonymous feedback back to the organisation, so leaders can manage the environment from the top-down, as changes are happening on the ground.

Chapter 16

Leading in Times of Change

C hange is nothing new – in fact, it's the only constant in life. What *is* new is the pace of change. Long-established leadership models for leading change are based on the assumption that each change has a clearly defined start and end point. What companies are facing now is ongoing 'bumpy change' with little or no time to adjust and adapt before the next wave of change hits them.

This chapter explores new ways of leading in a more mindful manner in times of change that will equip you to manage this constant ongoing change.

Understanding Change from Your Brain's Perspective

Every second of the day, your brain is hard at work keeping you alive and repairing and maintaining your body. Setting this aside, your brain's primary function is to maximise reward while minimising threat. To do this, your brain pays more attention to things it decides are potentially harmful. This stems back to ancient times when humans faced regular life-and-death situations. If we failed to see the 'tiger' in the bushes we would be dead.

The good things in life (shelter, food, friendship, and a sense of achievement) are good, and in most cases, they're unlikely to harm or kill you, so the brain tends not to linger on them. Instead, the brain focuses on the next goal, such as delivering a project on time and on budget, buying a new car, or getting a promotion. The brain initially treats anything that might get in the way of you achieving this goal or reward as a threat and pays it a lot of attention in an attempt to help remain safe and stay on track to achieve your goal.

Under normal circumstances when you're working in a calm and level-headed way, your brain learns by experience not to panic or activate your threat system when you encounter challenges along the way to achieving your goals. You engage your higher brain circuitry to plan, prioritise, make decisions and think of new and innovative ways of working. Your primitive brain makes good use of tried and tested ways of working that have served you well in the past for the more routine tasks at work.

Change creates uncertainty. The human brain hates uncertainty. In an effort to reduce uncertainty, your brain seeks information. The problem is that often this information is unavailable until later on in the change process. In a bid to create certainty where none exists, your brain starts to construct stories about what's happening and what's likely to happen. Due to the negativity bias, these are often catastrophic stories as the brain fills the information gap with the worst scenarios possible. It then treats these stories as facts and uses them as the basis for decisions and actions.

Think of a sudden or unexpected change that you encountered at home or work and answer these questions:

>> What happened initially?

>> How did you respond initially?

>> Were you aware of any initial thoughts or emotions in response to the change?

>> Did you make any assumptions of what was happening or was going to happen? If so, what were they?

>> What happened in the end?

When faced with a sudden or unexpected change, you can easily jump to conclusions or think the worst. You may initially experience what psychologist Daniel Goleman calls an 'amygdala hijack' – an immediate, overwhelming emotional response followed later by a recognition that the response was inappropriate. This is because strong emotional information travels directly from the thalamus to the amygdala without engaging the higher 'thinking brain' regions. This causes a strong emotional response that precedes more rational thought.

Mindful leaders can recognise and then accept this human response to threatening stimulus. Doing so helps them to bring conscious awareness to what's going on and reduces the likelihood of being sucked into negative thought spirals that trigger strong emotions and can result in inappropriate behaviours.

Being a mindful leader won't stop you from experiencing the pain and suffering that change can bring, but it will help you to reduce its impact and put your higher thinking brain back in the driving seat more quickly. It will also help you to take better care of yourself so you can be the best leader you can be even when under immense pressure.

Mindful leaders are more aware of what's going on inside themselves and around them moment by moment. This enables them to observe the impact of the change on their peers and team, helping them to decide what's most needed at any moment in time.

Becoming a more mindful leader doesn't suddenly turn you into a superhero. As a leader, you're still a human and are still likely to experience the same human responses to change as others around you. Mindful leadership is about being human, honest and authentic. At times, sharing with your colleagues or team that you feel scared or insecure may be appropriate. At other times, you may need to be a statesman, saying and doing the right thing to create some forward momentum. In this instance, it's still important to acknowledge and accept your own fears and insecurities and cut yourself some slack. Doing so is a sign of strength, not weakness, as it helps you to maintain an optimum state of mind that enables you to be the best you can be (see the model in Chapter 1).

Leading When Change Is the Norm

Change is no longer a short break from 'business as usual' – it's now the norm. We live and work in a world that's *volatile, uncertain, complex* and often *ambiguous* (VUCA). In a VUCA world, leaders need to adapt to and stimulate continuous organisational change.

Older models of change leadership are often top-down strategies for gaining buy-in and overcoming resistance to discrete initiatives. These models are designed with the aim to control change. They often fail to create shared, long-term ownership and engagement. Neither do they lead to a heightened readiness and flexibility in the face of continuous, emergent change – a symptom of the VUCA world. Traditional change models often result in employee cynicism and fear, reducing productivity and creativity and making an organisation even less resilient.

Learning is a process of change, and change is a process of learning. In order to manage change, you need apply a structured process and set of tools for leading the *human aspects* of change in order to achieve a desired goal. The next few pages explore your role in leading change, suggesting some new ways to consider, plan and lead the process.

Managing change or leading change?

Although you may hold a leadership role, it's important to ask yourself whether you're really leading change or simply trying to manage it. *Change management* is facilitating the change process, whereas *change leadership* empowers action that allows change to take off.

Change leaders work collaboratively and seek to inspire. Being a change leader isn't simply a case of making change initiatives efficient; change leaders need to be able to take risks to find new ways of working instead of merely seeking to control and contain the change. Change leadership initiates change on a large scale instead of making small changes or adopting a silo mentality

Good change leaders recognise the need for change and respond to it quickly, leaving their managers to create order, set timelines and manage budgets. They innovate and set engaging visions, leaving managers to integrate the visions so they become 'the way we do things round here'. Change leaders empower those around them to create change for themselves instead of simply encouraging them to adapt.

Change leadership isn't about working through a defined change process by using some tools and techniques while remaining organised and reporting on your project plan. Change leadership requires leadership skills. Leaders need to have an in-depth knowledge of their company and its customers and competitors, communicate effectively, taking into account individual and collective responses to change, and encourage creativity and innovation.

Observing the change continuum

Are you familiar with the change curve? The change curve, shown in Figure 16-1, is based on a model originally developed in the 1960s by Elisabeth Kubler-Ross to explain the grieving process.

The change curve model explains the emotional roller-coaster that people go through when experiencing a sudden or unexpected change. People pass through the different stages on the curve at different speeds. At the early stages, people need you to communicate with them as much as possible. In the middle stages, you need to be especially mindfully aware of people's need for emotional support, creating an environment that allows them to get this from their workmates, family or you. At the later stages, try to get your team as involved as possible in creating their new future, being there to direct and guide them towards it.

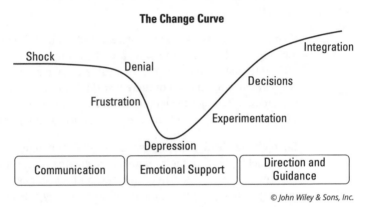

© John Wiley & Sons, Inc.

FIGURE 16-1: The change curve.

With today's bumpy change, I like to think of the change curve as more of a change continuum (see Figure 16-2). As each change 'bump' is encountered, people may remain static, move backwards or forwards on the continuum, with no distinct start or end point, as one change may 'hit' before another change is fully embedded.

The Change Ccontinuum

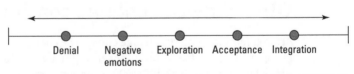

© A Head for Work Ltd.

FIGURE 16-2: The change continuum.

Using this model, mindful leaders need to constantly assess at what point on the continuum individuals and the majority of the team are, and flex their leadership style to help them to progress more rapidly towards a productive working state. Instead of thinking of each change as an individual entity, by accepting and embracing the fact that change is the norm, mindful leaders suffer less change fatigue, and their team becomes more accepting of the constantly changing nature of their work.

Exploring Models of Change Leadership

Although many companies claim to actively manage change, a recent poll indicated that 60 per cent of all companies use no specific change model to manage change. Of those who did, 20 per cent used Kotter's model and 17 per cent used the Prosci model. In the next few pages, we explore a few approaches to leading change, some well known, others less known, but worthy of consideration. You can then mindfully select the right approach for your organisation, or design one yourself.

Kotter's model of change leadership

In 1996, John Kotter introduced an eight-step transformation model based on analysis from 100 different organisations going through change, as outlined here:

>> Step 1: Establish a sense of urgency.

>> Step 2: Form a powerful guiding coalition.

>> Step 3: Develop a vision and strategy.

>> Step 4: Communicate the vision.

>> Step 5: Remove obstacles and empower action.

>> Step 6: Plan and create short-term wins.

>> Step 7: Consolidate gains.

>> Step 8: Anchor in the culture.

Although the model appears linear, it's best to think of it as a continuous cycle that maintains momentum for the desired change.

Prochaska and DiClemente's stages of change model

Unlike other change models, this model focuses on the human dimension of change. Change is a process that unfolds over time. It is a process that involves you passing through a number of stages, which may result in a change in your behaviour. The model defines these as precontemplation, contemplation, preparation, action and maintenance

Applied to organisational change it involves the leaders making a number of covert and overt moves to help employees adapt their behaviour and mindsets in the face of change.

The process starts with the leader making it clear to employees the things that need to done differently in the future – for example, using new technology appropriately, working collaboratively in a team, performing with total quality improvement guidelines.

At the precontemplation stage, individuals are not ready to act. They may feel demoralised from having failed to make changes in the past. They may not even be considering change. At this stage, leaders need to raise consciousness as to why it is important to make the behavioural changes and to raise the pros of doing so. They should acknowledge their lack of readiness but find subtle ways to encourage them to re-evaluation of current behaviour. A good strategy might be explaining and personalising the risk they face by not changing.

At the contemplation stage, individuals begin to think about or get ready to act or do things differently. They may still be ambivalent about the change or 'sitting on the fence'. At this stage, leaders need to reduce the 'cons' of doing the new behaviour and inspire the employee to work towards what the organisation can become with the move to action. They might consider getting the teams together to re-evaluate their group image through group activities, or identify and promote new, positive outcome expectations

At the preparation stage, individuals are ready to act. Some start to test the water and try to start changing their behaviour. At this stage, leaders need to prepare and encourage employees to make a commitment to perform the new behaviour, to take small steps, and to learn the behaviours that are needed to be in action. The leader needs to identify and promote new, positive outcome expectations in the individual and encourage taking small initial steps.

At the action stage, employees are performing the new behaviours, but the change is not yet embedded. Stimulus control is important, as well as rewards, helping guiding relationships, and using substitutes (substituting the new behaviour for the old behaviour). At this stage, people start to make deliberate actions moving towards the new desired behaviours. Leaders need to be cautious at this stage as it's easy for staff to slip back to old ways of doing things. They need to help the team to establish new social and cultural norms, overcome barriers and obstacles and deal effectively with feelings of loss and frustration.

Maintanance is gained after six months of repeating the new behaviour. At the maintenance stage, it's important to stay on track. Ongoing, active work is needed to maintain changes in behaviour and prevent a slip back to old ways of working or thinking. Stimulus control, rewards and helping relationships continue to be important. As the individual's confidence increases, the danger of returning back to old ways of working diminishes. At this stage, the leader needs to plan in follow-up support, and provide rewards (praise, recognition or financial) to continue with the new behaviour.

Prosci's ADKAR Model

Prosci developed the ADKAR model in 1998 based on research gathered from more than 300 companies who were undergoing major change projects. ADKAR is a goals-oriented change management model that encourages change managers and their teams to focus their activities around specific desired business results. The benefits and limitations of this model are as follows:

>> **Benefits:** It focuses on the business process element of change in addition to the individuals involved in the change process.

>> **Limitations:** It misses out the role of leadership in the process, which may lead to a lack of clarity and sense of direction.

Although many change management projects focus on the steps necessary for organisational change, the Prosci ADKAR model focuses on five actions and outcomes necessary for successful individual change and therefore successful organisational change. For change to be effective, individuals need the following:

>> Awareness of the need for change

>> Desire to participate and support the change

>> Knowledge on how to change

>> Ability to implement required skills and behaviours

>> Reinforcement to sustain the change

Knowledge and practice of mindfulness, together with some basic knowledge of how the brain works on the part of both the leader and employees, make this model even more effective. In the words of Jon Kabat-Zinn, founder of mindfulness–based stress reduction (MBSR), 'You can't stop the waves, but you can learn to surf'.

Practicing Mindful Strategies for Leading Change

When leading change, it's easy to focus on numbers and statistics. This sometimes overshadows the human aspects of change. The human need for safety, certainty and control is more likely to derail a carefully planned change project than a failure to accurately predict budgets or future profits.

Here are three mindful strategies for leading change:

>> Letting go of the illusion of control

>> Becoming more emotionally intelligent

>> Remaining rooted in the present moment

We discuss these strategies in detail in the following sections.

Letting go of the illusion of control

Irrespective of the position, power and influence you may hold, you never really have true control over your life, no matter how wealthy or educated you may become. Leaders commonly overestimate their ability to control or influence what's happening around them.

Instead of seeking to have more control in your life, it's often better to strive for more resilience. Merriam-Webster defines resilience as 'an ability to recover from or adjust easily to misfortune or change'. Times are always changing, and you can make yourself miserable by trying to cling to the past or reject your current circumstances. Mindful leaders learn to quickly identify the things they can't influence or change and then actively choose to accept them instead. This is particularly useful in times of change. Doing so allows you to focus your energy, time and attention on things that you can control or influence for the better.

Mindful leaders assess all the information at hand and make the decision about what to do now that will have the best likelihood of a desired outcome in the future. After you make the decision, you can use feedback to adjust and adapt as needs dictate. As to what you may do in the future or unpleasant outcomes that can happen, those are only relevant to the extent that it influences what you need to do now. If you can do nothing now to change potential future outcomes, then there is no point in thinking about them.

Becoming more emotionally intelligent

When leading through change, managing your physical assets is never the issue – the human response to change is. Leading change is about leading people, and change can be an emotive subject, so emotional intelligence (EQ) is key. A number of researchers have identified a positive relationship between EQ and mindfulness. Practicing mindfulness helps you to develop your emotional intelligence in three ways:

>> **Mindfulness helps you to identify and understand your emotions better.** Practicing mindfulness helps you to observe your emotions, moment by moment. This conscious awareness creates a small gap between the stimulus and your response. This gap or brief 'thinking space' allows you to choose how to respond, based on an assessment of facts as opposed to emotions like fear or anger.

People who practice mindfulness tend to have a higher awareness of their emotional state, noticing as emotions come, go and change. Other research concludes that the more mindful you become, the clearer your awareness is of feelings, resulting in lower distraction.

>> **Mindfulness helps you to develop the ability to detect and understand the emotions of others.** A research study concluded that being mindful allows you to focus your attention better on how other people around you are feeling and helps you to notice and decipher emotional cues of others more accurately. It can also improve your empathy. Another study demonstrated that those who attend mindfulness training have more empathy for themselves and others.

>> **Mindfulness helps you to enhance the ability of individuals to regulate and control their emotions.** Researchers discovered that people with a higher level of mindfulness tended to recover more quickly from emotional distress compared with those with a lower level of mindfulness – something that could give you the edge in times of change.

Mindfulness can help you to use your emotions more effectively. Mindfully observing your emotions while suspending judgment allows you to adopt an emotional state, which helps you to focus on and perform a task better and avoid performing a task that you can't perform well when certain emotions are present.

Mindful leaders are aware of their emotional state and over time develop sufficient EQ to select the optimum emotional state to get a task done well. Being in a positive mood is important for tasks that require creativity, integrative thinking, and deductive reasoning, but being in a negative mood tends to make people become more effective in tasks that require attention to detail, detection of errors and problems, and careful information processing.

Emotions aren't necessarily a bad thing, but they can have a major impact at inappropriate moments. When emotions become overwhelming, try the RAIN model developed by mindfulness teacher Tara Brach. You can use this model at work or home to help manage your feelings in a more mindful way.

Stop and focus on the present moment sensations of breathing.

R – Recognize the emotion you're feeling.

A – Accept the experience you're having.

I – Investigate. Become curious about your experience.

N – Non-identification. See the emotion as passing events, without the need for further response.

Remaining rooted in the present moment

Practicing mindfulness helps you to develop the ability to remain rooted in the present moment when you need to. This helps you avoid getting caught up with overanalysis of past mistakes and wild predictions of the future. It allows you to assess things as they are in the moment with clarity and decisiveness.

As a mindful leader, you can do a number of things to help encourage others to remain rooted in the present, including the following:

» Ban laptops, mobile phones and other devices during meetings. Many Silicon Valley workplaces already do this.

» Encourage single tasking. Stanford researcher Clifford Nass discovered that multitaskers get much less done because they use their brains less effectively.

» Encourage others to apply the 20-minute rule. Instead of switching tasks from minute to minute, dedicate a 20-minute chunk of time to a single task, and then switch to the next one.

» Encourage others to take breaks. Productivity diminishes if you work all the time. Taking breaks is good for you, not to mention essential to rebuilding your attention span.

5

Becoming a Mindful Organisation

Assess the suitability of mindfulness training for your organisation.

Improve the processes and outcomes of workplace practices, from meetings to decision-making to project management.

Chapter 17

Introducing Mindfulness to Your Organisation

You can introduce mindfulness to your organisation in a variety of ways. You can allow mindfulness to grow organically, plump for organisational evolution or revolution. This chapter contains the basics you need to know to get started.

Starting with the Outcome in Mind

When considering how to introduce mindfulness to your organisation, don't be tempted to rush immediately into *doing mode* –that is, contacting random mindfulness providers and asking them to pitch and re-pitch as your ideas take shape. Instead, first invest some time to identify and clarify the outcomes you want to achieve.

Defining desirable organisational outcomes

As a specialist in learning design and consultancy, I always start with the end in mind. Often what the client first asks me for is different from what they actually need. Busy people are prone to jump to solutions before they have adequately defined and explored what the issue is.

A good starting point is to examine the challenges your organisation is currently facing or is likely to face in the near future. Next, think of what staff may need to address these challenges. Use Table 17-1 to rank improvements in terms of importance at this point in time and within the next 6 to 18 months. Rank 1 for most important and 12 for least important.

TABLE 17-1 **Rank of Desired Improvements required by Your Organisation**

Improvements in . . .	Importance Now (Rank 1–12)	Importance in 6–18 Months (Rank 1–12)
Ability to see the bigger picture		
Communications		
Creativity		
Emotion regulation		
Health and well-being		
Kindness to self or others		

Improvements in . . .	Importance Now (Rank 1–12)	Importance in 6–18 Months (Rank 1–12)
Leadership capability		
Organisational working culture		
Personal productivity		
Relationships at work		
Resilience		
Self-management		

All the items in Table 17-1 are things that mindfulness could help you to achieve. You may find that ranking some of these items is difficult because they may seem equally important. The key is to try to identify your organisation's current top priorities that mindfulness may help you address. Here are some ways to do that:

» If you have a high staff turnover or low levels of staff engagement, you may want to focus on *relationships at work* and/or improving your *organisational working culture.*

» If you're in the midst of rapid, ongoing change, staff *resilience* and *leadership capability* may be high on your list.

» If your staff works in health and social care, *resilience, emotion regulation, self-management* or *kindness* may be high on your list.

» If your leadership team is suffering from change fatigue, with another major change round the corner, you may need them to be able to *see the bigger picture*, improve their *resilience* and/or improve their *productivity.*

» If you have high staff sickness and absence, it's worth checking out the causes because you may need to address HR, *leadership* or *organisational culture* issues first.

REMEMBER

Mindfulness isn't a Band-Aid or cure-all. It can be a part of a blended solution, or it can be a stand-alone programme. Well-designed, workplace-focused mindfulness programmes, such as WorkplaceMT or CBMT, have the potential to offer organisations much more than improvements on health and well-being.

Deployed well, they have the potential to transform working practices in a way that benefits both the employer and the organisation.

Assessing the risk of possible negative impacts

As we discuss in Chapter 2, mindfulness isn't a panacea for all ills. Many issues with staff engagement, sickness absence and productivity may be down to poor management or poor organisational processes and working practices.

The following sections explore a few examples of when mindfulness may *not* be the right solution.

When mindfulness training is compulsory

Mindfulness requires people to literally change the way they think. Behavioural change occurs only if individuals are willing to rewire their brain by engaging in the exercises with curiosity, self-compassion and discipline. You can't force someone to change – they have to want to. For this reason, mandating individuals to attend mindfulness training in the hope that they will change is, at best, optimistic and, at worst, a waste of time and money.

If difficult employees are open to learning about emotions and how they impact their behaviour and relationships at work, then mindfulness may help, but they may also need additional coaching, mentoring or training. Similarly, mindfulness may help improve poor working relationships within teams, but equally, mindfulness may bring matters to a head with explosive consequences.

When staff have to deal with unresolved issues at work

WARNING

Workplace mindfulness programmes are not designed to act as a therapy. On very rare occasions, unexpected effects may surface when you explore your experience using mindfulness exercises. Focusing attention on emotions and bodily sensations during mindfulness exercises may very occasionally bring up feelings of anxiety or even panic. This is why we always recommend that mindfulness training is facilitated by a suitably experienced, well-trained mindfulness teacher rather than just an employee who practices mindfulness. Properly managed, a mindfulness teacher can help minimise any negative impacts for individuals and the group as a whole and safeguard vulnerable employees.

When mindfulness training may be inappropriate or damaging

Workplace mindfulness programmes are designed for a healthy working population. The assumption is that if an employee is healthy enough to be at work, he's healthy enough to attend mindfulness training. Even when I (Juliet) have pre-screened staff attending training for contraindications, on occasions some people slip through the net. In these instances, I talk to them discretely after the course to decide a way forward or refer them to occupational health or other relevant support.

For a small minority of people, mindfulness exercises that focus on the breath may be disturbing, especially if they have a history of breathing difficulties such as asthma. We discuss ways to work around this in Chapter 2.

REMEMBER

Staff with a history of depression, alcohol or drug abuse, psychotic episodes, or PTSD should check with their doctor before attending mindfulness training. Alternative versions of mindfulness training, such as an eight-week MBCT or eight-week MBSR, may be more appropriate for some staff.

For the vast majority of individuals, mindfulness is entirely safe, and in our experience, when taught well, the organisational impacts and return on investment vastly exceed the costs involved, especially when compared with traditional management and personal productivity training, which usually cost much more.

Developing Mindful Individuals in Your Organisation

You can introduce mindfulness training on an individual basis or organisation-wide basis. In my experience, most mindful organisations start with developing a few mindful individuals. The following sections explore ways to focus on helping individuals to become more mindful.

Cultivating mindful individuals

Offering workplace mindfulness training to staff is a first step on a journey to becoming a more mindful individual. It doesn't happen overnight and requires dedication and practice.

A six-week mindfulness programme provides you with a good basic foundation. My teaching experience suggests that only when people reach the end of a six-week course do they fully grasp the benefits of practicing mindfulness. Many people decide that they want to work through the programme from Week 1 again because they feel that six weeks wasn't long enough for them to fully embed learning and change their mindset and behaviour. This is one of the reasons why Marina and I decided to include a six-week self-study WorkplaceMT course in Part 3 of this book. By including the full course in the book, you can recap your knowledge and consolidate learning at your own pace.

Others may gain a few tools and techniques that they find helpful and incorporate these informal everyday mindfulness techniques into their working day. They may not formally practice mindfulness afterwards. This is fine. People should be encouraged to take what they need from a mindfulness programme.

One doctor I recently trained simply uses a quick one-minute mindfulness technique at her desk between patients to clear her mind and refocus. She gets five minutes of mindfulness practice on some days while at home and none on others. And that's okay.

REMEMBER

There's no right or wrong outcome from a mindfulness course. For some, it's a life-changing experience; for others, it makes a small difference. Academic research studies indicate that the longer people spend formally practicing mindfulness, the more positive outcomes they report. This echoes research based on self-reported outcomes from participants. Those who practice for 10 to 15 minutes each day usually report a higher degree of desirable workplace outcomes than those practicing for less time.

A six-week mindfulness training course is a good starting point. Once completed, people can come back to it at any time to develop their mindfulness further, attend other forms of mindfulness training, or attend retreats if they wish. They can study the underpinning research and neuroscience or read books like this one that give practical guidance on how to apply mindfulness to their work.

The point is, how you develop mindfulness is a personal choice. An individual's willingness to engage with mindfulness will vary depending on personal circumstances, future aspirations and personal values. There is no one-size-fits-all mindfulness outcome, just like there is no right or wrong way to be a mindful leader.

Those who gain a lot from mindfulness training may become a formal or informal mindfulness champion within their company. Individuals with a passion for mindfulness are the best role models for other staff. A small number of these staff, supported by a good mindfulness teacher and a supportive management team, can be the catalysts for building a more mindful organisation over time. Their potential impact on others is much greater than any marketing activities or encouragement from HR to attend mindfulness training.

Making mindfulness more accessible to staff

Mindfulness taught in a group setting is a highly effective way to develop mindfulness. It may equally be taught one to one, via web conferencing technology in real time or via self-directed learning through books like this one or online learning. The following sections explore the practicalities of each of these learning options.

In a group setting

Mindfulness taught in a group setting can be very powerful. People learn from others' experiences and can form strong, supportive bonds. Knowing that others are struggling with the same thing as you or, like you, maybe don't quite get it, coupled with the trainer's advice and guidance can help you overcome barriers that may make you give up if you were studying alone.

>> **Pros:** The opportunity to learn from others' experience. Support from other learners. Trainer on hand to help you overcome difficulties.

>> **Cons:** Not everyone may be able to attend due to location, timing, or other constraints. Some may be able to attend only some of the sessions and may miss out on key learnings if the course doesn't have a process to cover for missed sessions.

One-to-one training or coaching

Mindfulness taught one to one is an excellent option for people in senior roles who may feel reluctant to share their personal experiences with other employees, who may include those they manage. It is also a good option for people with very specific things they wish to address as part of the training process.

>> **Pros:** The trainer can help the individual to delve deeper if desired and spend time focusing on individual needs. More time to unpack, reflect and learn from personal experiences. Very flexible and tailored.

>> **Cons:** Cost is much higher and no opportunity to learn from others.

Live web conferencing

Humans crave interaction and tend to learn better in face-to-face learning environments. However, this isn't always possible, especially when workers work remotely, on different sites or countries. Live web-based teaching can provide a viable alternative to face to face.

>> **Pros:** Good for small numbers of people working on multiple sites, who can receive live teaching responding to their needs without the need to travel. More cost effective than running multiple small group face-to-face sessions.

>> **Cons:** Lacks the group dynamic, which can hinder motivation. Also can experience technical issues. The opportunity to interact and ask questions is more limited than face-to-face courses, and trainers may not notice if learners become disengaged and be able to take steps to address this.

Self-directed learning

Self-directed learning is a very flexible and cost-effective option to help employees develop mindfulness but can have an exceedingly high dropout rate (60 to 70 per cent versus only 5 to 10 per cent on face-to-face courses). Self-directed learning options may include using a book like this or a web-based mindfulness course. It can work well as part of a blended approach with some face-to-face training and access to a suitably experienced trainer.

>> **Pros:** Cost efficient, very flexible, and learners can learn at their own pace. Courses such as Be Mindful (www.bemindfulonline.com), if studied exactly as directed over a four- to six-week period, can, in my experience, produce similar outcomes to a taught course.

>> **Cons:** Mindfulness e-learning programmes have a very high dropout rate as people encounter problems or barriers and then give up. No trainer is at hand to help and support if difficult things arise.

Making Your Organisation More Mindful

If you want to make your whole organisation more mindful, the next few pages are for you. In this section, you find practical examples, hints and tips on designing a mindful workplace and planning your implementation approach.

Designing a mindful workplace

The journey towards becoming a mindful organisation can be a lifetime's work. It's often easier to start with a blank canvas and design mindfulness into the organisation from the outset.

For example, a mindful entrepreneur of a fast-expanding successful small technology company based in London has introduced a mindful silent half hour at the start of the day. It aims to provide staff with the opportunity to start the day with an open mind. The staff has the flexibility to use the half hour in a number of ways, as long as they're silent, don't make phone calls or check emails. Some employees use the time to think about and prepare for the day ahead. Others clear their desks, and some practice mindfulness. This mindful strategy is proving popular with staff and is good for working relationships and productivity.

Trying to make a well-established organisation mindful at a later date can be harder work, but there are ways to achieve this. For example, Capitol One, a financial services company based in the UK, set up a small mindfulness room for staff to attend informal mindfulness drop-in sessions during their workday or to take a few minutes away from their desk to regain their focus.

Deciding on your approach

If you work within a well-established organisation and want to introduce mindfulness, you need to decide: will it be *evolution* or *revolution*?

>> If you choose evolution, you can encourage mindfulness growing organically within small pockets and support emerging mindful business practices, ensuring that they're appropriately shared and showcased with others. The advantage of this approach is that mindfulness can grow and evolve over time without the need for major culture change initiatives and all that accompany them. The disadvantage is that it can take a very long time, and small pockets of good practice may wither and die without adequate support and recognition.

>> If you choose revolution, you need to make a substantial investment of both time and money. Revolution can start only after you have sufficient staff at all levels trained in mindfulness who are actively applying it to their work. Only when people have direct experience of working mindfully will they be equipped to review and revise working systems and procedures.

Whichever approach you decide on, an experienced work-focused mindfulness teacher can help you support growth and overcome barriers, helping you find ways to incorporate mindfulness into organisational processes and practices.

REMEMBER

You simply can't force people to adopt mindful working practices – they have to see a benefit and genuinely wish to do so. However, making a concerted effort to make an organisation a more mindful place to work can help you move towards becoming a mindful organisation more quickly. Both evolution and revolution take time. Unfortunately, with mindfulness, there is no quick fix, but the return on investment is likely to be high.

TIP

At an organisational level, you can design mindful working practices into an organisation, especially when at start-up phase or following restructuring. In well-established organisations, mindful leaders can also start to introduce mindfulness into working practices such as at meetings, break times and meal times.

Getting Down to Practicalities

This section explores some of the practical aspects involved with workplace mindfulness interventions. You find information on how to gain support and buy-in, make the business case and pilot mindfulness, designing an evaluation at the outset.

Gaining support and buy-in

If you decide to introduce mindfulness into your company, you need to gather support and cultivate buy-in. Although many very successful organisational mindfulness initiatives start with one keen advocate, the more support and buy-in you have at the outset, the better.

Publications such as 'Making the Business Case for Mindfulness', available via Mindfulnet.org, may be of assistance to you at this stage. In a nutshell, start with the desired outcomes you identify earlier in this chapter (see the section 'Defining desirable organisational outcomes'). Link this to evidence from research studies. If possible, make a return-on-investment calculation to back up your proposal. If necessary, work to demystify mindfulness and dispel misconceptions. Provide examples of other individuals or organisations who offer staff mindfulness training or adopt mindful working practices and the benefits they've gained.

TIP

Work in partnership with an experienced, suitably trained workplace mindfulness training provider who may be able to help you make the business case and work with you to design a successful implementation approach.

Piloting mindfulness

Most mindfulness initiatives in organisations start with a pilot. Simply put, a pilot is a trial run, a small-scale version of your larger project. A program pilot is an important step that can help you test the effectiveness of a learning programme and make any necessary refinements before further roll out. A good pilot will help you to evaluate the potential organisational gain of introducing mindfulness, any barriers that need to be overcome, and how best to adapt the programme for your audience.

Carefully consider where and when training should take place. Timing can have a huge impact. It shouldn't just be a case of booking when rooms are available. Providing training during working hours sends out the right messages and encourages attendance.

TIP

So when should you schedule mindfulness training? The first part of the day or last part often works well. Lunchtime sessions can be very popular, or they can be hit or miss if people are rushing from place to place and are late arriving or preoccupied with their next meeting. Another possibility is having the course take place during work hours half of the time and during personal hours the other half. Following this schedule can cut costs for organisations and can encourage more personal investment from individuals.

Most organisations offer mindfulness training free for their employees, while others may subsidise the cost.

REMEMBER

Be sure to select your training provider carefully. Make sure the individual has attended appropriate training as a workplace mindfulness teacher, understands the sector your organisation operates in and the challenges faced, and can 'speak your language'. Ideally, the trainer should have experience with working in a similar environment, which encourages participant engagement and shapes her approach to the training.

TIP

Evaluation should be considered at the start of the training design process - don't try to tack it on at the end. Make it compulsory that people complete the pre-course evaluation before they attend. You can even use the incentive of offering staff post-course CPD certificates after they've completed their post-course evaluations. Consider asking a researcher to evaluate your data. Doing so may encourage participants to be more honest and may even end up being written up as a case study for a journal, if desired.

At the end of the programme, spend time on the evaluation. Learn from it, and use it to help you decide on next steps or to strengthen your business case, if applicable.

Practical Considerations

In this section, we explore some practical considerations when introducing mindfulness to your organisation. Is it best to use internal or external teachers in the long term? Should you provide a dedicated space of people to practice mindfulness in? Read on to find out.

Developing internal capacity

If your pilot was broadly a success and you want to roll it out further, you have to, of course, consider cost implications. If budgets allow, you can employ a number of experienced mindfulness teachers to help you roll it out.

TIP

A longer-term, cost-effective option is to identify a number of people within your organisation who have an interest in mindfulness and encourage them to develop into mindfulness teachers.

Is it best to use external or internal teachers? Again, there are pros and cons for both. External teachers are seen as independent, so participants may feel more comfortable to open up and gain more benefit as a result. On the other hand, internal teachers can use their detailed knowledge of the company to adapt the course to better fit the organisation's needs and culture.

WARNING

Unfortunately, some organisations try to save money by finding an employee who 'meditates' and asking him to design and deliver a course or introductory session. The efforts of enthusiastic employees like this often fail and can have a negative impact. This may be because they confuse meditation with mindfulness, add in a spiritual dimension absent from MBSR, MBCT or WorkplaceMT, or simply fail to translate their knowledge into an engaging learning experience. This is often compounded by the HR or learning lead being unable to assess its suitability because they don't know what 'good' looks like in mindfulness training terms.

TIP

If you have staff members who have experience with mindfulness or meditation, by all means involve them in pilots or future mindfulness rollouts. Consider developing them as mindfulness champions or sending them on mindfulness teacher training. Just don't expect them to be equipped to teach mindfulness to others.

Providing mindful practice space

Most mindfulness courses in the workplace are taught in standard meeting rooms. If that's the case, it's best to avoid glass-fronted meeting rooms because some people may feel embarrassed practicing in a room that feels like a fish bowl with others looking in.

If you want to embed mindfulness after initial training, consider setting aside a small room for people to practice in. The room should be reasonably quiet and provide places for people to sit. Consider including a CD player or MP3 player so people can benefit from using professionally recorded guidance for exercises.

Some organisations make their multi-faith room available for people who wish to practice mindfulness. This can work quite well.

If you can't find a spare room for this purpose, see if it's possible to book a meeting room at least once a week for an informal mindfulness drop-in session. A suitably experienced mindfulness champion can facilitate this session, or someone can simply switch on a guided mindfulness MP3 recording

TIP

After completing a mindfulness programme, some employees may identify moments in their day when they feel they need a little time for mindfulness. Despite attending training in work time, they often feel that they need 'permission' to leave their desks to practice the exercises. Try to create a working environment that trusts people and empowers them to take the necessary steps to manage themselves and safeguard their well-being. Doing so often increases staff engagement and results in increased work output.

Chapter 18

Integrating Mindfulness into Everyday Work Practices

I t's easy to fall into the trap of embracing the concept of mindfulness without actually practicing it or embedding it into your life. If you're serious about becoming a more mindful leader, you need to set a firm intent to integrate it into the way you work. This chapter helps you get started by exploring three key activities that all leaders are involved in – meetings, decision-making and project management. Before exploring each of them in turn, we start with the basics – improving the way you manage yourself.

Managing Yourself Better

WorkplaceMT formal training techniques, such as mindfulness of breath (Chapter 8), body scan (Chapter 9) and mindfulness of sounds and thoughts (Chapter 10), help you to use all your senses to progressively step out of autopilot. Noticing when your mind wanders and observing without judgment your unique patterns of thought and behaviour help you to manage yourself better.

REMEMBER

Give yourself permission to take time out to be mindful. This many sound simple, but many leaders find that taking time out to be mindful is hard to do at the outset. They worry about what others will think, or they don't think they have time.

Most leaders start by practicing formal WorkplaceMT mindfulness exercises in the privacy of their own home. They then start practicing at work with quick and easy techniques, such as the three-step breathing space (see Chapter 10). For many, this is sufficient to make a huge impact to their working day. Others graduate onto integrating ten minutes of 'me time' to practice mindfulness at lunch time or first thing in the morning.

As we discuss in Chapter 7, maintaining peak performance is simply a matter of noticing the moment that your performance starts to deteriorate and taking a very short mindful break to bring yourself back to peak performance. You don't even have to close your eyes! For example, you can make a cup of tea or brew some coffee and pause for a few moments to savour the flavour and aroma. Or you can take a short walk round the building or outside – or have a good stretch at your desk. The key is to find something that works for you, but give yourself permission to take a short mindful productivity break when you need it.

Mindful Meetings

Sonia, a mergers and acquisitions consultant, used to work for one of the big three consultancy firms. She spent most of her days attending meetings with top companies across the UK. She recounts that 'the majority of the meetings were totally pointless, mind numbing, and sucked the life out of me'. This is a common experience with leaders I work with. Some cynically tell me that meetings are actually a stalling tactic to avoid making important decisions. One meeting invariably turns into many meetings, making the person calling the meetings look productive, while in reality he's achieving little or nothing.

The good news is, it doesn't have to be like this. In the following sections, we help you understand why meetings are important and introduce ways to make meetings more effective and efficient.

Understanding why you should have meetings

The Internet is full of tips on how to make meetings more effective and general complaints about meetings. Most leaders complain of having too many poorly organised meetings and meetings straying off topic. What's rarely addressed is the reasons meetings have become a key feature of the business world.

Participation satisfies a basic human need to belong and have roles to occupy. Being a leader gives you a role and statue within your work community. This role gives you responsibilities and rights. The meeting of these roles and responsibilities define people within society, is the basis of personhood, and helps people create a sense of identity. By fulfilling the responsibilities that are associated with these roles, you claim a place in your society. This fulfilment requires visibility – that is, others have to recognise your contribution for it to count.

Starting at an early age and continuing on through school and university, you're taught to participate. Participating, or being invited to participate, reaffirms your place within the group, solidifies your role and communicates your value to other group members. Participation is part of social currency. The more people that notice and recognise your participation, the more important you become.

Meetings aren't confined to work – they happen in personal life, too. You meet for dinner or for coffee, at which time you may seek advice, catch-up or organise a shared event. In business meetings, senior team members may vie for visibility to preserve their place within the pack, creating convoluted discussions where decisions are delayed and time is wasted. At times, everyone seems to have his own objectives and goals and vigorously resists the consolidation or sharing of information. Why? Because doing so may detract from an individual's power and status within the pack.

Of course, meetings aren't all bad. If meetings were banned, people would still find ways to meet. They would linger by people's desks or offices, huddle in the kitchen, or gather around the water cooler. What needs to change if meetings are to be effective is the value placed on participation. At present, most companies subconsciously place more value on the quantity of meetings attended (being seen to be busy) than the quality of individual inputs and collective meeting outputs.

As a mindful leader, you can use this information to explore the dynamics at play within meetings and find new ways to share information and collectively make decisions.

Discovering when meetings are most effective

Cranfield University academic Andrey Pavlov set out to study the elements that make meetings effective. He sat in on a number of meetings within organisations to observe what was going on and to try to pinpoint the lightbulb moment when the meeting was truly productive and decisions were made. What he noticed was unexpected.

The moments when meetings were at their most productive were when people got into a frame of mind that closely resembled the state of mindfulness. In this state, they saw things more clearly and as a result made better decisions. Andrey Pavlov and fellow Cranfield academic Dr Jutta Tobias came up with a ten-point guide to making meetings more mindfully effective.

TIP

These ten tips guide you, as a leader and meeting chair, to help participants become more mindful during meetings, based on the work of by Dr Andrey Pavlov and Dr Jutta Tobias. These may sound obvious, but not necessarily the norm.

>> **Encourage openness.** Encourage everyone attending to speak openly without fear of repercussion or criticism.

>> **Establish trust.** Trust is a powerful tool in encouraging openness and sharing of information.

>> **Make sure everyone is physically comfortable.** Research shows that thoughts and emotions arise first as physical sensations. These thoughts and emotions influence decision-making.

>> **Make sure that there are different views among the group.** This will help you avoid the dangers of groupthink and bring different perspectives to the meeting.

>> **Allow participants to express emotions.** Expressing emotions is sometimes frowned upon in a business context. How you feel is an integral part of how you make decisions, so a mindful state can't emerge if expressing emotions isn't allowed.

>> **Meet face to face wherever possible.** Meeting face to face is important not only because it creates a personal connection, but also because it provides a stronger grounding in the present moment. Being in the present moment provides an environment in which mindfulness can thrive.

>> **Respect the fact that people have a limited attention span.** Focus and attention are crucial to maintaining mindfulness. They're also hard work and in limited supply. Keep meetings brief and to the point, and provide breaks and refreshments if necessary.

>> **The chair must maintain focus.** As the meeting chair, you need to stay present in mind as well as body, keeping the meeting focused by bringing it back on course and clarifying the structure if necessary.

>> **Allow new ideas and priorities to be discussed.** Mindfulness is all about the 'now', the present moment. Focus on what is needed 'right now'.

>> **Shape the structure of the meeting.** By paying attention to the structure of the meeting, everyone else can focus on the content and therefore make mindful decisions.

If you want to read more about this, search the Internet for 'Mindful meetings by Jutta Tobias and Andrey Pavlov'.

Improving meeting efficiency by creating the space to think

I recently attended a workshop on mindful meetings run by Debbie Jeremiah, Mindful Leaders Program Manager for GE's global leadership learning organisation, Crotonville. Debbie had been studying the effects of maximising employees' thinking ability within GE's meetings, on the basis that it is usually in meetings that the key business decisions are made. She believes that better meetings equate to better thinking, resulting in better decision making and thus improved corporate outcomes. She had been exploring redesigning meetings and meeting training, to take account of the impact on brain performance from social threats caused by others' words, behaviours or even just mere presence

To maximise meeting participation, engagement and outcomes, consideration was given to participants' mental threat state, using the SAFETY model.

Consideration is given to social drivers of motivation, or participants' SAFETY profile (ablsafety.com) – their need for security, autonomy, fairness, esteem, and trust and you (an in-depth look at the individual variables that impact these drivers). As a result meetings have been restructured to maximise participation.

If you want to try a new way of running meetings that's more inclusive, focused and less likely to get sidetracked, try out this meeting methodology that's based on a number of the ideas in Nancy Kline's book *Time to Think* (Cassell). Also, we encourage you to check out the book yourself to gain an understanding of the rationale for the method and how to implement it.

I have experimented with using 'thinking rounds' and, once I suspended my initial scientism, I found the method highly effective. Every time I use this method, it feels like a real luxury to be able to think out loud, uninterrupted, and allow my ideas to unfold without any pressure.

At your next meeting, try following these steps:

1. **Start by welcoming everyone, and then appreciate their coming.** Restate the purpose of the meeting. Propose an opening round to respond to this question: 'what is a success

you (or your team) have had recently?' Make certain that people know to be very brief in exchange for knowing that they will not be interrupted.

2. **Be sure that you have put every agenda item in the form of a question.** Begin each agenda item with a round of response and thinking from each person.

3. **Instead of having an agenda, start the meetings by clearly stating the question that needs to be considered and addressed.** Check in to ensure that everyone agrees that this is the question that needs addressing.

4. **Ask the question out loud that needs addressing then start a 'speaking round'.** Ensure that everyone is given an equal number of minutes (maybe two or three) to speak or think out loud. Brief everyone else to give their full attention to provide a supportive, encouraging environment for the individual talking. Participants should listen in the moment, without distraction, give good eye contact and display open body language The aim is to make the speaker feel safe to openly share his thoughts, ideas, and perspectives.

5. **As the chair, you need to summarise the thinking in the room between each 'round', sharing areas of consensus and difference.** You may then pose a new question for consideration to build on what has been shared so far. Repeat the thinking rounds until resolution or a way forward is found.

6. **Ensure the meeting always ends on time**. Make a conscious effort to finish the meeting on a positive note, with a sense of achievement and forward momentum.

REMEMBER

This method sounds as if it will take longer than conventional meetings, but those who are practiced in using the model report meetings taking on average a third less time to conclude.

TIP

Here are a few additional tips for making meetings as successful and efficient as possible:

>> **Pay great attention to the quality of 'listening' within the meeting.** No one listening should interrupt or speak, because it will negatively impact the speaker's ability to think and share ideas and thoughts.

>> **Ban laptops, mobile phones and devices to avoid distraction.** Ban the use of note taking by 'listeners' whilst listening – they can do this when the person stops speaking if absolutely necessary.

>> **Pay close attention to the body language of the listeners.** Closed body language and lack of eye contact can be perceived at a subconscious level as threatening, closing down higher brain creative thinking capability in the speaker.

Mindful Decision-Making

In this section, you discover that a lot more is involved in decision-making than simple logic. Concentrating and thinking is a very energy-hungry business. Tasks such as problem-solving and decision-making use up a lot of energy.

Because energy is a finite resource, in an effort to be efficient, the brain uses energy-efficient subconscious thinking whenever possible. This automation saves time and energy – it's estimated that around 95 per cent of brain activity is subconscious.

Conscious thinking can help you become more mindful and considered in how you think, feel and act. It takes more energy but helps you to take greater control and improves outcomes.

Exploring decision-making in the brain

In this section, you are invited to explore both the conscious and subconscious elements of decision-making.

Looking at decision-making at the subconscious level

Research by Libet in the 1980s concluded that the subconscious brain can make decisions seconds before the conscious brain becomes aware. Information processed subconsciously can influence the accuracy of your decisions without you knowing it.

Although you may think that your decisions are based on consciously evaluating all the facts, every type of decision you make includes unconscious elements – many more than you may think.

The busier you get, and the tighter your deadlines become, the more likely you are to default to using subconscious data processing and decision-making. It's your brain's way of helping you to maximise reward while minimising threat.

Your brain may interpret workplace pressures as a danger or threat to your well-being. In response, the brain automates your responses and thought processes as much as possible in an effort to save you by freeing up energy to help you escape from danger. That's great when you're facing a life-and-death situation but not so good when you're trying to make a multibillion-pound decision for your company.

Understanding the impact of fear on decision-making

Humans have evolved to be fearful for sound, pragmatic, evolutionary reasons. Fear is a strong driver of human behaviour, but few leaders ever admit to being fearful. The leadership ideal of being focused, calm, decisive and in control isn't always easy to maintain. Top leaders often give the outward appearance that they're calm, collected and everything is fully under control, while in reality (like a swan) they're paddling like hell underneath.

While in the grip of fear (due to a perceived immediate or future threat), creativity is reduced and options narrowed. This happens because the brain automates key elements of the decision-making process and can make decisions only based on information, memories and emotional responses already stored in the brain. In this fear-based state, you're likely to make decisions that feel safe or have worked well in the past instead of seeking out new perspectives or fresh, creative solutions. When under extreme pressure, some leaders may actually freeze and be rendered incapable of deciding on a wise course of action.

Over time, practicing mindfulness can help you to notice emotions as they arise and observe the impact they're having on your thoughts. Doing so can stop your thoughts or emotions or tension that you're holding in the body from escalating further, enabling you to pause, stand back and look at the situation you're facing more objectively.

Improving your decision-making

As a leader, you're employed to make decisions. A number of factors can impact the quality of your decision-making that have nothing to do with your intellectual capability, experience, and the information that you have to handle. When was the last time you considered the fitness of your working memory capacity or explored your cognitive bias when making decisions? The following sections give you the chance to consider both.

Working memory capacity

Decision-making requires your brain to use working memory capacity. Sonia, the leader you met earlier in this chapter, once had to make a decision that involved merging two newly acquired organisations with disparate working cultures into one. To make a decision on the right way to move forward, Sonia's working memory had to hold information about the two companies, their working culture, how they fitted within the acquiring company's portfolio and a whole host of other things.

The UK country lead for Sonia's company was putting her under immense pressure to get things moving. Sonia, who is normally calm, collected, organised and methodical, ended up walking out of a meeting after a very angry exchange with her manager.

Sonia wasn't 'losing it' – she was simply at the mercy of her working memory capacity, which, at this point, had reached capacity.

Working memory capacity is a scarce resource, and it's degraded by stress. It's also essential for emotion regulation, decision-making, innovation and creativity and cognitive control. The function of your working memory is to hold information and filter out the noise. In Sonia's case, the volume of information she was attempting to juggle combined with time pressure led to a working memory overload, which made her act out of character.

The good news is that mindfulness training has been shown to increase working memory capacity. This is one of the reasons the US Marine Corps became interested in mindfulness training for its soldiers.

Imagine this scene: You're a marine on patrol in the Middle East. You see a car speeding towards you. You have a split second to make a life-and-death decision that will impact you, the occupants of the car, and your fellow soldiers and may even cause an international incident.

With this scenario in mind, mindfulness training was adapted for the military and rebranded as Mind Fitness training. In this training, troops are trained in mindfulness before being deployed. The troops are asked to participate in realistic simulations (like the one above) of the situations they may encounter when deployed. The exercises are deliberately designed to put them under stress. Even though their levels of stress are high, their working memory capacity improves. If it works for the Marines, it can work for you, too.

Sunk cost bias

Have you ever bought a bargain suit on sale only to have it hang in your wardrobe for years without wearing it? This is an example of sunk cost bias – sticking by a decision even when it's not working. Because you've invested in the suit, you're reluctant to let it go even though it doesn't look good on you, or maybe doesn't even fit!

This bias can cost companies billions of pounds. Imagine that you're leading a project that isn't working. You may reason that further investment is warranted on the fact that the resources already invested will otherwise be lost. What you may fail to consider is the overall losses involved in the further investment.

Consider this example: Mark, a board member, was working on a major project to expand the business. The consultancy bills from a well-known consultancy firm were well in excess of £100,000. The consultants had reported back to Mark that he shouldn't move forward with his plans because the market he was looking to expand into was declining. Despite their advice, Mark decided to go ahead with the planned expansion, reasoning that he'd invested a year of his time in it and a large amount of the company's money. The results of this decision were disastrous, leading to a loss of market share, dented reputation and substantial financial losses.

Mark was a victim of sunk cost bias. He had invested heavily in the project both financially and in terms of time. Despite best advice not to go ahead with the planned extension, Mark continued to try to push it forward and try to make it work, reasoning at a sub-conscious level that he had invested too much to simply let it go.

In a recent ground-breaking research study, a group of managers were asked to practice mindfulness for a short period of time while another group didn't. All the managers were then given a business scenario to consider that involved an investment decision that was going wrong. The managers who had practiced mindfulness were more likely to let go of the bad investment and move on than the other group of managers, who were more likely to pour more money into the project in an attempt to make it work.

Practicing mindfulness, even for ten minutes each day can help you to reduce the impact of your subconscious bias and help you make better decisions.

Making decisions mindfully

In Week 3 of your WorkplaceMT training (Chapter 10), you discover the benefits from working in approach mode of mind. In approach mode of mind, leaders actively approach and explore a challenge with an open mind and a sense of curiosity, looking for new oppor-tunities and exciting possibilities. On the other hand, in avoidance mode of mind, leaders seek options that will minimise possible harm and keep themselves and their organisations safe from harm.

Dynamic, forward-looking leaders spend most of their time work-ing in approach mode of mind. Doing so maximises their options and encourages creative solutions. The same can be applied to decisions. Mindfulness helps you to cultivate an approach mode of mind, which is conducive to good decision-making.

Because many leaders are very good at portraying the outward appearance of being calm, collected and in control, it would be easy to think that they'd naturally default to working in approach mode, but this isn't always the case. As we discuss in the 'Looking at decision-making at the subconscious level' section, earlier in this chapter, subconscious fears may trip leaders into avoidance or safety mode of mind.

Consider the plight of a Mark (from the previous section), who was working on a company expansion project. Mark identified the need for some skilled work to be completed to a high standard within a tight time frame. His options were (a) use costly external consultants (an approach that had worked well for him in the past), or (b) deploy and upskill internal staff. Both approaches could result in a positive outcome, but under pressure, Mark's subconscious motivation to keep safe could be a deciding factor. In this example Option A is a safe bet, despite the cost implications. Option B, which costs less and is more beneficial in the long run, might not even be considered.

REMEMBER

Decisions made in avoidance mode of mind aren't necessarily bad decisions. They may be very good and produce the desired outcomes on time and budget. Conversely, decisions made in approach mode of mind may bring you outcomes you couldn't have dreamt of or may be flawed and ineffective. The important thing is to bring conscious attention to the drivers that influence your decision-making. Only by stepping out of autopilot and shining a spotlight on your hidden motivators will you become a truly fearless leader.

Mindful Project Management

If you've been steadily reading through this chapter one page at a time, you're now aware that your own biases, emotions, and preconceived notions can get in the way of clearly seeing things for what they are. (If you're jumping in to the chapter at this section, we encourage you to take a look at the rest of the chapter.)

It's easy to get projects into trouble when you make decisions based on perceptions of reality that your brain dreams up then treats as reality. The last part of this chapter is concerned with how to be a more mindful project manager.

If you work as a project manager, your job description likely says something like 'able to manage multiple conflicting priorities'. Of course, project management isn't the only thing that requires you to juggle a number of tasks simultaneously – that's a part of everyday life and work. Mindful project managers may look as if they are multitasking, when they are really single tasking.

Becoming a single tasker

Remember Sonia who we introduce in the section 'Mindful Meetings', earlier in this chapter? In an effort to become more efficient and squeeze more out of every working minute, she started to adopt different time and task management tips. Even though these tips helped her to increase her productivity, she didn't feel satisfied with her work, which started to feel pointless and never-ending. In the end, she went to her doctor for advice on how to handle her increasing levels of stress and anxiety. Her doctor recommended mindfulness taught on a one-to-one basis to fit in with her busy working life.

After six weeks of WorkplaceMT training, Sonia started to slowly, gingerly, apply mindfulness. She started having her morning coffee by the kitchen window, avoiding the temptation to scan emails or listen to the news. She learned to simply enjoy the coffee and the view out of her office window over open farmland. To her surprise, Sonia discovered that drinking her coffee in this way took her only five minutes, whereas in the past, when she multitasked, it had taken her around 15 minutes. Saving ten minutes that easily encouraged her to try to apply mindfulness to her project management work.

Sonia tried working on her tasks one at a time. She switched off the email notifications on her computer so she wasn't constantly bombarded with pings as emails flowed in during the day, choosing times that were right for her to respond to them. She switched her phone on silent for periods of the day, alerting others to this and ensuring that they knew when she would be available again. The end result was that she gained a sense of spaciousness in her work day. As time passed, she felt less and less like the walls and life were closing in on her. By single tasking and taking control of her technology, taking time out when necessary to re-charge, Sonia not only improved her efficiency as a project manager but also improved her health.

REMEMBER

Research shows that single taskers like Sonia get more done than multitaskers. Single tasking may feel counterintuitive at first, but in the long run you will get more done in less time.

Mindfully leading projects

In this section, you find a number of tips to help you become a more mindful project manager.

Be present

It's amazing how few project managers are fully present with what's going on around them. In meetings with stakeholders and team members, avoid dwelling on the past or wasting energy trying to predict the future. Focus on what is actually being said, and by whom, and what you can deduce by how they say it.

Be aware of what's going on

A common misconception about mindfulness is that it suppresses emotions. On the contrary, mindfulness is about recognising emotions and habitual behaviour patterns as they emerge without letting them hijack or control you.

The next time you have to have a difficult conversation with someone who has missed a deadline or isn't pulling his weight, don't be a victim of your emotions. Recognise emotions as they start to arise and smile at yourself inwardly. Acknowledge your emotional response, but don't let it drive you to an unhelpful response you may later regret.

Try to remain as calm as possible

Remaining calm in the face of chaos helps you to make better decisions. An added bonus is that when others see that you're calm, they'll remain calmer and more composed. By doing so, they're less likely to make emotion-driven decisions that just make things worse.

Keep focused

Projects can have hundreds, sometimes thousands, of elements, milestones and dependencies. Try to avoid the temptation to juggle your project management work with your other leadership responsibilities.

When working on projects one task at a time, your productivity will increase, and you'll make fewer mistakes.

Be serene

When working for the police as a project manager, I (Juliet) had the 'Serenity Prayer' tacked to the wall next to my desk. It read, 'Grant me the serenity to accept the things I cannot change; courage to change the things I can; and wisdom to know the difference'.

REMEMBER

This is wise advice for any project manager. Most projects involve a high level of uncertainty and a number of elements you have no control over. Although you may not be able to control some events that impact your project, you have total control over your reaction and response to it. When others see you accepting the bad with the good things that you have no control over and proceeding in a mindful manner, they're more likely to be calm and focused.

Be positive

If your project goes off track, don't panic. Panicking or getting angry will negatively impact your interactions with others. Try to accept that things are tough, but still greet the world with a smile.

Be kind to yourself and others

People are often their own worst critics. Beating yourself up when things are going wrong is unlikely to make things any better. The more stressed or fearful you become, the less objective and productive you're likely to be.

Research shows that being kind to yourself is a fast way to switch down your threat response and put your higher thinking brain back in the driving seat. Being kind to others has a similar impact. It can make you more productive and make you feel good, too.

The Part of Tens

IN THIS PART . . .

Discover practical hints and tips to improve your decision-making.

Practice mindful ways to reduce the risk of burnout.

Get familiar with simple everyday mindfulness exercises to improve your attention.

Check out more mindful leadership resources.

Chapter 19

Ten Mindful Ways to Make Better Decisions

A s a leader, you're employed to make decisions. A number of factors that have nothing to do with your intellectual capability, experience, or available information can impact the quality of your decision-making. In this chapter, you find ten mindful, handy tips that will help you to make better decisions. These include recognising the impact of fear, heuristics, and your place within your social group on the decisions you make.

Becoming Aware of Heuristics

A *heuristic* is a mental shortcut that you use when making a judgment or decision. Heuristics help you to reach conclusions quickly but can sometime lead you to make mistakes or misjudge situations. To avoid making poor decisions, you need to first be aware when heuristics are at play.

When investing in stocks and shares, you may judge the probability that your next investment will be successful based on whether your previous investments have been successful. In reality, the outcome of your new investments may not be connected in any way to the success of your older investments. In this instance, you're judging the probability of an event happening based on what happened in a similar situation in the past. This is an example of what psychologists call *a representativeness heuristic*.

You may believe that terrorist attacks in cities are more common than they really are, simply because you can quickly bring to mind several examples of terrorist attacks in cities. In this instance, you're judging the likelihood of an event happening based on your ability to recall similar events This is an example of what psychologists call *an availability heuristic.*

TIP

If you do discover that heuristics may be negatively influencing your decisions, apply a little mindfulness. Try following these steps:

1. **Accept that you're human and prone to these biases (reducing your threat reactivity).**

2. **Congratulate yourself on having noticed what was happening (igniting your brain's reward circuitry).**

3. **Make a conscious effort to separate facts from heuristics and assumptions about things that your mind makes up when information is absent.**

Avoiding Overconfidence

As a leader, it's easy to overestimate your own knowledge, ability or judgment. Researchers investigating overconfidence in decision-making in the 1970s discovered that when people stated that they were 100 per cent confident in their answers, they were correct only about 80 per cent of the time.

The tendency to overestimate your knowledge can lead you to make bad decisions. Overestimating your knowledge isn't necessarily a sign of arrogance. At times, you may not realise how uninformed you are about a subject because you don't know what you don't know. You may also have incorrect information drawn from an unreliable source.

Mindful leaders are aware of the potential impact of overconfidence and check their information sources carefully for accuracy. Practicing mindfulness also helps you to see more clearly the difference between facts and any assumptions being made – treating facts as facts and assumptions as assumptions. When mindful leaders do get it wrong, they acknowledge the error and swiftly move on to rectifying the situation, while being kind to themselves by not wasting too much time on negative emotions or beating themselves up.

Remembering That You Are a Social Animal

Mindful leaders make decisions based more on their emotions than logic. In a recent study, a group of experienced executives were asked to analyse a number of management scenarios and make recommendations. Their brains were scanned by using functional magnetic resonance imaging while they undertook the task. Instead of seeing a dominance of activity in the brain areas associated with planning and logical reasoning, researchers saw a dominance in the brain areas associated with social and emotional thinking. The group's top strategic thinkers displayed the most activity in these areas.

Decisions invariably have an impact on others. In a work context, a good decision can move you up the social hierarchy within your group. A bad decision can force you into the 'out group', ignored or shunned by your social group.

Mindful leaders are emotionally intelligent of their needs and the needs of others around them. They also take into account the impact of their decisions and actions on group dynamics. A high level of social cohesion and acceptance within your social group at work increases the likelihood that others will embrace your decisions.

Avoiding Linking Things That Aren't Connected

When making decisions, you may sometimes find yourself identifying relationships or patterns that don't really exist. For example:

> As a police officer, you may believe that two unrelated muggings are related simply because they occurred around the same time on the same day in the same place. You may also assume that two variables are somehow connected.

> As a driving instructor, you may encounter two young, rude, badly behaved learner drivers coming from the same housing estate. As a result, you may mistakenly believe that all young people from that estate are going to be rude and badly behaved.

In psychology, this is known as an *illusory correlation*. It can lead to faulty beliefs and poor decision-making.

REMEMBER

On WorkplaceMT mindfulness training, we refer to this affectionately as 'having a mind the gap moment'. *Mind the gap* refers to the gap between how you *think* things are and how they *really* are. Mindful leaders mind the gap by being aware of when they're filling in the gaps in their knowledge with assumptions or stories, and take this into account when making decisions.

Becoming Conscious of Your Unconscious

Scientists are currently unable to estimate exactly what percentage of brain activity is made by the conscious brain. What they do agree on is that only a tiny percentage of everything the brain does is conscious. Subconscious brain activity is fast and energy efficient, making decisions seconds before the conscious brain becomes aware. Information you process subconsciously can heavily influence your decisions. Although you may think that your decisions are based on consciously weighing all the facts, every decision you make includes unconscious elements.

When under pressure, you're more likely to default to using sub-conscious data processing and decision-making. Your brain's drive for efficiency will lead you to automate your responses and thought processes as much as possible. This can be bad news when you are trying to make important decisions, as your brain may draw conclusions based on patchy information and make assumptions that may not be correct.

Although you may default to subconscious information processing, mindfulness helps you notice more quickly and take steps to kindly and gently put your conscious brain back in the driving seat, helping you to make better decisions.

Making Fearless Decisions

Fear is a strong driver of human behaviour, and as a leader, you're not exempt from it. Feeling fear is natural at times. It's a healthy response to a perceived threat, but the fear response is often disproportionate to the threat actually faced. Creativity is reduced when you experience fear, and your options are narrowed. This is because the brain automates key elements of the decision-making process and can make decision only based on information, memories and emotional responses already stored in the brain.

In this fear-based state, you're likely to make decisions that feel safe or have worked well in the past instead of seeking out new perspectives or fresh creative solutions. When under extreme pressure, some leaders may actually freeze and be rendered incapable of deciding on a wise course of action.

Practicing mindfulness can help you to notice emotions as they arise and observe the impact they have on your thoughts. Doing so can stop your thoughts or emotions or tension you're holding in the body from escalating further, enabling you to pause, stand back and look at the situation you're facing more objectively.

Improving Your Working Memory Capacity

Decision-making requires your brain to use working memory capacity. Your working memory (sometimes called short-term memory) gives you the ability to hold information in your mind and mentally manipulate it over short periods of time. Think of it as mental workspace that you use to store important information in the course of your day. Working memory can accommodate only around seven items or less at any time, so it can slow down your thinking processes and, as a result, your decision-making.

For example, when in a budget meeting, your working memory may be holding last year's budget total and this year's budget total. If you wanted to work out the increase or decrease in your budget, you may do some mental arithmetic. To do this, you'd first need to hold the two numbers in your working memory. Next, you'd apply learned mathematical subtraction rules. Finally, you'd subtract last year's budget from this year's budget to calculate the total budget increase or decrease.

Without working memory, you wouldn't be able to carry out this kind of complex mental activity (keeping in mind some information while processing other material).

Working memory capacity is a scarce resource, which can be degraded by stress. Mindfulness training has been shown to increase working memory capacity.

Avoiding Sunk Cost Bias

Sunk costs are costs that are irrecoverable – for example, money or time already spent and that you won't get back, regardless of future outcomes. Imagine spending thousands of pounds and hours and effort on a project that simply isn't working. The wise decision would be for you to stop, but you may have developed an irrational attachment to cost (both effort and financial) and doggedly throw more time and effort at the project in an attempt to recoup your sunk costs.

Sunk cost bias can cost companies billions, and countries even more (for example, a country insisting on a war so the lives already spent 'are not wasted').

Practicing mindfulness can help you avoid sunk cost bias, overturning decisions that are no longer serving you well and making new decisions based on present-moment facts. For more information, see Chapter 18.

Approaching Decisions with an Open Mind

The human brain tends to work in either approach mode of mind or avoidance mode of mind. In approach mode of mind, leaders actively approach and explore a challenge with an open mind and a sense of curiosity, looking for new opportunities and exciting possibilities. In avoidance mode of mind, leaders seek options that will protect them by minimising possible harm to themselves and their organisation.

TIP

To check whether you're working in approach or avoidance mode, bring to mind a decision you need to make and ensure that the question that needs answering is absolutely clear in your head before following these steps:

1. **Tune in to your body for a few moments.**

   You may find it easiest to close your eyes to do this. Are you aware of any tension or discomfort in your body? Score 1 for yes, 2 for no.

2. **Tune in to your emotions for a few moments.**

   You may find it easiest to close your eyes to do this. Are you experiencing any emotions, such as fear, anger, frustration, or excessive worrying? Score 1 for yes, 2 for no.

3. **Consider possible solutions to your decision and answer the following questions:**

- Are you exploring these solutions with a sense of excitement and exploration, looking for new and exciting opportunities? Score 2 for yes, 1 for no.

- When you think about possible solutions, are you basing your decision primarily on things that worked well in the past? Score 1 for yes, 2 for no.

- Is the solution you're considering the ideal solution, or more of a 'safe' bet? Score 1 for 'safe bet', 2 for 'ideal solution'.

Add up your score. If your score is between 5 and 7, you're likely working predominantly in avoidance mode. A score of 8 or more indicates that you're working primarily in approach mode.

REMEMBER

Decisions made in 'avoidance mode of mind' aren't necessarily bad decisions – in fact, they may be very good and produce the desired outcomes on time and budget. Conversely, decisions made in 'approach mode of mind' may bring you outcomes you couldn't have dreamt of or may be flawed and ineffective. The important thing is bringing conscious attention to the drivers that influence your decision-making.

Managing Your Emotions by Tuning in to Your Body

Scientists have discovered that even the tiniest of negative emotions can cause the fascia to contract and become tense. This connective tissue fibre forms sheets or bands beneath the skin that attach, stabilise, and separate muscles and other internal organs.

When fascia is introduced to the stress hormone cortisol, it contracts and continues to hold the tension until it's released. Tension held in the body sends messages to the brain that all is not well and danger may be round the corner. How your body feels can have a profound impact on your decisions and actions.

As a leader, your emotional state influences others around you. It is therefore important to be aware of your emotions, noticing them as soon as they arise, identifying their trigger point, and accepting their presence. Many people find that the easiest way to detect and release emotions is by tuning in to their body.

TIP

Most people attending WorkplaceMT courses can quickly identify the areas of their body where they typically hold tension. Some people clench their jaw; others hold tension in their hands or shoulders or stomach.

Identify the areas of your body where you most frequently hold tension and check in with these areas on a regular basis. If you do detect any tension, spend a few moments focusing on the tension, accepting its presence and kindly letting it go. Doing so will help you to maintain the optimum brain state for making good decisions.

Chapter 20

Ten Mindful Ways to Reduce the Risk of Burnout

B urnout is a state of emotional, mental, and physical exhaustion caused by excessive and prolonged stress. It occurs when you feel overwhelmed and unable to meet constant demands. Burnout has both a human cost and a business cost and is better prevented in the first place than managed when it does occur.

As a leader, you need to spot the signs of burnout in yourself and others at an early stage and take steps to address both the symptoms and the causes. In this chapter, you find ten mindful ways to reduce the risk of burnout in yourself and those around you.

Identifying the Symptoms of Burnout

The best way to reduce the risk of burnout is to identify the symptoms and take action before things escalate to burnout stage.

In a report published in 2001 ('Job Burnout' by Christina Maslach, Wilmar Schaufeli and Michale Leiter), three key symptoms lead to burnout (see also Figure 20-1):

» **Exhaustion:** Depletion of emotional resources to cope with the current work environment leading to a stressed-out, overwhelmed employee

» **Cynicism:** A distant attitude toward a job leading to a disgruntled employee

» **Inefficacy:** A reduced sense of personal accomplishment leading to a stressed-out employee with a cynical attitude who has given up trying

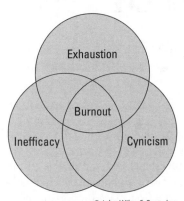

© John Wiley & Sons, Inc.

FIGURE 20-1: When these symptoms combine, the result is burnout.

Answer the following questions to see whether you or those around you may be suffering from burnout.

>> Does every day feel like a bad day?

>> Does it feel like a waste of energy to care about your work or home life?

>> Do you feel exhausted all the time?

>> Do you feel that the majority of your day is spent on mind-numbingly dull tasks and activities?

>> Do you feel that the majority of your day is spent on tasks that are overwhelming or feel never-ending?

>> Do you feel that nothing you do makes a difference or is appreciated?

If you answered yes to the majority of these questions, you may be experiencing or approaching burnout and need to seek some professional support and help.

Regularly practicing mindfulness has been proven to reduce the risk of burnout and may make you aware of the signs at an earlier stage. However, if you're acutely suffering from burnout and haven't practiced mindfulness before, you may not be in the best state of mind to benefit from it and may need to take steps to regain your balance and equilibrium before starting to learn mindfulness.

Recognising the Causes of Burnout

A number of work-related factors (see Table 20-1) can lead to burnout. The good news is that you can activity manage most of these factors and reduce their risk.

TABLE 20-1 Work-Related Contributors to Burnout

Contributory Factor	Identification	How to Reduce the Risk
Overwhelming job demands	People with stacks of papers on their desk, a huge to-do list and a look of panic or manicness on their face	Ensure that job demands aren't excessive or unreasonable and/or provide support to help them regain a sense of control.
Conflicting job demands	Employees who work hard but often achieve little, constantly juggling tasks, often 'losing the plot', becoming distracted and unable to focus	Encourage employees to plan their work better, working through one task at a time rather than attempting to unsuccessfully multitask.
Role ambiguity – a lack of adequate information to do the job well	Employees who are constantly working hard but fail to meet targets and/or achieve what's expected of them	Review employee job descriptions and amend if unclear. Provide a mentor if appropriate. If no job description exists, involve the employees in writing one.
Lack of appropriate resources	Employees who may have had improper training and/or inadequate resources to do their job effectively and who may be struggling to get work done, using outdated equipment	Provide training and appropriate resources to help employees work more efficiently.
Lack of social support	Employees new to the role with an absent line manager or co-workers who don't support them, or those who feel ignored or ostracised	Lack of support from managers is a major cause of burnout. Ensure that all employees receive adequate and appropriate support.
Lack of feedback on performance	Employees who don't know how well or badly they're performing and don't know what's expected of them and how to achieve it	Informal or formal feedback is important – ensure that all employees know whether they're on track, and if they're not, what they need to do to rectify matters.

Contributory Factor	Identification	How to Reduce the Risk
Lack of control of work	Employees who are told what to do and are unable to mold or shape the way in which their work is done, or employees who are never or rarely involved in the decision-making process.	The less involved employees have a sense of control over their work and decision-making processes, the higher the rates of burnout. Involve employees as much as you can in decisions that directly impact their work

REMEMBER

Burnout costs associated with prolonged staff absence are much higher than the cost of temporary staff to cover the absence. Prevention is better than cure.

Providing mindfulness training and weekly drop-in sessions on a voluntary basis can help employees manage themselves better and reduce their risk of burnout.

Avoiding Work Mismatching

Work mismatching (see examples below) can be a major contributor to burnout.

Common work mismatching includes

>> Employees being overloaded with work

>> Employees working hard on tasks they're ill-equipped to perform

>> Employees with insufficient control over the resources needed to do their work effectively

>> Employees with insufficient authority to pursue their work in the most effective manner

Keep a mindful eye out for work mismatching, and take steps to redress the balance as soon as possible to reduce risk of burnout.

Making Work More Rewarding

For staff to feel engaged and motivated, they need to feel that their work is sufficiently rewarding. A lack of appropriate recognition or reward for work can lead to burnout.

If an employee feels that they're receiving insufficient financial rewards (salary or benefits commensurate with their achievements), they may start to look for alternative employment. If they can't find alternative roles that reward them better financially, they may feel trapped, and resentment and frustration may escalate, leading to burnout.

Employees who feel that their hard work is ignored or not appreciated by others may suffer from a lack of social rewards. Even the least sociable, most introverted employees still need to feel that they're a part of a larger social group and that their work is appreciated by others. Feeling ignored or unappreciated can be a cause of great unhappiness, and their effectiveness will suffer as a result.

Even the most hardworking and committed employees may quit or experience burnout if they feel that their work is underappreciated having once again been routinely denied a pay raise or promotion due to budget cuts. In times of financial austerity, companies may not be able to offer staff the pay raises and financial rewards they'd like to.

Mindful organisations find other ways to reward employees, This may include the freedom to work at times and locations that suit them, providing training, secondments, or mentoring to help them develop. Mindful organisations may also publically recognise and celebrate success and strive to provide a stimulating and fun working environment that promotes both productivity and well-being.

Increasing Your Self-Efficacy

Self-efficacy is concerned with your belief in yourself and your ability to successfully accomplish and manage goals and tasks that have meaning for you. The stronger your perceptions of self-efficacy, the less stress you're likely to encounter, even in challenging situations. Situations will cause you less stress if you believe that you can cope.

The most effective way to enhance your self-efficacy is through performing tasks that give you a sense of mastery then pausing to fully acknowledge your achievement and the emotions, thoughts and bodily sensations this evokes. The successful achievement of goals, however small, ignites your brain's reward circuitry, releasing feel-good hormones into your bloodstream and encouraging your brain to seek new challenges and ways to excel.

You may also wish to try simply observing a work colleague accomplishing something meaningful. Doing so can make you feel more positive and can help you to increase your ability to meet any challenges you may face.

Identifying the Essentials You Need from Your Work

It's worth spending a little time to consider to what extent your current job fulfils your needs. The happier and more fulfilled you feel, the less risk you have of suffering burnout.

The *Harvard Business Review* recently surveyed hundreds of executives, identifying six key things that a dream company would provide. The following six questions are inspired by their responses:

- >> Does your current job allow you to be yourself?
- >> Does your current job keep you fully informed as to what's really going on?
- >> Does your current job magnify your strengths?
- >> Does your current job give you daily work that is rewarding?
- >> Do you work for a company where stupid rules don't exist?
- >> Does your company stand for something meaningful?

How does your company measure up? Few companies meet all the above criteria, but this list is a useful starting point that will help you to carve out your ideal job role.

Encouraging Creativity

Burnout has a negative impact on your performance, increases your tendency for rigid thinking, and decreases your ability to think accurately, flexibly, and creatively. Forward-thinking companies encourage creativity, even amongst those staff that aren't formally in 'creative' roles.

For example, Google lets its employees work on anything they want for one day a week so long as they're still in the office. Google call this 'Innovation Time Off'. By giving employees the freedom to work on their pet projects for one day a week, they encourage staff to be creative. As a result, many new product launches have originated from Innovation Time Off, and Google has been listed many times at the very top of *Fortune* magazine's list of best companies to work for.

Mindful leaders encourage creativity in their own work and the work of others. If work temporarily provides you with no form of creative outlet, it's important to find one at home – whether it's gardening, completing DIY projects, dressmaking or painting landscapes. Be creative with your creativity – try something new and have fun!

Taking Good Care of Yourself

At work, it's easy to feel as if you're on a treadmill and always have something to do. Sitting down and 'doing nothing' may not seem like the answer, but it can be.

When you become infected with the busyness virus, you gobble down your lunch without even tasting it while you keep on working. You arrive at work earlier and earlier 'to avoid the traffic' and stay late because 'it's vital I get this finished'. In the long term, this is unsustainable.

Although thinking that you must always be seen sitting at your desk and working hard may seem seductive, your body isn't a machine. It doesn't matter how much caffeine and sugar you pump into your body as fuel, eventually the abuse of sitting down for long periods of time each day, or dashing around for 18 hours a day will catch up with you and physically stop you from working.

Mindful leaders know when to take a break to recharge themselves and regain equilibrium. It may look like they're 'doing nothing', but in reality, mindfulness exercises increase your brain activity and can be hard work! However, their investment pays off by making them more productive when working and getting more done in less time.

Getting Support

Leadership can be a lonely job. It can be difficult to find people to confide in, and you may at times feel that asking for support is a sign of weakness.

The closer you get to burnout, the more you may want to bury yourself in your office and avoid contact with workmates. Maintaining social connections takes time and effot, but supportive people are the best way to protect yourself from burning out.

TIP

Many mindfulness evangelists who used to have high-powered demanding jobs are keen to share their burnout story with others to prevent others from the same fate. Mindfulness can certainly help you to recover after experiencing burnout, but it's better that you get professional support to learn mindfulness *before* your experience burnout.

Taking Time Out to Appreciate the Good

As you discover in Chapter 3, humans tend to suffer from a negativity bias. In simple terms, your brain pays more attention to things it perceives as potentially harmful or threatening, but the good things in life pass you by unnoticed. Smiling triggers a release of feel-good hormones into your bloodstream, rapidly reducing your blood pressure and releasing stress.

TIP

The next time you experience something nice, pause to appreciate it and take a few moments to fully benefit from it. Paying additional conscious attention to the good things in life, however small or trivial they may seem, can help you gain balance and perspective in your working life. What's more, it's free of charge and takes very little time. Enjoy!

Chapter 21

Ten Ways to Improve Your Attention with Mindfulness

This chapter brings together a number of useful mindfulness techniques that will help you improve your focus and attention. The best way to train your attention is via formal mindfulness exercises as we outline in Chapters 8 through 13. These exercises can feel repetitive (your mind wanders, you notice and bring it back, and then your mind wanders again . . .). This is intentional because the repetition helps you get better at managing your wandering mind and hardwires new pathways in your brain that strengthen attention.

Many leaders we've worked with find it difficult to practice formal mindfulness exercises while at work, which is why the WorkplaceMT mindfulness training we teach includes informal everyday mindfulness exercises that are easy to slip into your day.

In this chapter, you find both formal and informal everyday mindfulness exercises, which help you to hardwire the ability to manage your attention over time. The only difference is that formal mindfulness exercises are like taking your brain to the gym for an intensive workout, while everyday mindfulness takes less time and is less intensive.

Noticing When Your Mind Wanders

Harvard research suggests that, on average, the human mind wanders for around 50 per cent of the day. Each time your mind wanders, a period of time elapses before you recognise that it's no longer where you had intended it to be. Only when you recognise that your mind has wandered can you bring it back to where you want it to be.

Formal mindfulness exercises, such as mindfulness of breath (Chapter 8) or body scan (Chapter 9), require you to focus your attention on one thing. Doing this helps you notice more quickly when your mind has wandered and bring your attention back. Over time this improves your ability to remain focused.

For example, if you're focusing your attention on your breath and you find yourself thinking about the report you have to write, a family excursion, or that promotion you hope to gain, your mind has wandered. You then kindly and gently focus your full attention back on your breath. Why *kindly* and *gently*? Because blaming yourself or beating yourself up for your inability to remain focused doesn't help – it only makes things worse.

Negative emotions like anger can trigger your threat response, releasing the stress hormone cortisol into your bloodstream, making it even harder to focus your attention. By making light of the fact that your mind has wandered, accepting that you're only human and this is what human brains do, or even congratulating yourself on having noticed your mind has wandered, makes it much easier to regain and maintain your focus.

Noticing that your mind has wandered and accepting it are critically important to improving your focus and attention.

Focusing on Breath

This formal exercise isn't about controlling your breath. There is no right or wrong way to breathe. Simply observe, without judgment, the natural rhythm and sensations of breathing, from moment to moment. Newcomers to mindfulness usually find it easier to use the guided MP3 provided (Track 1A or 1B). (If you want more information about this exercise, see Chapter 8.)

1. **Settle yourself in a chair where you can sit in a comfortable upright position.**

2. **Plant both feet firmly on the floor, relax your shoulders with the chest open and your head facing forward with the chin dipped slightly to your chest.**

Your upper body should feel confident and self-supporting, embodying a sense of wakefulness and alertness. Close your eyes.

3. **Direct your attention to the contact points between your body and the chair and floor.**

Spend a few minutes exploring how your feet, legs, bottom and any other areas in contact with the chair and floor feel in this moment in time. Briefly scan each area of your body in turn, starting at the feet and finishing at the crown of your head. If you detect any tension, experiment with breathing into the area on the in breath and imagine releasing the tension on the out breath.

4. **Focus your attention on the breath.**

Notice how the chest and abdomen feel as the breath enters and leaves the body. If this is difficult, focus first on wherever your feel the breath most vividly.

5. **Place your hand on your abdomen and focus your attention on the sensations of the abdomen rising and falling in its own natural rhythm.**

6. **Allow your hand to gently return to your side and shift the focus of your attention to the short pause that occurs naturally between the in breath and out breath.**

7. **Refocus your attention to the tip of your nostrils.**

   Observe the sensation of the breath entering and leaving the body through the nostrils. Notice any subtle differences between the temperature of the air as it enters and leaves your nostrils.

8. **Refocus your attention back to the body.**

   Tune in to your body and notice how it feels in this moment in time.

9. **At the end of the practice session, gently stretch your fingers and toes and open your eyes.**

REMEMBER

If your mind wanders away from focusing on your breath, it's okay – you are human after all! Simply kindly and gently bring your attention back to where you want it to be.

Focusing on Your Body

It's recommended that you practice the body scan formal exercise somewhere you're sure not to be disturbed for around 15 minutes. Newcomers to mindfulness usually find it easier to use the guided MP3 provided (Track 2A or 2B) rather than attempting to guide themselves.

If you're practicing this at home, you may like to try this lying on a bed, but beware – doing so may send you to sleep. If it does, no problem – you probably needed the sleep, but try it in a chair the next day.

TIP

If you want more information about this exercise, check out Chapter 9.

REMEMBER

If at any point during the exercise you feel any discomfort, treat it as an opportunity to explore what's going on. Approach the discomfort with kindness and curiosity. What does it feel like? What sensations arise? What thoughts enter your mind? What emotions are you experiencing? Then try letting go of the discomfort as you breathe out.

1. **Sit on a comfortable chair, with your feet firmly on the floor.**

Sit with your back upright, your knees slightly lower than your hips, and your arms supported and resting comfortably. Make sure your whole body feels balanced and supported. Close your eyes, and try to remain aware of your posture throughout the exercise, and realign yourself if you notice that you're slouching.

2. **Focus your attention on your breath.**

Feel the sensations of your breath coming in and your breath going out. Do so for approximately ten breaths.

3. **Focus your attention on your toes.**

Start with your right foot, and identify whether you can feel any sensations in your toes, such as hot, cold or tingling. See whether you can feel your toes in contact with your socks or shoes. Spend a few moments exploring your toes, and then repeat the process with your left foot. Don't try to create any sensations or make it be any different from how it is; just notice what is there in that moment. If you can't feel any sensation at all, just notice the lack of sensation – that's absolutely fine. Compare your right and left toes. Do they feel any different?

4. **Focus your attention on the soles of your feet.**

Start with your right sole, and identify what you feel. Repeat the process with your left sole, and then compare the sensations you experienced with your right and left soles.

5. **Focus on your lower legs.**

Spend time exploring the right lower leg then the left, and then compare the two.

6. Focus on your knees.

Examine the sensations in your right knee then your left knee, and then compare the two.

7. Focus on your thighs and bottom.

Explore how they feel when in contact with the chair.

8. Explore the sensations in your internal organs.

Focus on your liver, kidneys, stomach, lungs and heart. You may not notice any sensation at all, and that's okay – just see what you can notice.

9. Focus on your spine.

Move up your spine slowly, focusing briefly on one vertebrae at a time, noticing any or no sensations.

10. Focus on your arms.

Identify the sensations in your right arm then your left arm, and then compare the two.

11. Focus on your neck and shoulders.

If you experience any tension or discomfort, try letting it go as you breathe out.

12. Focus on your head

Notice any feelings and sensations in your jaw and facial muscles. Notice how your nose feels, how your eyes feel, how your scalp feels.

13. Expand your attention to gain a sense of how your whole body feels at this moment in time.

14. Open your eyes and return to your day.

Focusing on Sounds

This formal exercise is a shortened variation of the sounds and thoughts exercise in Chapter 11.

1. **Settle yourself into your chair, sitting in a comfortable upright position that embodies the intention to practice mindfulness.**

2. **Close your eyes, or hold them in soft focus gazing downwards.**

3. **Gently direct your attention inwards towards your breath.**

   Tune in to the sensations of the breath entering and leaving your body. Allow your breathing to fall into its own natural rhythm. You don't need to change your breathing in any way – your body knows exactly how to breathe. Focus on the sensations of breathing for around two minutes.

4. **Shift your attention to the sounds that surround you.**

   As you notice each sound, let go of the habit of naming and judging it. Treat everything you hear as equal – beyond being pleasant or unpleasant. See if you can notice more subtle sounds or sounds within sounds.

TIP

   If your mind wanders, kindly guide it back to focusing your full attention on the sounds that surround you. Simply allow sounds to enter and exit your conscious awareness. Practice this for around five minutes.

5. **Gently move your attention back to your breath.**

   Remember: you don't need to change your breathing in any way. Focus on the sensations of breathing for around two minutes.

6. **Shift your attention back to your body, spending the last two minutes observing (and if you wish, releasing tension), working from the tips of your toes to the crown of your head.**

7. **When you're ready to do so, open your eyes. Have a stretch if you wish to, and reconnect with your day.**

Using Your Body as an Early Warning System

People commonly hold tension in areas of their body. Where they hold that tension varies from person to person. I (Juliet) tend to clench my jaw when under pressure, closely followed by hunching my shoulders. Some people clench their hands; others feel a knot on their stomach.

Which areas of your body do you feel tension when working under pressure? After you identify the one or two areas of your body where you commonly hold tension, you can use it as an early warning system.

By checking in with these areas on a regular basis, you can detect and release tension before it impacts your performance. You can also use the presence of tension as an indicator that your performance is dropping off and you need to do something to bring yourself back to peak performance.

Avoiding Falling into the Zone of Delusion

At some point each day, you reach a state of flow. You're in a state of flow when you're completely immersed in an activity. Time flies. Every action, movement, and thought follows inevitably from the previous one. You're using your skills to the utmost.

If you experience excessive pressure, you may fall out of this state of flow and enter the zone of delusion. The zone of delusion is that state where you're working hard but achieving little. Your ability to focus diminishes, and you repeat work because you're making mistakes. Your mind may be telling you to work harder and push on to get things done, but despite your hard work, you actually achieve very little.

TIP

Although it may sound counterintuitive, the best thing to do when you enter the zone of delusion is to stop what you're doing and do something that takes your mind away from the task. Take a short walk. Drink something hot or cold slowly and mindfully, enjoying every mouthful.

REMEMBER

To avoid entering the zone of delusion, use your body as an early warning system, and take action at the first sign that you have fallen out of flow and into delusion. A few minutes of informal mindfulness at this point can bring you straight back to a state of flow.

Minding the Gap

Your mind can easily wander into focusing on the coulds, shoulds and oughts. To maintain focus and attention, you need to 'mind the gap'. Mind the gap between the stories that your mind creates about how things 'should' or 'ought' or 'could' be and how things really are in any given moment in time. Doing so will help you keep focused for longer, or get back on track. For more on minding the gap, see Chapter 10.

Enjoying Mindful Coffee and Chocolate

Pausing to fully appreciate the present-moment experience of eating or drinking can be a great way to regain your focus. Eating is something that many busy people do on autopilot. People bite, chew and swallow often without noticing the texture or flavour of what they're eating.

Try paying mindful attention to that next cup of coffee or square of chocolate that you eat. Notice its colour, appearance, and aroma. Notice your body's response – does your mouth salivate? Notice how it feels to chew or swallow.

TIP

You can treat anything you eat or drink in this way – for a few bites, sips or for the whole snack bar, meal or cup. Being fully immersed in doing so can help you to refocus your attention. It can also make the experience of eating a more pleasurable one. You can find out more about this in Chapter 8.

Engaging in Mindful Walking

However desk-bound you are, there are always certain points in your day when you walk. For example, you may walk from the Underground, bus stop or car into work. You may walk from office to office or up and down stairs.

See Chapters 5 and 6 for examples of how mindful leaders Tim and Marion incorporate this mindful activity into their day.

TIP

Every step you take can be an opportunity for some mindful walking. Doing so is really easy. Simply tune in to the sensations you experience as you walk. Notice how your weight shifts from side to side as you walk. Notice which parts of the foot move with each step. Fully tune in to the experience of walking.

If you have time, have a walk outside and connect with nature. Whether it's a 5- or 15-minute walk, try to fully focus on the walk – the sensations of walking and the texture or the surface you're walking on. Notice the architecture or nature surrounding you and the colours and smells you experience. Doing so can be enjoyable, release tension and improve focus thereafter.

Doing the Three-Step Body Check

This exercise is a really quick version of the body scan exercise (see Chapter 9). Many people find this exercise useful and easy to do while sitting at their desk – and appearing to be staring at their computer screen.

You can do this exercise with your eyes open in soft focus (just slightly opened and looking downwards) or closed. Sit in a comfortable, upright position with your feet firmly on the floor. Centre yourself by focusing on the sensation of taking three slow breaths.

1. **Focus on your feet, legs and lower body (area 1 in Figure 21-1).**

Notice the sensations you experience, such as heat, cold or tingling, when you focus your full attention on your feet. Pause to observe, and then repeat with your legs, followed by your bottom.

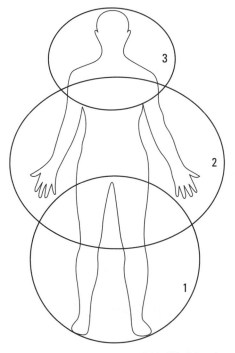

FIGURE 21-1: Focus on each of these three separate areas of the body.

2. Repeat as above, focusing on your chest and internal organs, followed by your arms (area 2 in Figure 21-1).

3. Repeat as above, focusing on your neck and shoulders. Follow this with your jaw, nose, facial skin and scalp (area 3 in Figure 21-1).

4. Finish by centring yourself by focusing on the sensations of taking three slow breaths.

Chapter 22

(More Than) Ten Sources of Info on Mindful Leadership

I n this chapter – the final chapter of the book – you find lots of valuable sources of information to help you move forward on your mindful leadership journey. Instead of confining the contents of this chapter to websites and books focusing specifically on mindful leadership, we include information on brain-based leadership and ways to create thinking spaces within organisations. We believe that gaining awareness of how your brain works and learning how to work with it rather than against it is essential for any aspiring mindful leader.

The Academy of Brain-Based Leadership

Your brain controls everything you do. By gaining an understanding of how it functions, setting an intent to optimise its strengths and minimise its limitations, you improve not only your performance as a leader but also your relationships at home and work, not to mention your health and well-being.

Managing a business, organisation or government agency in the 21st century can be challenging, and constant technological disruption and distraction are becoming the norm. For the last seven years, our work has focused on bringing practical brain science coupled with mindfulness into the board room as an aid to resilience and productivity.

In the last 15 years, we have seen improvements in brain scanning technology and an increase in neuroscience research as a result. Research into working with mental obstacles, such as stress or change, and finding new ways to learn and store information are just two examples. Insights gained from this research can help you improve the way you lead and live your life in general.

The Academy of Brain-Based Leadership (ABL; www.academy-bbl.com) translates, evaluates and distils relevant neuroscience findings into useable learnings and real-time applications to provide answers to tough challenges. The ABL aims to 'introduce you to the fundamentals of the brain with scientifically validated tools for learning, providing you with access to an expanding pool of cutting-edge research and resources', with the aim that you can 'become an expert on you'.

As well as many free resources, the ABL provides practical tools, techniques, and coaching and training to help you apply these insights to your work.

TIP

Coupling knowledge of how the brain works with mindfulness is a powerful combination. By getting to know how and why your brain functions the way it does, you'll be able to manage your mind better and improve your overall experiences in life.

Institute for Mindful Leadership

The Institute for Mindful Leadership (`www.instituteformindful leadership.org`) is a non-profit organisation dedicated to training and supporting leaders in the exploration of mindfulness and the fundamentals of leadership.

Janice Marturano founded the Institute in January 2011, after ending her 15-year tenure as vice president, public responsibility and deputy general counsel for General Mills, Inc. While fulfilling her duties as a corporate officer at General Mills, she also co-developed the very first mindful leadership curricula at the University of Massachusetts Medical School's Center for Mindfulness, where she served as a member of the advisory board.

In the media section of the website, you find a useful blog, links to articles, videos and podcasts. The website also provides information on mindful leadership training and retreats.

Time to Think

The power of effective listening is recognised as an essential leadership and management tool. Nancy Kline developed an elegant, practical model that creates the right environment for thinking by encouraging active listening. Her simple but powerful techniques can help you become a better leader by leading meetings more productively, by creating the space for others to think more creatively and solve business problems, and by helping you to forge stronger relationships by enhancing the quality of your listening.

Nancy identified ten behaviours that form a system called a 'Thinking Environment', a model of human interaction designed to improve the way people think and thus the way they work and live. She is author of the best-selling book *Time to Think: Listening to Ignite the Human Mind* (Cassell).

Nancy is the founder and president of Time to Think, an organisation she began in 1984 from her consulting and teaching work. On the Time to Think website (`www.timetothink.com`) you can find information on courses, registered coaches, books and resources.

The Mindful Globe

A recently launched website, The Mindful Globe (www. themindfulglobe.org) is an independent, interactive platform that provides information on mindfulness for business, along with research-based content from the world's leading mindfulness-at-work practitioners and commentators.

The Mindful Globe aims to orient companies towards the best solutions for their organisations by bringing mindfulness specialists, leadership professionals and companies together.

The site includes the Mindthropology Blog – articles from the specialists on different approaches to teaching mindfulness as well as the latest research and thinking on the subject.

Mindfulnet.org

Mindfulnet.org is an independent website that was set up in 2010 to provide information on mindfulness. Over the last six years, it has had over a million hits and has been influential in increasing the popularity of mindfulness in medicine, schools, the workplace and the judicial system.

The website is designed for busy people and covers all the main things newcomers and researchers want to know. It contains links to hundreds of other sites for more information. Mindfulnet. org includes information on the applications of mindfulness, its research base, teachers, teacher training, resources and events.

A Head for Work

A Head for Work (www.aheadforwork.co.uk) is my (Juliet Adams's) business website, which focuses on mindful approaches to leadership, change, performance improvement and mindfulness at work.

The website includes information about adapting mindfulness for use in the workplace, mindful leadership training and coaching, WorkplaceMT mindfulness training, and programmes for those who wish to teach mindfulness in the workplace. Do feel free to contact me via this website.

Dr Rick Hanson

Dr Rick Hanson, a psychologist who combines knowledge of modern brain science with mindfulness and ancient contemplative practices has a great website at www.rickhanson.net.

With Rick Mendius, MD, he founded the Wellspring Institute for Neuroscience and Contemplative Wisdom. The Institute publishes the monthly *Wise Brain Bulletin* and hosts the www.WiseBrain.org website. This website is full of resources to help you train your brain.

In 2009, Dr Hanson wrote *Buddha's Brain: The Practical Neuroscience of Happiness, Love & Wisdom* (New Harbinger), which shows you a number of effective ways to light up the brain circuits that relieve worry and stress and promote positive relationships and inner peace.

Dr Hanson's more recent book *Hardwiring Happiness: The New Brain Science of Contentment, Calm, and Confidence* (Rider) is a *New York Times* bestseller. It shows you how to tap the hidden power of everyday experiences to change your brain and your life for the better. In this book, he describes the human negativity bias and strategies for correcting this human bias

Hardwiring Happiness is also the fundamental text for his online experiential Foundations of Well-Being program, which uses the science of positive neuroplasticity to grow the '12 Pillars of Well-Being' – key inner strengths, including self-caring, mindfulness, intimacy, courage, and service. You can find information about this program on his website.

Daniel Goleman

Be sure to check out the website and blog (www.danielgoleman.info) of psychologist Daniel Goleman, PhD, author of *Leadership: The Power of Emotional Intelligence (More than Sound)*.

Goleman is an internationally known psychologist who lectures frequently to professional groups, business audiences, and college students. Working as a science journalist, Goleman reported on the brain and behavioural sciences for *The New York Times* for many years.

Goleman's 1995 book, *Emotional Intelligence: Why It Can Matter More Than IQ* (Bantam Books), was on *The New York Times* bestseller list for a year-and-a-half, with more than 5 million copies in print worldwide in 40 languages and has been a bestseller in many countries.

The *Harvard Business Review* called emotional intelligence – which discounts IQ as the sole measure of one's abilities – 'a revolutionary, paradigm-shattering idea' and chose his article 'What Makes a Leader' as one of ten 'must-read' articles from its pages.

Emotional Intelligence was named one of the 25 'most influential business management books' by *TIME Magazine.* The *Financial Times, Wall Street Journal* and Accenture Institute for Strategic Change have listed Goleman among the most influential business thinkers.

Goleman writes in an accessible, practical manner, and I regularly recommend his books and articles to leaders.

Mindful Work

Although the book *Mindful Work: How Meditation Is Changing Business from the Inside Out*, by David Gelles (2015), isn't specifically about mindful leadership, it's definitely worth a read – especially if you want to convince others within your company about the positive impacts of mindfulness from a business perspective.

David Gelles is a *New York Times* reporter who writes in this book about how mindfulness is key to fostering a happier, more productive workplace. He also includes many real-world examples of how mindfulness has benefited companies that have adopted it — from the millions of dollars Aetna has saved in healthcare costs to the ways Patagonia has combined leadership in its market with a pervasively mindful outlook.

Mindful Work attempts to explain how a wide range of businesses and workers can benefit from mindful techniques.

Mindfulness in Organizations

The book *Mindfulness in Organizations: Foundations, Research, and Applications*, edited by Jochen Reb and Paul W. B. Atkins (2015), isn't explicitly about mindful leadership but is a really good book to have by your side if you want to cite the evidence base for mindfulness in a workplace context.

As interest in the role of mindfulness in organisational settings continues to increase, this book provides an overview of the latest theoretical and empirical research on workplace mindfulness. It brings together world-leading scholars to explore the foundations, key discussions, diversity of approaches and applications of mindfulness in organisations.

It also provides valuable ideas for implementing mindfulness programmes in organisations, for teaching mindfulness in business contexts, and for coaching with mindfulness.

Resonant Leadership

The bestseller *Primal Leadership: Learning to Lead with Emotional Intelligence*, by Daniel Goleman, Richard E. Boyatzis, and Annie McKee (Harvard Business Reiew Press), introduced the concept of 'resonant' leaders-individuals who manage their own and others' emotions in ways that drive success. Leaders acknowledged the validity of the concept of resonant leadership but struggled with how to achieve and sustain it amid the relentless demands of work and life.

In *Resonant Leadership: Renewing Yourself and Connecting with Others Through Mindfulness, Hope, and Compassion*, by Richard E. Boyatzis and Annie McKee (Harvard Business Review Press, 2005), the authors provide practical guidance on how to become a resonant leader. Drawing from extensive multidisciplinary research and real-life stories, *Resonant Leadership* offers a framework for creating the resonance to improve your leadership capabilities. The book reveals that the path to resonance is through mindfulness, hope, and compassion and shows how intentionally employing these qualities creates effective and enduring leadership.

Neuroscience for Leadership

Neuroscience for Leadership: Harnessing the Brain Gain Advantage, by T. Swart, K. Chisholm, and P. Brown (2015), is a valuable volume for any aspiring mindful leader. This book is well researched and highly accessible for those who aren't scientists or PhD scholars. It skilfully links scientific brain network research with solid advice on decision-making, employee motivation, and organisational growth.

It argues that leadership can be learned; and new evidence from neuroscience clearly points to ways that leaders can significantly improve how they engage with and motivate others.

This book provides leaders and managers with an accessible guide to practical, effective actions based on neuroscience.

The Mindful Brain

The Mindful Brain: Reflection and Attunement in the Cultivation of Well-Being, by Daniel J. Siegel MD (W. W. Norton & Company, 2007) blends personal experience with scientific research and was one of the first books to integrate neuroscience research with mindfulness.

The book outlines an approach to improving mental health and life in general. It shows readers how personal awareness and attunement can actually stimulate emotional circuits in the brain, leading to a host of physiological benefits, including greater well-being, resilience, emotional balance, and improved cardiac and immune function.

Siegel's illuminating discussions of the power of the focused mind provide a wealth of ideas that can transform your life and deepen your connections with others and with yourself.

Mindfulness: Finding Peace in a Frantic World

No reading list on the subject of mindfulness would be complete without giving a mention to the bestselling book *Mindfulness: A Practical Guide to Finding Peace in a Frantic World*, by Professor Mark Williams and Dr Danny Penman (Piatkus).

The eight-week MBCT-based mindfulness course detailed within the book formed the basis for our approach to teaching mindfulness in a workplace context. It was also the model of mindfulness teaching used to teach MPs and UK parliamentary staff (see Chapter 4).

This book was the first book written as a self-help guide specifically for a healthy population (as opposed to a clinical population), outlining a shortened approach to teaching mindfulness, with practice requirement of 10 to 20 minutes a day.

Although the book doesn't focus specifically on the workplace or on leadership, it's a really accessible self-help book on the subject of mindfulness that almost anyone can pick up and apply, and we highly recommend it.

Index

T

U

V

W

Y

Z

About the Author

Juliet Adams, MSC, FCIPD, is the founder of Mindfulnet.org and director of A Head for Work Ltd. She is a learning and development professional who has worked for more than 25 years in HR, OD and consultancy roles. She was awarded a master's degree in training and performance management in 2008. She specialises in leadership development and performance improvement.

Juliet has been at the forefront of work to develop mindfulness training that meets the needs of busy people working in demanding roles. Juliet has helped organise three international conferences on mindfulness in the workplace and has written three books on the subject.

Since 2012, Juliet has been developing mindfulness training designed to enhance well-being, productivity and resilience in the workplace. WorkplaceMT takes 60 per cent less time than traditional mindfulness training, making it much more accessible. Juliet teaches and mentors individuals and groups wishing to develop their workplace mindfulness teaching skills.

Juliet works internationally with a team of associates to deliver leadership, productivity and WorkplaceMT training for organisations ranging from the Bank of England to CIPD, and individuals including CEOs to GPs, teachers, social workers, investment bankers, accountants and council workers.

Juliet lives in Cambridgeshire near the beautiful city of Ely.

For more information on Juliet's mindfulness programmes, coaching and mentoring, visit www.aheadforwork.com. To follow Juliet on Twitter, her ID is @A_Head_for_Work. For information about WorkplaceMT mindfulness training, visit www.workplacemt.com.

Technical Editor Marina Grazier, BA Hons, BSc Hons, MBPsS, is the owner of The Mindfulness Exchange Ltd. With over 30 years' business development, marketing and HR experience in the IT and business consulting sectors at companies including KPMG Consulting and IBM, Marina is no stranger to the challenges of sustaining success in high-performing roles.

Marina retrained as a psychologist to provide a platform to teach MBCT and trained and taught at the Oxford Mindfulness Centre (OMC). She joined Prof Mark Williams's Development Board in 2010 to support the Mindfulness in the Workplace project, which was spun off as The Mindfulness Exchange (TME) in 2012.

Marina is a thought leader in the application of mindfulness to help people master their minds and flourish at work. WorkplaceMT is an evidence-informed approach to delivering mindfulness in the workplace, robustly tested over four years in TME's client base. She also pioneers mindfulness trainer training, for mindfulness teachers and corporate professionals taking mindfulness into the workplace.

Building on her successful corporate life, Marina is passionate about bringing the benefits of mindfulness to the workplace to manage the evolving challenges of modern working life. She believes that the cognitive scientific understanding of mindfulness is highly relevant to the workplace needing to deliver sustainable success in business.

Marina lives in Devon in Symondsdown House in the beautiful Axe Valley. Symondsdown House is the base for TME WorkplaceMT teacher training programmes. You can find out more at www.symondsdownhouse.co.uk.

For more information on TME's mindfulness programmes, WorkplaceMT trainer training and mentoring, visit www.mindfulness-exchange.com or check out Marina on Facebook at The Mindfulness Exchange.

Authors' Acknowledgments

Juliet: I would like to thank Jeremy Hunter and Jutta Tobias for their support, encouragement, belief in me, help and suggestions that motivated me to complete this book. My thanks to Lord Stone, Tim Neild, and Marion Furr for agreeing to share their experiences of mindful leadership. My thanks to Marina Grazier for her technical expertise and support, without which I wouldn't have completed the book. My thanks also to Sid who mindfully told me to 'stop talking about it and get it written' when I was procrastinating, and my amazing partner, Jim, who kept the home fires burning and entertained the cats while I sat in front of the computer for months on end. Without all of you, this book would not have been possible.

Marina: I would like to thank Professor Mark Williams for suggesting that I train to become a professional mindfulness teacher and for supporting me through my training. I would like to thank my husband, Stuart, for supporting my career change and enabling me to flourish, for the beach walks with the dogs and his hard work running Symondsdown House. Many thanks to Juliet Adams for helping me to develop the successful TME WorkplaceMT trainer training week, which she co-teaches, and imparting her L&D knowledge to make the programme more effective.

Publisher's Acknowledgments

Executive Commissioning Editor:
Annie Knight

Editorial Project Manager:
Christina Guthrie

Development Editor:
Christina Guthrie

Copy Editor: Jennette ElNaggar

Production Editor:
G. Vasanth Koilraj

Cover Image: jgroup/iStockphoto